Praise for Eve Kosofsky Sedgwick

"It is difficult to calculate the impact of Sedgwick's scholarship, in part because its legacy is still in the making, but also because she worked at a skew to so many fields of inquiry. Feminism, queer theory, psychoanalysis, and literary, legal and disability studies— Sedgwick complicated and upended them all, sometimes in ways that infuriated more anodyne scholars, but always in ways that pushed the established parameters."—RICHARD KIM, the *Nation*

"Sedgwick had a special gift for handling power-tool theory lightly, porting continental thought into subcultural, everyday idioms. . . . To a generation reared on disembodied theory and an ethic of philosophical impersonalism, this blur of the theoretical and the auto-referential granted permission to make bodies matter."
—EMILY APTER, *Artforum*

"As [Sedgwick] wrote in *Epistemology of the Closet*, 'Axiom 1: People are different from each another.' She went on, 'It is astonishing how few respectable conceptual tools we have for dealing with this self-evident fact.' In the face of the dazzling and dizzying ways in which people differ from each other (and themselves), sexual orientation is a pretty blunt instrument. That is a deceptively simple argument, which Sedgwick went on to unfurl without ever losing sight of how and why self-identifying as gay or lesbian in the face of a homophobic world does vitally, urgently continue to matter."
—ANN PELLEGRINI, the *Chronicle of Higher Education*

"[Sedgwick's] largely symbolic role in [the culture wars] meant that criticism of her work seldom did justice to the subtlety and searing wit of her writing, nor to her sensitivity to the social and sexual bonds that tie us to each other and to the world."
—MACY HALFORD, the *New Yorker*

"Eve Kosofsky Sedgwick's gift is to electrify intellectual communities by reminding them that 'thought' has a temperature, a texture, and an erotics. With a generosity that is at once self-abnegatingly ascetic, and gorgeously, exhibitionistically bravura, she opens door after door onto undiscovered fields of inquiry."
—WAYNE KOESTENBAUM, author of *Andy Warhol*

"One of the most extraordinary critics of her generation."
—MAUD ELLMANN

"Sedgwick is such a powerful critic of literary studies and of sexuality because she recognizes where interpretive possibilities have been foreclosed and points to how they might be reopened."
—ANDREW ELFENBEIN, *Modern Philology*

"Sedgwick is one of the smartest and wittiest critics writing. The play of her mind as it goes from Henry James to John Waters and Divine, from AIDS to Jane Austen and women's anal eroticism, is dazzling. . . . Her work is often as moving as it is acute: Like the best of the gay male writers whose work has been her principal subject, in her prose flawless surface lures the reader to explore new depths."
—MARILYN HACKER, the *Nation*

"Eve Kosofsky Sedgwick is deservedly recognized as the primum mobile of lesbian and gay studies. Yet her real achievement lies not so much in the creation of a new academic discipline, as in the profound implications her work carries for the rest of the academy, and the wider world beyond. For she assigns an absolutely fundamental, constitutive role to homophobia in the construction of Modernity, and its myriad institutions, discourses, pleasures, and pains."
—SIMON WATNEY, author of *Policing Desire*

"Eve Kosofsky Sedgwick presents a way of counterknowing that pries open, merrily deconstructs, exposes the terrors of impossible double binds we live by, and holds out a promise of better things that might be." —JAMES R. KINCAID,
the *Journal of English and Germanic Philology*

"Loving and wise teacher, groundbreaking and controversial scholar, scared but resilient breast cancer survivor, utterly fabulous queer icon, skilled weaver of gorgeous fabrics, shy daughter of middle-class Jews — Eve Sedgwick is all of these, but most importantly . . . she is truly a poet of incomparable courage, insight, and power."
—RAFAEL CAMPO

"Sedgwick's remarkable power to define the field of gender and sexuality studies over the past couple of decades can be traced to a number of causes: her undeniable brilliance; her apparently infinite will to read — and especially to read against the grain of a deadening common sense; [and] her generosity, to which nearly all who write about her attest." —HEATHER LOVE,
the *Women's Review of Books*

"In her search for what enables Proust's unmatched skill for reawakening the vitality of the world, Sedgwick assembles an entirely new Proust and offers him up for our active daily use so that we might better experience his sustenance. And, in doing so, Sedgwick also rebuilds *herself* differently: witness the optimistic, expansive movement . . . in her later work towards themes of refreshment and rebirth. Her art is perhaps the best place to see the contours not just of the Proust she recasts for us, but of the late Sedgwickian mode she simultaneously refines. . . . Everywhere, and particularly clearly in her art, Sedgwick theorizes a practice of mindfulness. . . . [A] mindfulness practice rooted in creative work is the spine, the nexus, that holds together Sedgwick's late work."
—KATHERINE HAWKINS, *Criticism*

The Weather in Proust

Edited by Michèle Aina Barale,

Jonathan Goldberg,

Michael Moon, and

Eve Kosofsky Sedgwick

Eve Kosofsky Sedgwick

The Weather in Proust

JONATHAN GOLDBERG, EDITOR

Duke University Press Durham & London 2011

Printed in the United States of America
on acid-free paper ∞
Designed by C. H. Westmoreland
Typeset in Monotype Fournier
by Tseng Information Systems, Inc.
Library of Congress Cataloging-in-
Publication Data appear on the
last printed page of this book.

"Anality: News from the Front"
originally appeared in the Routledge
journal *Studies in Gender and Sexuality*
11, no. 3: 151–62.
"Thinking Through Queer Theory"
originally appeared in the *Journal
of Gender Studies*, no. 4 (2001) from
Ochanomizu University.

Duke University Press gratefully
acknowledges the support of the College
of Arts and Sciences, and the James T.
Lancy School of Graduate Studies, both
at Emory University, which provided
funds toward the production of
this book.

for Panda

Contents

xiii   *Editor's Introduction*

1   The Weather in Proust

42   Cavafy, Proust, and the Queer Little Gods

69   Making Things, Practicing Emptiness

123   Melanie Klein and the Difference Affect Makes

144   Affect Theory and Theory of Mind

→→

166   Anality: News from the Front

183   Making Gay Meanings

190   Thinking through Queer Theory

→→

206   Reality and Realization

217   *Figure Credits*

219   *Index*

Editor's Introduction

The Weather in Proust gathers, in its first five chapters, the writing toward a book on Proust that occupied Eve Kosofsky Sedgwick in the last years of her life. I've titled the entire volume after the opening essay, the only one in which Proust is always her central focus, but which, in its capacious concerns with subjects as diverse as Neoplatonism, Bette Davis, affect theory, and puppet theater, suggests that under that title much can be safely subsumed. "Cavafy, Proust, and the Queer Little Gods," which follows, records Eve's discovery of a madeleine moment: responding to an invitation to speak about C. P. Cavafy afforded her the chance recognition that Cavafy's periperformative invocations of the "queer little gods" were the inspiring force behind her realization of their role in Proust. What is "in Proust," indeed, is likewise but differently in question in "Making Things, Practicing Emptiness." There, her textile practices, while resistant to verbal translation, nonetheless involve texts, often by Proust; text and textile are warp and weft woven together in such forms as accordion books and looms. "Melanie Klein and the Difference Affect Makes" underscores one important theoretical strand in the Proust project. It is measured in "Affect Theory and Theory of Mind." Those theoretical relations are instantiated in this chapter by a reading of the difficult fifth volume of Proust's *A la recherche du temps perdu*.

The next group of essays opens with "Anality: News from the Front," which contains what may have been the last sentence Eve composed, a parenthetical remark about the hope inspired by the inauguration of Barack Obama, which took place less than three months before her death on April 12, 2009. It is followed by two much earlier pieces, "Making Gay Meanings" and "Thinking through Queer Theory," valuable now for the ways in which she reviews her career as a queer theorist, and revealing for the citations from earlier work that she chooses. Each piece also makes interventions into the scenes of their delivery, showing that her career as a queer theorist continued to the end of her life, as "Anality: News from the Front" certainly demonstrates as well. The final essay, "Reality and Realization," written soon after her breast cancer had metastasized to her spine, provides the ground note encounter with impending death, and with Buddhism, that subtends much that comes before, including, centrally, the work on Proust.

This collection does not represent all of Eve's unpublished and un-collected work. There are early poems, MLA papers, even class syllabi and assignments, not to mention advice to job seekers, that may appear or reappear (a previously unpublished early essay on James Merrill, for example, is slated for publication in GLQ in 2011). Only one piece of late writing is not reprinted here, a talk titled "Come as You Are." It reworks virtually all of "Reality and Realization" in the characteristic way in which Eve treated her own writing as a series of movable modules. (Those practices guided me in making one chapter out of three separate yet overlapping and diverging talks on Cavafy; I detail such editorial decisions and procedures in the notes to each piece. [Notes that I have added appear in brackets.]) To "Reality and Realization," "Come as You Are" adds several pages used again later in "Making Things, Practicing Emptiness." At appropriate points I have inserted as notes to "Reality and Realization" and "Making Things, Practicing Emptiness" virtually all the passages from "Come as You Are" that do not appear in those two pieces. Omitted, however, are two poems of Eve's (previously published in *Women and Performance* 16, no. 2 (2006): 327–28) that initially were part of "Come as You Are." It seems apt to close this editor's introduction with them.

Death

isn't a party you dress up for, man,
it's strictly come-as-you-are, so don't get too
formal, it's useless. *Don't* grab that prosthesis,
those elevator shoes, or girdle to jam your tummy
in, for your interview with Jesus or
forty-nine days in the bardo of Becoming.
The point's not what becomes you, but what's you.

Why did I buy those silk PJs with feathers
so long before the big affair began?
I've always slept in the nude. Now I sleep in the nude forever.

Bathroom Song

I was only one year old;
I could tinkle in the loo,
such was my precocity.
Letting go of Number Two
in my potty, not pyjama,
was a wee bit more forbidding
—and I feared the ravening flush.
So my clever folks appealed
to my generosity:
"What a masterpiece, Evita!
Look! We'll send it off to Grandma!"

Under the river, under the woods,
off to Brooklyn and the breathing
cavern of Mnemosyne
from the fleshpotties of Dayton—
what could be more kind or lucky?

From the issue of my bowels
straight to God's ear—or to Frieda's,
to the presence of my Grandma,
to the anxious chuckling
of her flushed and handsome face
that was so much like my daddy's,
to her agitated jowls,
Off! Away! To Grandma's place!

As, in Sanskrit, who should say
of the clinging scenes of karma,
"Gaté, gaté, paragaté"
(gone, gone, forever gone),
"parasamgaté; bodhi; svaha!"
(utterly gone—enlightenment—
svaha! Whatever svaha means),
Send the sucker off to Grandma.
Gaté, gaté, paragaté;
parasamgaté; bodhi; svaha!

In editing this collection, I have turned for advice and help to a number of people. I am happy to acknowledge them here: Lauren Berlant, Jason Edwards, Lynne Huffer, Nina Katzander, pii, Ernst J. Van Alphen, J. Keith Vincent, Erik Wirth. Sarah McCarry deserves her own sentence for her tireless assistance. David Kosofsky got me started by providing me with the files on Eve's computers and the unique typescript of "Come as You Are." Monroe Hammond worked as my assistant, giving expert attention and thoughtful care to getting the manuscript into final shape. J. Hal Rogers kept me on track in other important ways. Michael Moon was, as ever, ever supportive. Hal Sedgwick lent his remarkable love at every stage.

The Weather in Proust

Early in the fourth volume of *A la recherche du temps perdu*, Proust's narrator goes to a party at the home of the Prince de Guermantes, where he sees a fountain designed by the eighteenth-century architect Hubert Robert. His description of the fountain is one of the novel's (admittedly many) descriptive set pieces:

> It could be seen from a distance, slender, motionless, rigid, set apart in a clearing surrounded by fine trees, several of which were as old as itself, only the lighter fall of its pale and quivering plume stirring in the breeze. The eighteenth century had refined the elegance of its lines, but, by fixing the style of the jet, seemed to have arrested its life; at this distance one had the impression of art rather than the sensation of water. Even the moist cloud that was perpetually gathering at its summit preserved the character of the period like those that assemble in the sky round the palaces of Versailles. But from a closer view one realised that, while it respected, like the stones of an ancient palace, the design traced for it beforehand, it was a constantly changing stream of water. . . . [Its] continuity, apparently complete, was assured, at every point in the ascent of the jet where it must otherwise have been broken, by the entering into line, by the lateral incorporation, of a parallel jet which mounted higher than the first and was itself, at a greater altitude which was however already a strain upon its endurance, relieved by a third. From close to, exhausted drops could be seen falling back from the column of water, passing their sisters on the way up, and at times, torn and scat-

tered, caught in an eddy of the night air, disturbed by this unremitting surge, floating awhile before being drowned in the basin. They teased with their hesitations, with their journey in the opposite direction, and blurred with their soft vapour the vertical tension of the shaft that bore aloft an oblong cloud composed of countless tiny drops but seemingly painted in an unchanging golden brown which rose, unbreakable, fixed, slender and swift, to mingle with the clouds in the sky.[1] (4:75–76)

This conspicuously emblematic description seems to offer a crux for articulating a number of issues — architectonically as well as thematically important ones — in *A la recherche du temps perdu*. Hayden White has analyzed this paragraph as a miniature demonstration of the tropes of historiographic rhetoric *tout court*.[2] Again, considered generically, the description represents a brash manifesto for the *roman-fleuve*, the fictional form in which destinies high and low are relayed and transmuted through a series of generations and where, for example, a single character may recycle under serial names or titles, while a single name or title can be forwarded by a series of distinct characters.[3]

From the point of view of iconography, the Robert fountain links to earlier fountains in European literature, art, and landscape to invoke a tradition that is specifically Neoplatonic. Originating with Plotinus in the third century AD, the philosophical and spiritual discourse of Neoplatonism holds that, in Proust's words, "there exists but a single intelligence of which everyone is co-tenant" (2:195), toward the plenitude of which souls ceaselessly rise and merge, and from which they just as naturally fall and individuate. To quote Plotinus: "The cosmic content is carried forward to its purpose, everything in its co-ordinate place, under only one Reason-Principle operating alike in the descent and return of souls and to every purpose of the system."[4] The Neoplatonic fountain offers an emblem for the possibility of non-oppositional relations of many important kinds: between pattern and contingency; the eternal and the ephemeral; the universal soul and that of the individual.

That Proust tends to have reincarnation on his mind is clear from his mention of it in the opening paragraph of his novel; and among the Neoplatonic associations of this fountain perhaps the most pointed, in the career of the individual water drops anthropomorphized by Proust in terms of their exhaustion and transmutation, involves a narrative of reincarnation. As Plotinus describes the reincarnation narrative, "The sufferer, all unaware, is swept onward towards his due, hurried always by the restless driving of his errors, until at last wearied out by that against which he struggled, he falls into his fit place and, by self-chosen movement, is brought to the lot he never chose."[5] Among the series represented by this fountain is the possibility of souls' enacting serial lives.

And at the most literal level, the Guermantes' fountain, like any fountain, is a machine for animating and recirculating water. Simultaneously a spring and a fall, and with the narrator's repeated emphasis on the state-changes of condensation and cloud formation, it offers a stylized, artificial epitome of the unending processes by which water is propelled through its life-giving round of physical metamorphoses.

Both as a representation of the rebirth cycle and of the water cycle, then, the Guermantes' fountain, with all its eighteenth-century elegance, might be taken as representing a novelistic vision that combines flexibility with an extraordinary economy, in an endlessly mutable but ultimately closed system where what goes around comes around, where linear narrative is propelled through a perpetual recycling of elements, lives, positions, structures, and desires that honors the conservation of matter and energy, that operates according to law. In the framework of reincarnation, such a system might be called strictly karmic; in a more familiar Western mythology, Oedipal. But compelling as this vision may be, it is no sooner finely articulated than it goes wastefully, farcically off course. The full-scale weather system comes athwart the fountain's condensed and elegant version: as Mme d'Arpajon crosses the garden in search of her errant lover, suddenly "a strong gust of warm air deflected the jet of water and inundated the fair lady so completely that, the water streaming down from her low neckline inside her dress, she was as thoroughly soaked as if she had been plunged into a bath" (4:77). Sometimes things that come around don't go around, and vice versa.

The important question in Proust of how open systems relate to closed ones, or perhaps better put, of how systems themselves move between functioning as open and closed, seems like an invitation to explore some literary and psychological connections to the scientific insights that are nowadays popularly grouped under the rubrics of chaos and complexity. The weather has a privileged place in discussions of complexity. By the mid-nineteenth century, there was a full array of accurate mechanistic laws and measurements for understanding what one critic refers to as "the heat/water/steam machine we call *weather*."[6] Not until the late twentieth-century study of chaos and complexity, however, following the increasingly sophisticated understanding of feedback processes that developed leapfrog-fashion with the computer's vast increase of human computational powers, has it been possible for science to conceptualize together the absolutely rule-bound cyclical economy of these processes, on the one hand, and on the other hand the irreducibly unpredictable contingency of the actual weather. Yet this kind of juncture is the matrix, the growing point, of narrative and reflection in Proust.[7]

Rather than trying to bring Proust into explicit relation with the science of chaos and complexity, however, or with the science of his own day, I'm trying in the present project to use these topics in contemplating some characteristically Proustian modes of being, of relation to self and the world. Like, I think, many readers of Proust, I especially want to understand his continuing access to a psychology of surprise and refreshment, as well as his nourishing relation to work.

Despite the Plotinian emphasis of passages like the one I began by quoting, it may seem like an unearned provocation to refer to these subjects together as his mysticism. But it is just the quotidian, unspecial, reality-grounded structure and feel of Proust's mysticism that draw my attention. It becomes visible less through set pieces of "mystical experience"—though of course these occur—than through a habitual relationality in the novel as a whole. And while the surprise and refreshment in Proust may respond to this logic of mysticism, so too do the deeply motivating experiences of desolation and of dread. Certainly we can say, to begin with, that Proust's mysticism—if that's the right term—owes nothing at all to the occult or esoteric. There is a whole history of esoteric offshoots of Neoplatonic thought, but in these—and unlike, for example, Yeats—Proust displays no interest. And rather than calling on belief of any kind, his mysticism emphasizes, instead, the transformative potential of the faculties of attention and perception.

At the same time one would need to ask about the relation of such a mysticism to Proust's unresting practice of demystification. Proust is famous for his scouring determination to unearth what he calls "laws" or "truths" of human desire, self-deception, and limitation.[8] But the order of these distinct, propositional laws and truths, delineating at most a grid on which to map the ground of reality, seems distinct from the non-propositional, environmental order of Proust's reality orientation, which coincides with his mysticism. I note the radical narrowing of focus, the stereotypy of terms that characterize Proustian demystification—most tellingly, as when any character's search for "the truth" about a lover always and only means demanding to know one single thing: whether or not that person is unfaithful. No one is better than Proust at giving the sense that the true interest of a psyche, a landscape, or indeed a sentence may be actually inexhaustible. Yet that grounded reality-level of surprise and plenitude, like the fullness of his sense of place, is radically different from the demystifying, propositional level of knowingness and lack.[9]

At a methodological level, at least in a certain ongoing critical allegory of psychoanalytic theory, it seems to make some kind of sense to understand Proust's demystifying "laws" and "truths" through a version, however queer, of an Oedipal narrative. I am using "Oedipal" as shorthand here for a cluster of closely linked assumptions, by now the commonsense of Freudian and Lacanian approaches to psychic life and textuality, for which the Proustian "laws" and "truths" have offered such an irresistibly good fit. Oedipality in this sense is a closed system, like the Robert fountain, whose function or destiny is to reproduce itself. Its primary motives are sexual rivalry, sexual desire, and the near-impossibility of their direct satisfaction; its most visible assumptions include the centrality of dualistic gender difference and the primacy of genital morphology and desire. Underpinning these are less explicit but even more important structural and logical assumptions. Freud's insistence on understanding psychic life through what he called the "economic point of view," involving the systemic transformation and circulation of defined amounts of drive energy, underlines what a later vocabulary would call the zero-sum nature of this game, where, for example, one person's getting more love means a priori that another is getting less. Oedipality also necessarily invokes the either/or logical laws of noncontradiction and the excluded middle term, where inside is the opposite of outside, passive is the opposite of active, and, for another example, desire is the opposite of identification.

Yet the psychology of surprise and refreshment, desolation and dread, to which I've alluded, so compelling to many Proust readers, falls outside such an Oedipal logic.[10] Not only the mysticism of Plotinus, but mysticism as a phenomenon is all but defined by its defiance of the closed system of either/or and the zero sum. In these pages I am going to be using a different strand of psychoanalytic thought, organized around object relations and most closely identified with Melanie Klein, to explore the meaning and structure of these more complex energies in Proust. It is striking also that the issues of mysticism and of object-relations psychology seem to be closely intertwined. In the comments that follow, discussing a conjunction of rebirth and of the meteorological cycle, I am not aiming to arrive at a synthesis of Proust's or his novel's propositional laws or truths. Instead I'm hoping to pursue a meditation on Proustian reality, through the changeable medium of his novel's cosmologies and weathers.

Rebirth, transmigration, metempsychosis, metamorphosis, reincarnation, and one might add, as Proust certainly would, resurrection: these terms form a Venn diagram of concepts whose overlaps cluster around two sometimes-conjoined notions: the soul's survival after death, on the one hand, and on the other hand its occupation of differing bodies at different times. As surely as this space of insistent reference in Proust exceeds Christianity, it also exceeds a conventional French classicism and his own less conventional Ovidian preoccupation. And, as we'll see later, it fits in with a Proustian atmosphere in which every act and landscape brims with a proliferation of genii, demigods, Norns, and other such ontologically exceptional beings: no shadow or spring without its nymph, no phone exchange without its goddesses. Proust is unusual among French modernists, not in the frequency or suavity with which he invokes Christian and classical ontologies of death and the soul's survival and transfer, but in also explicitly bringing in dozens of Celtic, Persian, Egyptian, northern European, and Asian citations among others on the same subjects.

Reading Proust over the last few years with something of a Buddhist eye, I've continually been surprised by what seemed like invocations of and meditations on Hindu or Buddhist notions of reincarnation, karma, samsara, Buddha nature, and enlightenment. Actually it would be no more surprising to find them in Proust's very Orientalizing cultural context than in our own. What seems truer, though, as in the example of the Hubert Robert fountain, is that the Neoplatonic tradition remained for Proust the profoundest reservoir of such ideas and images, as it also was for such of his favored authors as Emerson, Bergson, and the Hardy of *The Well-Beloved*.[11]

It's been hard for twentieth-century and later readers to know how to take Proust's irrepressible interest in rebirth. The scientistic certainties of modernity have undermined any space in which a notion of literally successive lives could be reflectively received. Christian humanism, the principal form in which Neoplatonic philosophy survives in mainstream modern thought, jettisoned the belief in reincarnation many centuries ago. And in many ways Proust reflects a modern refusal to take reincarnation "seriously." One kind of acid test: although there are scores of invocations of metempsychosis throughout the *Recherche*, the narrator never responds to the two deaths most closely affecting him—his grandmother's and Albertine's—with so much as a speculation that the souls of those whom he has lost might reincarnate in new bodies.

The main reason it is easy to de-supernaturalize Proust's interest in reincarnation, though, is that he finds such a wealth of uses for it in describing the psychology of one lifetime. As Hardy does in *The Well-Beloved*, Proust's narrator describes the different people with whom he falls in love as successive embodiments of the same spirit, "the apparition which . . . , each time, leaves . . . [our heart] overwhelmed by fresh incarnations" (5:79). Family resemblance—any resemblance, in fact, including those between people and animals or objects—is a ground for invoking some version of transmigration. And while Proust describes different beings as incarnations of the same soul, he also envisions an individual's lifetime as a narrative encompassing many deaths and many unrecognizable rebirths. Not only the end of a love but every self-alienating aspect of the passage of time, through processes both acute and chronic, points to "the death of the self, a death followed, it is true, by resurrection, but in a different self, to the love of which the elements of the old self that are condemned to die cannot bring themselves to aspire" (2:340).

Besides love, Proust writes in this way especially often about sleep and dreams, the regular punctuation of oblivion and strangeness structuring the illusion of the everyday. The epitomizing version of Neoplatonic rebirth for the nineteenth century is surely Wordsworth's use of this image in the "Intimations" ode:

> Our birth is but a sleep and a forgetting:
> The Soul that rises with us, our life's Star,
> Hath had elsewhere its setting.[12]

Proust, more rococo, describes "that deep slumber in which vistas are opened to us of . . . disincarnation, the transmigration of souls, the evoking of the dead, the illusions of madness, retrogression towards the most elementary of the natural kingdoms . . . , all those mysteries which we imagine ourselves not to know and into which we are in reality initiated almost every night, as into the other great mystery of extinction and resurrection" (2:545).[13]

Another great engine of transmigration for Proust's narrator, maybe more surprising than sleep or romantic love, is a change in the weather, "sufficient to create the world and ourselves anew" (3:472). Some readers find the narrator's father a rather underdrawn character, since most of what we see him do is examine the barometer and speculate on when the weather will change. But he defends his obsession — "As if there could be anything more interesting!" (1:127) — and in adulthood his son inherits it, "to the extent of not being satisfied like him with consulting the barometer, but becoming an animated barometer myself" (5:96). This is quite a startling but, apparently, true remark. In particular, for the narrator, waking from sleep to find changed weather is a way of being "born again" (3:472). And paradoxically, the very ordinary seriality of weather offers a kind of daily, ground-tone pulsation of the *mémoire involuntaire* — anachronistic by definition — that elsewhere sets off a very few moments of gemlike preciousness: "Atmospheric changes, provoking other changes in the inner man, awaken forgotten selves" (5:662); "we relive our past years not in their continuous sequence, day by day, but in a memory focused upon the coolness or sunshine of some morning or afternoon" (3:544). It would be more than a pun, though not an equivalent, to translate the title of this novel *In Search of Lost Weather*.

What does the narrator mean in calling himself an animated barometer? For one thing it feels, he says oddly in *La Prisonnière*, like having a little mannikin inside him, "a certain intermittent little person" (5:1), "very similar to another whom the optician at Combray used to set up in his shop window to forecast the weather, and who, doffing his hood when the sun shone, would put it on again if it was going to rain" (5:5). This "little person inside me, the melodious psalmist of the rising sun" — and let's note here that to *be* an animated barometer seems to involve *containing* an animated barometer inside oneself — this mannikin, however mechanical and comic, has no superficial relation to the narrator's ontology. In fact, it may be a more enduring feature than is his faculty for metaphor itself.

> Of the different persons who compose our personality, it is not the most obvious that are the most essential. In myself, when ill health has succeeded in uprooting them one after another, there will still remain two or three endowed with a hardier constitution than the rest, notably a certain philosopher who is happy only when he has discovered between two works of art, between two sensations, a common element. But I have sometimes wondered whether the last of all might not be this little mannikin. . . . I know how selfish this little mannikin is; I may be suffering from an attack of breathlessness which only the coming of rain would assuage, but he pays no heed, and, at the first drops so impa-

tiently awaited, all his gaiety forgotten, he sullenly pulls down his hood. Conversely, I dare say that in my last agony, when all my other "selves" are dead, if a ray of sunshine steals into the room while I am drawing my last breath, the little barometric mannikin will feel a great relief, and will throw back his hood to sing: "Ah, fine weather at last!" (5:5–6)

And while the animated barometer may represent some last residue of supra-individual identity that persists at the moment of death, it is also a site of metempsychosis where, within a single lifetime, "a change in the weather outside" becomes "the substitution [for myself] of another person" (5:25). No casual invention, then, the happily impersonal "little person" pops up several times in the latter volumes of the *Recherche*.

What can we make of the Proustian narrator's self-description as an "animated barometer," crystallizing in the image of this buoyant internal homunculus? To begin with, it's interesting that the narrator, qua barometer, responds specifically to atmospheric pressure. Compared to the much more obvious alternatives — temperature, wind, precipitation, even humidity — air pressure is a subtle, invisible, and indivisibly systemic index of weather. A thermometer responds to a quality, heat, that's easy to perceive and interpret in isolation. The measure of barometric pressure, on the other hand, means nothing at all outside a dynamic interpretive context: it requires a full sense of how changes in the weight of a given column of air, relative to the weight of other near and distant columns of air, will affect both the vertical movement of heat and thus the air's temperature and ability to hold moisture, and also the horizontal travel of air masses that circulate "fronts" of pressure difference, and thus major weather systems, across the earth's surface. Attending to air pressure to any extent at all seems to presume an expert sensitivity — however amateur — to the entire working of "the heat/water/steam machine we call *weather*" (in Farnsworth's phrase). In fact, among the myriad descriptive tours de force that so give the note of Proustian inexhaustibility, it's remarkable how many invoke the air as a site of alchemical state change: the air and its light are described as "melted" (5:100), "glazed" (5:553), "unctuous" (5:553), "elastic" (5:555), "fermenting" (5:555), "contracted" (5:803), "distended" (5:803), "solidified" (6:19), "distilled" (2:387), "scattered" (2:387), "liquid" (2:565), "woven" (3:474), "brittle" (3:474), "powdery" (2:567), "crumbling" (2:567), "embalmed" (2:730), "congealed" (4:721), "gummy" (1:88), "flaked" (1:88), "squeezed" (1:120), "frayed" (1:214), "pressed" (1:235), "percolated" (1:387), "volatilised" (2:656), or even "burning" (4:534).

Invisible for all its pervasiveness, atmospheric pressure—like the air itself—is easy for most people most of the time to take for granted. But under some circumstances it is also possible or compulsory not to. Proust's narrator offers at least one reason for his own barometric aptitude: he is prone to "attacks of breathlessness" that also respond to atmospheric pressure. An asthmatic crisis both feels and in fact is life threatening. Evidently the mannikin is not a direct proxy for the narrator's asthma, since the same pressure drop that delights one exacerbates the other. Still what might be called the mannikin's aesthetic response, an access to happiness, is intimately linked with the narrator's simplest drive, the drive to breathe, and the threat to its satisfaction.

In this connection I can borrow an image from the Hungarian-born psychoanalyst Michael Balint (1896–1970), who studied with Sándor Ferenczi and was, following Ferenczi, a pioneer in what is now called object-relations psychology. In his final book, *The Basic Fault* (1968), Balint distinguishes between two forms of transferential relation, one malignant (in his terminology) and the other benign. The one he calls malignant is essentially the transference described by Freud: Oedipally structured, seductive, essentially rivalrous, "aimed at gratification by external action" of the transferential object, and based, like neurosis, on the conflicts surrounding an already salient genital desire. I assume the reason Balint calls it malignant, given the medical implication of that word, is that it is, like cancer cells, immortal, self-replicating, and insatiable, involving the "constant threat of an unending spiral of demands or needs, and of development of addiction-like states"—resembling Oedipal dynamics, at least a Lacanian version of them, in each of these respects.[14] Freud prescribes that this transference must be frustrated; in fact, being insatiable, it's unable to be other than frustrated. This malignantly spreading, Oedipal transference corresponds in many ways to the excruciating erotic situation of Proust's narrator, who—as in his relationship with Albertine—can desire another only as she makes him jealous, but experiences jealousy as the spiraling demand for a total control that cannot be achieved and would terminate his desire if it ever were. Swann's desire for Odette and Charlus's for Morel seem, as both René Girard and Roland Barthes make clear, to follow the same laws as the narrator's desire for Albertine.[15]

While for Freud the only model of transference is this malignant one, Balint envisions an additional kind of transference that he calls benign. Like a nonmalignant growth, it is benign because its requirements do not expand: it is satiable. Once its needs have been met, this kind of transference allows the subject's attention to turn elsewhere, including inward and toward possibilities of change. Neither competitively nor genitally organized, the benign transference does not demand to be gratified by "external action" on the part of its object. Instead, Balint writes, what it requires from its object is a mode of being, specifically the mode of being that characterizes the natural elements. It "presupposes an environment that accepts and consents to sustain and carry the patient like the earth or the water sustains and carries a man who entrusts his weight to them. In contrast to ordinary objects, especially to ordinary human objects, no action is expected from these primary objects or substances; yet they must be there and must — tacitly or explicitly — consent to be used, otherwise the patient cannot achieve any change: without water it is impossible to swim, without earth impossible to move on." [16]

It's worth noting here that in requiring support from the elements, the subject also lays a claim on their reliable ability to resist pressure from it or damage by it. In Barbara Johnson's paraphrase of Winnicott, "The object becomes real because it survives, because it is outside the subject's range of omnipotent control." [17] Elsewhere in his book Balint uses air and even fire, in addition to water and earth, to exemplify the "friendly substances" for this purpose. "It is difficult to say," for example, "whether the air in our lungs or in our guts is us, or not us; and it does not even matter. We inhale the air, take out of it what we need, and after putting into it what we do not want to have, we exhale it, and we do not care at all whether the air likes it or not. It has to be there for us in adequate quantity and quality" — adequate, Balint would emphasize, as opposed to infinite. [18]

The human need for air is satiable because, like the needs to drink, eat, and excrete, but unlike the libido, it is a biological drive in the strongest sense of the term: unlike sexual desire, for example, its satisfaction is necessary to sustain individual life. [19] And unlike Oedipally structured sexuality, it is not intrinsically organized around rivalry or mediation. The need to breathe, to eat and drink, to have one's weight supported are nonnegotiable, but being finite and satiable, they are not zero sum: except in extreme situations, one is rarely deprived by the satisfaction of another's need. Balint's interest in existential or survival-implicating functions, which he links to the weather elements — air, water, earth, and fire — is held in common by the pioneers of object-relations psychology. Like Ferenczi and Winnicott, Balint likes to attach friendly language to such "benign" or satiable object relations — what he also calls "the harmonious mix-up,"[20] and Winnicott calls the "holding environment" — the one where, as Winnicott hauntingly points out, it becomes possible for the infant to think about *something else*, something beyond the mother's care.[21]

But as the work of Melanie Klein, among others, reminds us, the truth or phantasy that the conditions of actual survival are at stake can also inject the kind of terror attached to survival into situations that traditional psychoanalysis would read in the more structurally mediated, less affectively drenched terms of anxiety. Using the leverage of more recent theories of affect, you could say that there is a gain in distinguishing, as Freud does not, between affect and drive. It is exactly by taking these existential functions, rather than libido, to represent drive in its existential urgency, that object-relations psychology becomes free to do justice to the qualitative intensity, the all-encompassing experience of the affects themselves.

Hence, the lacerating quality of Proust's narrator's inability to sleep in an unfamiliar space — as though the environment threatened not his desires but his life — feels less like the fear of having to share someone's sexual favors than like the asthmatic's fear of being unable to breathe. I would argue that even the mortal dread he feels, in childhood, at having to go to bed without his mother's kiss derives its quality and rhythm much more from a threatened existential function, such as breathing, than from a frustrated second-order drive, such as libido. Klein uses the phrase "total situation" to name the global, exclusive permeation of experience by the affective states of desolation or well-being:

> Quivering with emotion, I could not take my anguished eyes from my mother's face, which would not appear that evening in the bedroom where I could see myself already lying, and I wished only that I were lying dead. And this state would persist until the morrow, when . . . I would leap out of bed to run down at once into the garden, with no thought of the fact that evening must return, and with it the hour when I must leave my mother. And so it was . . . that I learned to distinguish between these states which reign alternately within me, during certain periods, going so far as to divide each day between them, the one returning to dispossess the other with the regularity of a fever: contiguous, and yet so foreign to one another, so devoid of means of communication, that I can no longer understand, or even picture to myself, in one state what I have desired or dreaded or accomplished in the other. (1:258)

Which is to suggest that even the undoubted centrality of Oedipal issues in Proust may owe much more than has been obvious to an unattenuated emphasis on the existential functions, the simple need for the elements of life "to be there for us in adequate quantity and quality," in Balint's words — "to consent to be used." [22]

What kind of intersubjectivity — of object relation — is apt to characterize a human barometer like Proust's narrator? To begin with, as we noted earlier, *to be* a human barometer seems to involve *containing* a human barometer, the little mannikin inside. And even the simplest mechanical barometer, with its pressure-indexing column sequestered by a vacuum, reproduces this structure of "X within X" or "an X surrounded by X." In this respect the barometer, whether mechanical or human, is like "the glass jars which the village boys used to lower into the Vivonne to catch minnows . . . filled by the stream, in which they in their turn were enclosed, at once 'containers' whose transparent sides were like solidified water and 'contents' plunged into a still larger container of liquid" (1:237). In a certain Gothic tradition and in, for example, the parts of Proust that emphasize the closet melodramas of sexual privacy, there is a lot of uncanny stress attached to a rigid, nearly impassable barrier between the inner X and the outer. [23] More characteristically in Proust, though, a creature is seen as plunging vitally into, navigating through, or resting in the midst of an element — water, air — that constitutes as well as surrounds and supports it. The intervening membrane represents a minimal obstruction if any. In this more relaxed view, as Balint says, "It is difficult to say whether the air in our lungs or in our guts is us, or not us; and it does not even matter." [24]

There's a powerfully resonant instance of this inner/outer flow when the narrator's dying grandmother, struggling to breathe, is attached to an oxygen tank:

When I returned I found myself in the presence of a sort of miracle. . . . [M]y grandmother's breath no longer laboured, no longer whined, but, swift and light, glided like a skater towards the delicious fluid. Perhaps the breath, imperceptible as that of the wind in the hollow stem of a reed, was mingled in this song with some of those more human sighs which, released at the approach of death, suggest intimations of pain or happiness in those who have already ceased to feel, and came now to add a more melodious accent, but without changing its rhythm, to that long phrase which rose, soared still higher, then subsided, to spring up once more, from the alleviated chest, in pursuit of the oxygen. (3:463–64)

But it isn't only the release of near death that stimulates such a flow; the grandmother has been identified as a fresh-air fiend (and fellow animated barometer) in innumerable ways since we first met her "pacing the deserted rain-lashed garden, pushing back her disordered grey locks so that her forehead might be freer to absorb the health-giving draughts of wind and rain. She would say, 'At last one can breathe!' and would trot up and down the sodden paths . . . her keen, jerky little step regulated by the various effects wrought upon her soul by the intoxication of the storm" (1:12).

At once stoutly distinctive as a personality and endowed with an unusual osmotic gift, the grandmother is far from being only a consumer of natural forces — at least in the narrator's eyes. She embodies an entire ecology of loving energy that animates *him* from both inside and out, assuaging his vulnerable sense of bodily borders not by consolidating his borders but by supporting their flexibility and permeability. When he first arrives at the hotel in Balbec, for example, "Having no world, no room, no body now that was not menaced by the enemies thronging round me, penetrated to the very bones by fever, I was alone, and longed to die. Then my grandmother came in, and to the expansion of my constricted heart there opened at once an infinity of space" (2:334). "To the expansion of my constricted heart there opened at once an infinity of space" — picturing this space, one places it internally and externally at the same time. And as grandson and grandmother are staying in adjacent hotel rooms, the wall between them, on which they knock softly to communicate in the mornings, becomes as eloquent a membrane as if it demarcated the chambers of single ear, or heart: "sweet morning moment which opened like a symphony with the rhythmical dialogue of my three taps, to which the thin wall of my bedroom, steeped in love and joy, grown melodious, incorporeal, . . . responded with three other taps, eagerly awaited, repeated once and again, in which it contrived to waft to me the soul of my grandmother, whole and perfect, and the promise of her coming, with the swiftness of an annunciation and a musical fidelity" (2:338).

Whatever else we make of such elastic, permeable boundaries of individuation in Proust, they are exactly the right medium in which to articulate the Plotinian understanding of a universal soul, reality, nous, or good that, like Buddha nature, both surrounds and animates the individual, both directly and through the mediation of tutelary spirits. "The Universal circuit is like a breeze, and the voyager, still or stirring, is carried forward by it."[25] It's true that the Neoplatonic universe is characterized by an un-Proustian hierarchy of levels of derivation and value.[26] But the most distinctive thing about Neoplatonic hierarchy, like its Buddhist parallels, is that it arises from the very fullness of its highest terms as they permeate the universe, rather than—as in Gnosticism or Christianity—from a scarcity of the good or a struggle between good and evil.[27] And as we'll see, Proust has an unusual aptitude (shared, for that matter, with Plotinus) for replotting linear, genetic, or hierarchical narratives as images, instead, of synchronic profusion and companionship—most especially, self-companionship.

Like Buddhism, Neoplatonic thought can be framed in terms associated with atheism, deism, monotheism, polytheism, or pantheism, depending on how one understands deity. Proust makes the most of all these possibilities except monotheism. After Plotinus's death some of his followers, consciously trying to construct a syncretic pagan metaphysics, further proliferated and further distinguished more-or-less-divine entities at multiple ontological levels, including the non-sentient: "a stone, a plant, a smell, or a song."[28] Within, around, and also against Christianity, this complex, cosmopolitan field of divinity became influential again in the Renaissance through the humanism of the Florentine Academy, through iconographies of architecture and art, and through poets like Ronsard, who welcomed "all divinities—whether from Asia, Greece, Rome, or Egypt, whether primitive, classical, or decadent."[29]

It's hard to convey through a few examples how this vast and varied divinity-field, the unsystematized proliferation of ontologically intermediate beings loosely attached—at once inside and outside—to places, persons, families, substances, ideas, music, buildings, machines, emotions, and natural elements, feels as one immerses oneself in reading Proust. Surprisingly pervasive, surprisingly easy to lose sight of, like the weather, the divinity-field characterizes the vital atmosphere of Proust reading more than its landmark moments. Neither omniscient nor omnipotent, local rather than omnipresent, these beings lack the somber sublimity of monotheistic deity. Theirs is not the dimension of "laws" or "truths" or of truth or the Law. Sometimes their invocation sounds like a kind of throwaway erudition, a sublimed version of the honking, mock-heroic cant that emanates from the narrator's friend Bloch. Sometimes it sounds like a fine French gallantry, where every woman is a goddess and most men too. Often it makes a shimmering play of capturing as if in motion the very processes of condensation and precipitation that animate any imaginative project of writing. As when

> I suddenly discerned at my feet, crouching among the rocks for protection against the heat, the marine goddesses . . . , the marvellous Shadows, sheltering furtively, nimble and silent, ready at the first glimmer of light to slip behind the stone, to hide in a cranny, and prompt, once the menacing ray had passed, to return to the rock or the seaweed over whose torpid slumbers they seemed to be keeping vigil, beneath the sun that crumbled the cliffs and the etiolated ocean, motionless lightfoot guardians darkening the water's surface with their viscous bodies and the attentive gaze of their deep blue eyes. (2:689)

This embodied divinity-field overlaps in a myriad of ways, at many different angles, with both the Neoplatonic and the even more varied Proustian understandings of transmigration. It shows, in fact, that for Proust the interest in transmigration is often fed much less by a focus on succession and causation than by one on simultaneity, recognition, and an unimaginable diversity of companionship and self-companionship. Among the ontologically exceptional beings, besides plain vanilla gods and goddesses, that the divinity-field comprises in Proust are giants (2:168), phantoms (1:326), sirens, devils (both 1:494), demigods (2:356), fairies (2:358), Nereids (2:387), Oceanides (2:408), witches, Norns (both 2:407), monsters (2:423), nymphs (2:724), peris (2:511), shawabti (3:39), sorceresses, Danaides, Furies (all 3:174), fire spirits, magicians (both 3:122), Arabian rocs (3:548), ghosts (3:178, 468), sphinxes (3:711), sibyls (5:334), dryads (5:345), household gods (5:705), river gods (6:244), druids (6:520), Pythian priestesses (4:119), Parcae (3:263), Brahmas (4:481), Eumenides (2:103), prophets, apostles, angels, the incarnate Word, the Eternal Father (all 4:597), and the universal spirit (6:301) — to name only a few.

In addition, there is a family of particularly interesting beings that can be traced through a cluster of words around *daimon* in Greek, *genius* in Latin, and the obviously but obscurely related *jinni* in Arabic. Over many centuries of transmission and displacement, these terms have come to indicate varied, even contradictory meanings — think of how *daimon* stands for both a malevolent demon, on the one hand, and on the other the tutelary spirit that repeatedly materializes to warn Socrates of hidden danger. Plotinus, like Proust, has a special interest in these spirits, especially in their guardian or tutelary functions. In Plotinus, each individual in each new incarnation, whatever its spiritual level, has an accompanying *daimon* or genius who represents the next higher spiritual level. "The *Timaeus*," he writes, "indicates the relation of this guiding spirit to ourselves: it is not entirely outside of ourselves; is not bound up with our nature; is not the agent of our action; it belongs to us as belonging to our Soul." [30]

The Latin phrase *genius loci*, or spirit of the place, is the only form in which English speakers still hear "genius" used in this sense: a spiritual familiar, like the "guardian" shadows in the passage I've quoted above, who, like the air and water that we breathe and drink, both animates from within and stands as distinct from the place or person to whom it belongs. These tutelary beings may manifest themselves only for the blink of an eye, or may develop a sustained and modulating presence. Their ontology is like that of the internal object in Melanie Klein: in the words of one Kleinian, "a part of the world lodged within, which both becomes identity and yet differs from what the individual feels to be himself." [31] A few examples of the many: the wind that is the "tutelary genius" of Combray (1:204); the invisible familial "genie" who, in the face of the Duchesse de Guermantes's socialist beliefs, nonetheless "reminded the servants of this woman who did not believe in titles to address her as 'Madame la Duchesse'" (3:602); the "Venus Androgyne" (4:434) that, for the likes of M. de Charlus, "is always the spirit of a relative of the female sex, attendant like a goddess, or incarnate as a double, that undertakes to introduce him into a strange drawing-room" (4:414). There are even genii to explain the mystery of gaydar: "Each man's vice . . . accompanies him after the manner of the tutelary spirit who was invisible to men so long as they were unaware of his presence. . . . Ulysses himself did not recognise Athena at first. But the gods are immediately perceptible to one another, like as quickly to like, and so too had M. de Charlus been to Jupien" (4:18).

And if our familiars consent to such quotidian offices of courtship, it is no surprise that they also continually mediate our experience of art. As when, recognizing the "little phrase" of Vinteuil's sonata, "Swann felt its presence like that of a protective goddess, a confidante of his love, who, in order to be able to come to him through the crowd and to draw him aside to speak to him, had disguised herself in this sweeping cloak of sound. And as she passed, light, soothing, murmurous as the perfume of a flower, telling him what she had to say, every word of which he closely scanned, regretful to see them fly away so fast, he made involuntarily with his lips the motion of kissing, as it went by him, the harmonious, fleeting form" (1:494). Characteristically, too, while the tutelary presence of the little phrase condenses outside of him, it affects his internal geography as well. "The little phrase, as soon as it struck his ear, had the power to liberate in him the space that was needed to contain it; the proportions of Swann's soul were altered; a margin was left for an enjoyment that corresponded no more than his love for Odette to any external object and yet was not, like his enjoyment of that love, purely individual" (1:335).

II

The French word *génie*, which Proust uses a lot to designate such divinities, is much more elastic than any one of its English cognates or equivalents. It continues to yoke together the modern English meanings of "genius" — unique brilliance, or someone uniquely brilliant — with the meaning, still current in French, of tutelary spirit, such as the *genius loci*. But *génie* bears in addition all the meanings that English assigns to genies or genii, from the Arabic *jinni* or djinn — very much including the strong association of those terms with the *Arabian Nights*. Now, critics have noted how the *Arabian Nights* mobilizes all kinds of meanings in the *Recherche*. It is the formative reading of the narrator's childhood; the all-but-native mythology of the French folk, as illustrated by the much-loved Aladdin, Sinbad, and Ali Baba cake plates belonging to his great-aunt; the very emblem, at the same time, of Oriental exoticism; and finally a significant model for the narrative task of the *Recherche* itself.[32] But it seems true additionally, so pervasive is this genius/genie figure in Proust's universe, to say that the novel's Neoplatonic element and that of the *Arabian Nights* become nearly coextensive in the figure of the *génie*.

Even though their worlds overlap so substantially, two tendencies often distinguish the *Arabian Nights*'s genie from the tutelary genius of Neoplatonism. The Oriental genie, for all its exoticism, is earthier, not disdaining the most pragmatic or even vulgar forms of magic. A shape-shifter itself, the genie is good for making people invisible, guiding them through labyrinths, teleporting them around the world, transforming their appearance or even species, and endowing them with fabulous wealth (all feats performed by genies in the allusive prose of the *Recherche*). And its reason for performing such services also tends to be more explicit: it has no choice in the matter. For all their extraordinary powers, genii are caught up, like people, in the cycle of strength and weakness, death and rebirth.[33] Genii are especially prone to get entrapped in objects—flasks, stone pillars, signet rings, and, notoriously, brass lamps—and whoever comes to own the object also comes into ownership of the genie and its powers.[34] Thus a distinctive psychopolitical, master-slave dimension of relationality opens up. The tutelary genius, unmotivated except by the universal Good, occupies an economy of plenitude, of gifts without exchange, and of nondualistic relations between internal and external. To the genie, on the other hand, giving its godlike support to a person may also signify its servitude. It is firmly external rather than internal to the person whose wishes are its command. It can be resistant: truculent or actively malicious in interpreting those wishes. Even where that is not the case, it becomes clear that genies are available, unlike tutelary gods, to be viewed through the lens of motivation. The nature of their ties to "their" people and places, once those ties are not metaphysically self-evident, can become an affectively potent space for speculation, longing, and *ressentiment*.

The enslaved genie, displaying its distinctive mix of superpowers with radical subordination, is also fertile ground for exploring an important dynamic of omnipotence and powerlessness that emerges from the work of Melanie Klein. In Freud's view, notoriously, our relation to omnipotence is pretty simple: we want as much power as we can get and start out thinking we are omnipotent; everything after that is the big, disillusioning letdown called reality. Yet in a sense, Freudian analytic theory, especially in its more structural or Lacanian aspects, never lets go of an implicit view that power of any sort or degree is equivalent to omnipotence. What changes with maturity and Oedipalization is the view of whom or what you have power over, rather than the understanding of power per se *as* omnipotence. Okay, maybe you can't own Mommy, but once you figure out about substitution, you can own some other woman substituted for her; and if you get as far as sublimation, you can have that same relation to a field of achievement. One Freudian way of reading Proust: he can't own Mommy; he can't own the succession of women he falls in love with, not even the last one, Albertine, whom he imprisons and keeps subject to his will; but he finally finds that in the world of his art, he can be omnipotent. I think this explains why psychoanalytically structured readings of Proust have often found the novel's ending stiflingly marmoreal: the story of a successfully consolidated omnipotence.

For the Kleinian subject, however, unlike the Freudian one, omnipotence is a fear at least as much as it is a wish. It is true here that the infant's self and its constituent parts, like others and their parts, can only be experienced as either helpless or omnipotent. The problem is that the infant's desires are passionately experienced but intrinsically self-contradictory. Instead of the undifferentiatedly blind, pleasure- and power-seeking drives of the Freudian infant, which encounter no check but the originally external ones of prohibition or lack, the Kleinian infant experiences a greed whose aggressive and envious component is perceived as posing a mortal threat both to her loved and needed objects and to herself. Thus the perception of oneself as omnipotent is hardly less frightening than the perception of one's parent as being so.

In fact, this all-or-nothing understanding of agency is toxic enough that it is a relief and relaxation for the child to discover a different reality. The sense that power is a form of relationality that deals in, for example, habits, negotiations, and small differentials, the middle ranges of agency — the notion that you can be relatively empowered or disempowered without annihilating someone else or being annihilated, or even castrating or being castrated — is a great mitigation of that endogenous anxiety, although it is something that requires to be discovered over and over.

By analogy, think how you feel when somebody who arrives on an overwrought scene you're involved in tells you, "It's not all about you." If you're like me, you may experience this as a strong rebuke. At the same time — or at least not too very long afterward — you can feel with gratitude how these words open up a more spacious view of relations than you had been acting from, and can free you from the grip of a painfully infantile sense of how you had been threatened and how you could respond.

It is not surprising, then, that the ontologically intermediate, tutelary spirits in Proust have this chastening, merciful reality principle, the extenuation of omnipotence, among the good things in their gift. In volume I, for example, when the narrator has fallen in love with Gilberte, he convinces himself that his desire to be loved is powerful enough to compel her to avow her love for him. Yet this sense of omnipotence is feverishly agitating and self-dividing. "Every evening I would beguile myself by imagining . . . [her] letter [avowing her love], believing that I was actually reading it, reciting each of its sentences in turn. Suddenly I would stop in alarm. I had realised that if I was to receive a letter from Gilberte, it could not, in any case, be this letter, since it was I myself who had just composed it. And from then on I would strive to divert my thoughts from the words which I should have liked her to write to me, for fear that, by voicing them, I should be excluding just those words—the dearest, the most desired—from the field of possibilities" (1:581).

But another being, and one with a different kind of creative skill, is lodged invisibly inside of him and taking no part in this manic defense via omnipotence. "While my love, incessantly waiting for the morrow to bring the avowal of Gilberte's for me, destroyed, unravelled every evening the ill-done work of the day, in some shadowed part of my being an unknown seamstress refused to abandon the discarded threads, but collected and rearranged them, without any thought of pleasing me or of toiling for my happiness, in the different order which she gave to all her handiwork. Showing no special interest in my love, not beginning by deciding that I was loved, she gathered together those of Gilberte's actions that had seemed to me inexplicable and her faults which I had excused. Then, one and all, they took on a meaning" (1:583). Their meaning is simply Gilberte's indifference to him. And while in one view the unknown seamstress may be an avatar of the fatal Clotho or Atropos, in another she is a more modest servitor entirely; and her effect on the young narrator is to offer a modestly relaxing clarification of reality.

The figure of the servant-god, then, is full of possible meanings that involve both omnipotence and helplessness, and their mitigation. To detour from Proust for a moment, I encountered one distilled vision of servant-god relationality in William Kentridge's production of Monteverdi's opera, *Il ritorno d'Ulisse in patria*, performed, bunraku style, with near-life-size puppets manipulated by dark-clad but quite visible onstage puppeteers.[35] Leaving aside the singing, the instrumental music, and Kentridge's concurrent video projection—this was quite a densely spectacular production—the puppeteering itself, by the Handspring Puppet Theater of South Africa, gave an almost unbearable immediacy to the sense at once of the puppeteers' complete power over the puppets, and at the same time their radical subordination to them. For instance, in this production the entire action seemed meant to be a hallucination of the dying Ulysses on the beach of Ithaca. The only way this was indicated was that, during the whole time the other characters (including a second Ulysses puppet) went through the opera's robust action, the first Ulysses lay onstage, invisible to them and almost to the audience, speechless and songless, occasionally struggling to move or turn over, in an unchanging state of illness and exhaustion. That is: unchanging except for the barely perceptibly smoothing and roughening tides of breath imparted to his abandoned frame by the puppeteer, who, with the humility and absolute absorption of a *stabat mater*, devoted every atom of his attention throughout those hours to maintaining the tenuous thread of the dying man's illusionary life.

Any bunraku performance features the puppeteers as tutelary deities in thrall to the material creatures to which they give life. Indeed, the puppeteers' immersion in this field of devotional skill is a defining plea-sure of seeing bunraku: the way their faces are mostly a mask of somber absorption in the exercise of their art, but very occasionally, uncon-sciously become expressive of the emotion they are trying to convey to the insentient body of the puppet, as a mother will gape her mouth invitingly when she conveys a spoonful of food to the lips of her child. But as Lee Breuer writes on the same topic, the black-hooded pup-peteers also "symbolize the fates in the image of a medieval 'Death' controlling every movement of the 'man-puppet.'"[36] And in this early opera derived from Homer, where the other hands that (figuratively) manipulate these adult characters' fates are those of the fond or vindic-tive gods—literal gods, quarreling childishly over their human favor-ites—the play of absolute dependency with power, tenderness, and envy unfolded in many dimensions.

Over the volumes and decades of Proust's *Recherche*, the being who crystallizes these servant-god relations most starkly is the longtime family cook and housekeeper, Françoise. If readers haven't been eager to think much about Françoise, I conjecture it's a result of the em-barrassment of encountering the narrator's condescension toward her and, much worse, his praise. There are passages that reduce the liveli-est students in my Proust class to a sullen silence. "Of thought," Proust writes for example, "in relation to Françoise, one could hardly speak. She knew nothing, in that absolute sense in which to know nothing means to understand nothing, except the rare truths to which the heart is capable of directly attaining. The vast world of ideas did not exist for her. But when one studied the clearness of her gaze . . . one was dis-quieted, as one is by the frank, intelligent eyes of a dog" (2:309–10).

In the context of Proustian high cogency I can only think of a pas-sage like that as a kind of stink bomb of banality, defensively lobbed to keep intruders away from an otherwise unsecured entrance to primi-tive levels of psychic dread. These dynamics are especially prominent in the less-read middle volumes of the novel. Françoise, who is offered to us through a series of conventionally "placing" archetypes of servi-tude and nationality—salt of the earth, artist in the kitchen, a comical rustic, fount of malapropisms, pure blood of France, unconscious philosopher and philologist, loyal across generations, perversely stubborn, a servant more protective of her masters' status than they are—is also the most subjectively dangerous character in the novel's world. While there is little actual hatred in Proust's novel, Françoise, the loyal retainer and very embodiment of dependency, hates and is hated. Her servitude is finally almost all there is about her, but the sense of ontological difference that wants to compare her to a dog seems a defensive displacement of another truth: her servitude makes of her a god. I think the narrator could increasingly say of her what he says of Habit, another domestic servant, recognized at last as "a dread deity, so riveted to one's being, its insignificant face so incrusted in one's heart, that if it detaches itself, if it turns away from one, this deity that one had barely distinguished inflicts on one sufferings more terrible than any other and is then as cruel as death itself" (5:564–65).

The narrator could say such a thing about Françoise, but actually he does not. She strangely persists as a cognitively disruptive force in the novel—that is, she makes it stupider—evoking litanies of "facetious" complaint or sugary tolerance on the topic of Servant Trouble that repeatedly disorganize the narrative. Here is a sample of some narrative tonalities on the subject:

> What compassionate declamations I should have provoked from Françoise if she had seen me cry. I carefully hid myself from her. Otherwise I should have had her sympathy. But I gave her mine. We do not put ourselves sufficiently in the place of these poor maidservants who cannot bear to see us cry, as though crying hurt us; or hurt them, perhaps. . . . We dislike high-sounding phrases, asseverations, but we are wrong, for in that way we close our hearts to the pathos of country folk, to the legend which the poor serving woman, dismissed, unjustly perhaps, for theft, pale as death, grown suddenly more humble as if it were a crime merely to be accused, unfolds, invoking her father's honesty, her mother's principles, her grandmother's admonitions. It is true that those same servants who cannot bear our tears will have no hesitation in letting us catch pneumonia because the maid downstairs likes draughts and it would not be polite to her to shut the windows. . . . Even the humble pleasures of servants provoke either the refusal or the ridicule of their masters. For it is always a mere nothing, but foolishly sentimental, unhygienic. And so they are in a position to say: "I only ask for this one thing in the whole year, and I'm not allowed it." And yet their masters would allow them far more, provided it was not stupid and

dangerous for them — or for the masters themselves. To be sure, the humility of the wretched maid, trembling, ready to confess the crime that she has not committed, saying "I shall leave tonight if you wish," is a thing that nobody can resist. But we must learn also not to remain unmoved, despite the solemn and threatening banality of the things that she says, her maternal heritage and the dignity of the family "kaleyard," at the sight of an old cook draped in the honour of her life and of her ancestry, wielding her broom like a sceptre, putting on a tragic act, her voice broken with sobs, drawing herself up majestically. That afternoon, I remembered or imagined scenes of this sort which I associated with our old servant, and from then onwards . . . I loved Françoise with an affection, intermittent it is true, but of the strongest kind, the kind that is founded upon pity. (4:239–40)

The severely disorganized structure of this passage only barely conceals the transition from the narrator's adamant refusal of Françoise's pity, as it begins, to his claim that pity is the strongest basis of love — his for her — with which it ends. It does obscure the complete factitiousness of the mawkish scenes by whose rehearsal he works up his pity. There is no question of Françoise's ever having been anything but honest, and if the narrator "remember[s]" "scenes of this sort" they are borrowed from the senescent, cruel, and sadly transparent fantasies of his Aunt Leonie, many years before. What deranges such a passage is more than anything its repudiatory overkill. She doesn't pity me, I pity her. She doesn't accuse me, in fact I accuse her. Perhaps falsely, perhaps maliciously. But, never cruel, in fact unusually compassionate, I put myself in her suffering place. And you ought to, too — even though everything that concerns her is laughably insignificant. Except that, as it happens, she could actually kill me and happily would. And again through the identical round of self-canceling protestations to the final declaration of love.

In Kleinian terms, these sentences seem to be largely at the mercy of the paranoid/schizoid position and haplessly exhibit its primitive defenses. The paranoid/schizoid position, founded in the terrible anxiety and dependence of early infancy, with its unmodulated fantasies of powerlessness and omnipotence, of greedy destruction and looming revenge, is dominated by the paired defenses of projection and splitting. I'm not abject, she is; she doesn't accuse me, I accuse her; I don't want to kill her, she wants to kill me — the purest distillates of projection. Where the splitting comes in (aside from the way it structures the stark dichotomies of projection itself) is less obvious but, I think, even more important, and I'll get to that in a minute. If we continue looking at this passage through Kleinian eyes, though, we can see that the primitive defenses of the paranoid/schizoid position are actually being invoked in the service of strengthening the narrator's hold — apparently tenuous at this point — on what Klein calls the depressive position. The depressive position, first experienced in later infancy, is a developmental achievement that helps the infant or adult calm the awful storms of the paranoid/schizoid world. To mitigate the paranoid/schizoid terror of actually destroying the source of nurturance through one's greed and aggression, there comes the depressive resource of pitying it, and holding it protectively inside of one in order to try and make it better. In Klein's understanding, this discovery opens up, along with a significant assuagement of the original dread, both new anxieties — including open ambivalence and the preconditions for severe depression — and also the whole world of creative possibility.

At the moment of this paragraph, however, the opening to creative possibility seems very distant. From his repetitive and weirdly homiletic evocations it's clear that the narrator's access even to the initiatory experience of pity, hard as he tries to compass it, is forced and brittle under the pressure of paranoid/schizoid fears and defenses.

While there are other passages in which the subject of Françoise has a similar fragmenting and degenerative effect on the writerly fabric of the *Recherche*, of course it's more characteristic for Proust to write from the security of his achieved, elastic style, sparkling with speculation and insight, and more securely located within the depressive position, about the paranoid/schizoid effects that stream between the narrator and Françoise. Her local omniscience and malice become a joke, but a persistent one. He writes about her "clairvoyant hatred" (5:493), and her moral code in which "to wish for the death of an enemy, or even to inflict it, is not forbidden" (5:11). Relishing the suggestion of cannibalism he writes, "I never in my life experienced a humiliation without having seen beforehand on her face the signs of ready-made condolences. . . . For she knew the truth. She refrained from uttering it, and made only a slight movement with her lips as if she still had her mouth full and was finishing a tasty morsel" (3:79).[37]

A minute ago, talking about the intensely projective dynamics between the narrator and Françoise, I deferred the question of how their relation embodied that other primitive defense of the paranoid/schizoid position, splitting. Klein saw the threatened self as prone to split both its objects and itself into very concretely imagined part-objects that can only be seen as exclusively, magically good or bad—where these are not in the first place ethical designations but qualitative judgments perceived as involving life or death. The most famous version of splitting is the infantile defensive separation of good mother/bad mother, or good breast/bad breast. (A friend suggests that in middle age this turns into good back/bad back.) This is where I would place Françoise: it seems clear that in many places in Proust, Françoise rather starkly represents the bad mother, and one whose presence in the novel, like that of the mother herself, persists well into the narrator's artistically productive adulthood.

In a way, nothing could be less surprising than to find the servant-god as Bad Mother in this novel that proceeds so intently under the sign of idealized maternal love. If my way of understanding Françoise's role is not already a critical commonplace—though I don't think it is—that's probably testimony to the stupefying efficacy with which Proust confuses his readers by releasing that thick fog of a painful class anxiety. The first part of this chapter discusses the beautiful language attached to the narrator's grandmother, her unusual osmotic giftedness, which seems to inhale the fiercest weather and exhale it in the form of a sustaining and space-making maternal devotion to her grandson. As I said then, she seems to concentrate in herself the possibility of a dependency without anxiety, the "benign transference" described by Michael Balint, offering in herself (in his words) "an environment that accepts and consents to sustain and carry the patient like the earth or the water sustains and carries a man who entrusts his weight to them," or like the air that we breathe without caring whether it is inside or outside of us.[38]

If this elemental mode of love and sustenance is the novel's version of good mothering, then it seems natural enough that the narrator receives it from not one but two good mothers—his grandmother and his mother—insofar as transindividuality marks its very nature. There is no reason why the Neoplatonic oversoul, all plenitude, should not precipitate any number of tutelary deities. Over the first couple of volumes of the novel, moreover, only one human figure usually performs the full maternal goddess function at a time. Like the tag team of Cordelia and the fool in *King Lear*, the grandmother and mother can be suspected of being played by the same actor—at least, we hardly see them together. And seeing each of them under the aspect of her maternal relation to the narrator, we have no reason to imagine a complexity of dynamic between the two of them. While Françoise grows into her parallel role of the antimother, the mother and grandmother, under the aegis of Mme de Sévigné, take turns embodying and redoubling the magnetic field of (what Winnicott will call) the maternal holding environment.

The crisis of the grandmother's illness and death in *The Guermantes Way* shatters this apparent benign equilibrium. Grandmother, mother, narrator, and Françoise in the same space, and under pressure of the grandmother's own debility, depression, and dependence—it's no wonder the latent fault lines of that earlier "harmonious mix-up" (to borrow Balint's phrase) suddenly emerge with devastating clarity. Silence, shame, and pity are the form of their visibility.

If you'll forgive a quick Hollywood detour, anybody who's seen Bette Davis in her 1939 weepie, *Dark Victory*, will have been struck by the mysterious imperatives of silence that drive this narrative of terminal illness. Playing the wealthy young socialite Judith Traherne, Davis experiences dizziness and double vision while jumping her horse, whereon her immediate instruction to her best friend Ann (played by Geraldine Fitzgerald) is that her doctor—of all people—must not be informed of her neurological symptoms.

When she is finally diagnosed by a specialist, he finds that she has an inoperable brain tumor and will die within months. Nevertheless, he tells her she has recovered completely. When her friend Ann suspects he is hiding something, he confesses, but only to Ann: "I can't save her, nothing can, *nothing*. . . . She's going to die. . . ."

"Would she have no warning, no chance to be ready?"

"There may be a moment towards the end, when her sight may not be quite as good as usual, a dimming of vision. Then, a few hours—perhaps three or four. . . ."

"Oh, I don't believe it."

"Ann, *she must never know*." [39]

During the period of Bette Davis's ignorance, she and the specialist (played by George Brent) fall in love, and even after she accidentally learns of her bad prognosis they get married and move to Vermont, where he continues his brain cancer research. The inevitable climax arrives on a day when he has to return to New York in triumph to give a definitive presentation of his research. At the same time Bette Davis suddenly realizes that her eyesight is failing by the minute. Her final, beautiful achievement is, with the omnipresent connivance of Ann, to muster every artifice to send him away in perfect ignorance of the fact that she is now altogether blind and within a few minutes of her death.

Judging by *Dark Victory*, terminal illness has the function of circulating an imperative that somebody, somewhere has to be kept in the dark. In this case the doctor is kept in the dark by the patient, then the patient by the doctor, then climactically, the doctor once again by the patient. What illness pointlessly generates is the someone, the series of someones, about whom it can be urged that they *must never, never know*. You could call it a matter of hysterical blindness except that, Medusa style, it is others, not oneself, on whom this hysteria inflicts its blindness.

There's always someone who *must never, never know*: in *A la recherche du temps perdu* that is the epistemology of illness, as well, during the grandmother's final weeks. Compared to the Warner Bros. movie, the scale of time and gesture in these scenes of *The Guermantes Way* is refined almost to the subliminal. On their walk in the Champs Élysées, for example, when the narrator's grandmother has her first stroke, she speaks to him afterward only because "she thought that it would be impossible . . . not to make some answer without alarming *me*"; yet on the next page, "I was afraid of *her* noticing the strange way in which she uttered these words." Then, "she had realised that there was no need to hide *from me* what I had at once guessed"; but again a page later, "I was obliged to keep *from her* what I thought of her condition" (3:423–25; emphases added). What would this pair have thought or said on their walk if they were not occupied with such futile transactions?

During the grandmother's harrowing last illness, the circuit of projective blindness only intensifies. She struggles to conceal from her family her loss first of sight, then of hearing, then of speech. "Then came a state of perpetual agitation. She was incessantly trying to get up. But we restrained her so far as we could from doing so, for fear of *her* discovering how paralysed she was" (3:453; emphasis added). And throughout, in paranoid mode, "my mother and I . . . would not even admit that my grandmother was seriously ill, as though such an admission might give pleasure to her enemies (not that she had any)" (3:435–36).

In addition to this circulating, projective blindness, the narrator's mother brings a new imperative to the scene of illness: not only must she hide what she sees from the patient as well as vice versa, but she herself is enjoined against viewing it. On their return from the Champs Élysées, for example,

> my mother went up to my grandmother, kissed her hand as though it were that of her God, raised her up and supported her to the lift with an infinite care . . . , but not once did she raise her eyes and look at the suf-

ferer's face. Perhaps this was in order that my grandmother should not be saddened by the thought that the sight of her might have alarmed her daughter. Perhaps from fear of a grief so piercing that she dared not face it. Perhaps from respect, because she did not feel it permissible for her without impiety to notice the trace of any mental enfeeblement on those revered features. . . . So they went up side by side, my grandmother half-hidden in her shawl, my mother averting her eyes. (3:433)

But there is one member of the household who transgresses against this hygiene of projective blindness with an abandon that is all but violent: the demoniacally gifted Françoise, who has "a power, the nature of which I have never been able to fathom, for at once becoming aware of anything unpleasant" in the lives of the family (3:76). Françoise at this juncture "never took her [eyes] from what could be discerned of my grandmother's altered features at which her daughter dared not look," gaping at the patient instead with "the unfeeling roughness of the peasant who tears the wings off dragon-flies until she gets a chance to wring the necks of chickens, and lacks that sense of shame which would make her conceal the interest that she feels in the sight of suffering flesh" (3:433–34). Her exacting, unresting care for the sick woman nonetheless betrays an officious relish,[40] while for the larger family an excruciatingly complex interplay of fear and hope concerning the dying goddess emerges in and around the bumptious ministrations of Françoise.[41]

In these wracking scenes Françoise's projected role as the bad mother coalesces with a role as the bad, profaning, even murderous child. For it is only here, with the narrator's grandmother and mother onstage together at last, the mother facing demands as both mother and child, that this cluster of relationships demands to be read as triangular and rivalrous rather than being one of Plotinian plenitude. It is only from this retrospect in the third volume that one can arrive at the Oedipal formulation that Elisabeth Ladenson offers flatly in *Proust's Lesbianism*: "Rather than displaying the standard positive oedipal situation . . . the narrator both desires and identifies with the mother. The mother, too, situates desire and identification in a single object; that object, however, is not her husband, father, or son, but her own mother."[42] With the grandmother dying or dead, it becomes true—and can be read, as Ladenson unconsciously does, as a retrospective truth—that the narrator has to see himself as rivaling both his grandmother for his mother's love, and his mother for (at least the memory of) his grandmother's love. The pressure of continuing to show each of these mothers in a sacralizing light, even as both they and the narrator come under the stress of triangular rivalry, seems itself to generate Françoise, the bad mother and impious child, as a demonic precipitate.

After the grandmother's death, the mother's form of mourning becomes the most potent sign of this new Oedipal exclusivity within the now-bifurcated maternal function. The narrator's mother not only grieves for her own mother but, the narrator says, actually turns into her: "As soon as I saw her enter in her crape overcoat, I realised — something that had escaped me in Paris — that it was no longer my mother that I had before my eyes, but my grandmother" (4:228). Far from resisting, in her grief the mother treasures and cultivates her own transformation; she especially cultivates her late mother's habit of constantly quoting from Mme de Sévigné, a byword for devoted, exclusive, indeed jealous and romantically formulated mother-daughter love. In fact, the mother's mourning is a textbook illustration for Freud's analysis of melancholia, in that her conflicts around the grandmother cause the grandmother to be introjected specifically in the form of a severely inhibiting superego. Fused, "congealed into a sort of imploring image," the mother seems "to be afraid of affronting by too sudden a movement, by too loud a tone of voice, the sorrowful presence that never left her. . . . Perhaps," Proust continues, "in our regret for her who is no more, there is a sort of auto-suggestion which ends by . . . a cessation of our most characteristically individual activity": in his mother, he specifies what is lost as her "common sense and . . . mocking gaiety" (4:228–29). *Only* her common sense, and her gaiety.

In Freudian psychoanalytic theory, the melancholic introjection of a lost object in the form of the prohibitive superego remained *the* defining instance of an internal object. Internalized objects in general interest Freud much less than the internal psychic structures, such as the unconscious, that develop as a result of repression. This is one of the most consequential ways in which Klein departs from Freud. For, as we have seen, Klein's understanding of the psyche proceeds almost entirely through the relations among multiple, semi-anthropomorphic objects — what, following Proust, we have been treating in terms of deities and daemons — that are introjected plurally from the outside, projected from the inside, and constantly reintrojected and reprojected, able in themselves to damage and be damaged, to renew and be renewed. The traffic of projection and introjection is the vehicle for the primitive defenses of the paranoid/schizoid position — but also for the forms of reality orientation and creativity, through the treatment of the good internal object, that can mitigate or transfigure those defenses. The fully melancholic, Oedipal, monotheistic form of mourning practiced by the narrator's mother, with its permanent sacrifice of "common sense" and "gaiety" to the exigent new superego, is indeed what the *Recherche* offers as *the* image of mourning. But it remains to be noted that this is not the path followed by the narrator or Proust.

If anything, in this Oedipal framework, the less-mutilated narrator seems like an exemplar of the failure to grieve. But from a Kleinian perspective, the mother's own grief looks like a continuing failure to internalize the grandmother in the form of a good object, a source of nurturance or possibility, one that could foster the kind of holding environment that would allow her to think of something *else*. For the narrrator, his mother's melancholia remains a kind of pressure for the duration of the novel, a reproachful and exclusive pressure. Around his mother the new questions seem to arise: Did his grandmother care more for his mother than for him? Was his sense of his grandmother's unswerving focus on his own welfare (her "desire to preserve and enhance my life . . . altogether stronger than . . . my own" [2:335]) in fact mistaken? And can his mother, absorbed almost to distraction in her filial task of mourning, spare enough attention to care for her own son?

There are times when the narrator is assailed by both wracking grief and guilt about his grandmother's loss, as well as the additional guilt of knowing that this is his mother's constant condition. But for him such attacks represent "the heart's intermittences." He uses this phrase not to trivialize them, but to acknowledge, however sadly or guiltily, that the grandmother in this aspect is a presence among other internal presences — an object, however riveting, or even a family of objects, that comes and goes. Even after the Oedipal crystallizations that are precipitated by the scenes of his grandmother's death, his mourning for her is not a failed Oedipalized mourning. Rather it is a stubbornly successful version of an animistic, Kleinian dynamic of multiple objects, projected and internalized at many levels, encompassing new possibilities of surprise.

Both during and after the grandmother's death, as I've suggested, the complex ontological status of Françoise seems to involve her functioning not only as the narrator's split-off evil mother, but also as the split-off self of the mother in her nightmare role of impious daughter. It seems telling that the mother and Françoise disappear from the novel at around the same time — both of them before the final volume, in which the now middle-aged narrator embarks on his ambitious project of writing. But as we'll see, the maternal function, in all its creative pride and humility, is far from disappearing from the novel along with these two characters.[43]

In the early reception of the *Recherche* there was a mainstream critical consensus according to which Proust, exemplifying many writers in a modern secular world, was seen as smuggling the remnants of a repudiated religion into his work under the name of Art.[44] In fact, as I have been trying to show, there is no question of smuggling. Proust is overt in his mysticism, not despite but through the bubbling current of different tonalities and contexts in which he invokes it.[45] But while art is certainly a distinguished term in Proust, it is not, as we have seen, set apart as a focus of mystical relationality. Even its distinction depends on a view of the entire universe, whether in its sublime or quotidian aspects, as instinct with value and vitality.

That the universe along with the things in it are alive and therefore good: here, I think, is a crux of Proust's mysticism. Moreover, the formulation does not record a certainty or a belief but an orientation, the structure of a need, and a mode of perception. It is possible for the universe to be dead and worthless; but if it does not live, neither do the things in it, including oneself and one's own contents. So put it comparatively: the universe itself is *as* alive as anything it holds. This formulation is always true for Proust, and for the reason we have discussed: the beings *in* the universe are filled, in turn, like human barometers, with the stuff *of* the universe. This is as true for art as it is for the irreducibly complex systems and substances that constitute the weather.

In terms reminiscent of Melanie Klein, you could say that everything in Proust depends on the ratio or relation between an internal object and an ambient surround. Inequality between them, or a collapse of either of them, leads to a collapse of the whole ecology of value and vitality. For example, the debacle of the narrator's first attempt to kiss Albertine occurs because his manic excitement has "destroyed the equilibrium between the immense and indestructible life which circulated in my being and the life of the universe, so puny in comparison" (2:700). Similarly during his breakdown in Venice, "I saw the palaces reduced to their basic elements, lifeless heaps of marble with nothing to choose between them, and the water as a combination of hydrogen and oxygen, eternal, blind, anterior and exterior to Venice." The direct result of this vastation of his surroundings is a vastation of self. "I could no longer tell it anything about myself, I could leave nothing of myself imprinted upon it; it contracted me into myself until I was no more than a beating heart and an attention strained to follow the development of *O sole mio*" (5:884).

That the universe is as alive as anything it contains: the sustained story of the narrator's vocation, far from representing a wishful or sacralized exception in Proust's view of the universe, has just the same structure. What's most notable about the "problem" of his vocation is that it is never simply about his internal faculties—his wealth or littleness of talent, his ability to focus or the apparent waste of his early years. With the persistence of these questions he always hungers to know at the same time that art itself has a life and value that are independent of him and beyond the direct will of any artist. In fact, it is impossible—not metaphysically but, for Proust, psychologically so—for either of these questions to stand alone in the *Recherche*. The narrator's always double anxiety is that art "is something I am not . . . made for and perhaps does not even correspond to any reality" (6:240). Nor, evidently, can the sense of art as an inward supply imply rivalry with the vitality of an artistic surround; the narrator never shows the slightest fear of being diminished by art that is not his. His fear, again, is of his own talent, unliving, being held within a dead ecology of art.

For Proust, the ultimate guarantee of the vitality of art is its ability to surprise—that is, to manifest an agency distinct from either its creator or its consumer. A consummated fantasy of omnipotence would be the precise opposite of such ability to surprise and be surprised. "It pre-exists us" is one of the ways he describes the autonomy of the work (6:277), and only for that reason is it able to offer "celestial nourishment" to our true self (6:264). At the same time, that already existing, maternal plenitude is also gestated internally like a child: "I felt myself enhanced by this work which I bore within me as by something fragile and precious which had been entrusted to me" (6:513–14). Reincarnation is one way to delineate this balance of agency between the internal and external, where the true self becomes, perhaps uncannily, "this being that had been reborn [with]in me" (6:264). "The writer feeds his book, he strengthens the parts of it which are weak, he protects it, but afterwards it is the book that grows, that designates its author's tomb and defends it . . . for a while against oblivion" (6:508).

Readers of object-relations psychology will recognize in these passages of Proust the subtle crisscrossings of agency, interiority, and priority that also characterize certain crucial situations in accounts of early, generative object relations. Winnicott's good enough mother, holding environment, and transitional object, like the benign transference described by Balint, each outside the omnipotent control of the subject — each nonetheless, or for that reason, involves a vital way of environing the subject, one that inspires and permits the subject's ability, in turn, to hold its own vital contents and support a wealth of self-relation.[46] Correspondingly, for many readers of Proust, the textual experience of the *Recherche* seems to give access to a radically fruitful double movement: into an acutely enriched space of reverie, and outward with an enriched interest in the daily-changing climates of reality.

Hence also the double function of surprise in the argument I've been making about Proust. Surprise is the mark of reality, insofar as what is real — what surrounds the subject, the weather of the world — has to exceed the will of the subject, including its will to arrive at truth. At the same time, surprise with its promise of an ever-refreshed internal world is the mark not only of reality, but of the mystical orientation that allows Proust to cherish that reality. It's in this context that one might compare Proust's love of the weather with the more overtly philosophical *amor fati*, the love of fate or necessity, that Nietzsche declared to represent his own "inmost nature."[47]

Perhaps it isn't feasible to say whether a reader of Proust assumes a position inside or outside the world of the *Recherche*, held by its amplitude or supporting *it* in a web of continuous attention. Pierre Hadot's study, *Plotinus, or the Simplicity of Vision*, offers some elementary formulations that together give a good idea of how these osmotic differentiations work in Proust:

"When it passes from one inner level to another, the self always has the impression that it is losing itself."[48]

"Yet these levels do not cancel each other out; rather, it is the interaction of all of them together which constitutes our inner life."

"Although the spiritual world is within us, it is also outside us."

Like the weather.

NOTES

"The Weather in Proust" was first delivered at the English Institute on September 9, 2004. The expanded version, parts 1 and 2, was first given on November 9 and 10, 2005, at Harvard University, in conjunction with Sedgwick's (EKS's) art show "Works in Fiber, Paper, and Proust" (which opened on October 19 and closed after the Proust lectures) and a lecture on Melanie Klein (given on October 20) that lies behind "Melanie Klein and the Difference Affect Makes." The text here draws on these initial versions but depends most on the versions delivered in 2007 in Seville and at Tufts University; part 2 incorporates a section that had been tentatively titled "A Proustian Medusa." In Seville, the chapter was delivered over two days. At the end of part 1, EKS forecast part 2 in these words: "In the next installment of this project . . . , I'm going to go further in discussing Proust's divinity-field, including the demon or genie along with the *genius loci* and the tutelary companion. The servant-god will emerge as an especially interesting figure, and we'll see how Françoise comes to fill the position of not only the resentful but even the murderous servant-god. She is an underside of the buoyant guardian spirits that propel the weather elements of the *Recherche*; of the hilariously overdevoted, elemental servant goddesses Marie Gineste and Céleste Albaret;[49] and especially of the narrator's grandmother, whose 'desire to preserve and enhance my life . . . was altogether stronger than was my own' [2:335]. We'll explore the way Françoise's *ressentiment*, emerging through a female version of the Oedipal narrative, offers a figure for the zero-sum issues that seem to be deferred alike by mystical vision of a Buddhist/ Plotinian sort, on the one hand, and on the other hand by the object-relations psychology of benign transference, in Balint's phrase, or the holding environment, in Winnicott's."

Opening part 2 the next day, she summarized part 1 this way: "In yesterday's lecture, part 1 of 'The Weather in Proust,' I tried to braid together three concerns in *A la recherche du temps perdu*. The first of these concerns is the weather, a constant force of fascination, regeneration, and even transmigration in Proust. The weather is an important crux both of his preoccupation with deriving systemic, zero-sum laws from the phenomena of the world, and at the same time of his tropism toward the irreducibly contingent — the saving inexhaustibility of surprise. For the second strand, at a methodological level, I was interested in framing that weather dynamic between closed systems and open ones as a conversation between a Freudian version of psychoanalysis and Oedipal law, on the one hand, and on the other hand, the non-zero-sum, affect-based psychology of Melanie Klein and the British object-relations school. The third element in the mix is the strange and little-noted proliferation of divinities in Proust's novel — of gods and goddesses, Norns and sibyls, fairies and Brahmas, hundreds of them everywhere, drawn from a great range of cultures and attaching to every manifestation of nature and the weather, technology, and the human psyche. I argued that the profusion of such ontologically unplaceable beings seems to represent a flowering of Proust's Neoplatonic mysticism — a Neoplatonism that is neither esoteric nor occult, compassing the possibility of nondualistic relations of many important kinds: between law and contingency, the eternal and the ephemeral, the universal soul and that of the individual. Proust's multiple divinities, neither quite universal nor quite individual, at once ambient and internal, are also like the weather elements–cum–biological elements of air and heat and water. And we explored some connections between these ubiquitous divinities and the multiple, semi-anthropomorphized part objects that populate both the interior and the surround of the subject in object-relations psychology. The Plotinian notion of the tutelary genius offered us an initial way into this braid of relations."

In the longer versions of "The Weather in Proust," EKS included these acknowledgments: "I'm indebted to many people in my work on this essay, which is part of a book in progress. Among them are Michael Moon, Joshua Wilner, Hal Sedgwick, and especially two current Ph.D. students at CUNY Graduate Center: Jenny Weiss, for the stimulus of her unpublished 2003 essay 'Toward the Writing Moment,' a close reading of several passages in *The Captive*; and Gregory Mercurio, who is working on a dissertation on the Ovidian motive in Proust, among other subjects, and has been kind enough to share many of his ideas with me."

1. All citations from Marcel Proust are to book and page number in the six-volume *In Search of Lost Time*, trans. C. K. Scott Moncrieff and Terence Kilmartin, rev. D. J. Enright (New York: Modern Library, 2003).

2. See Hayden White, "The Rhetoric of Interpretation," *Poetics Today* 9, no. 2 (1988): 253–74, especially: "In a word, in the sequence of tropological modes which leads from an original metaphorical characterization of an *interpretandum*, through a metonymic reduction and a synecdochic identification, to an ironic apprehension of the figurality of the whole sequence, we have something like the plot of all possible emplotments — the meaning of which is nothing but the process of linguistic figuration itself" (271).

3. As Proust writes, "for ever and ever, without interruption, there would come, sweeping on, a flood of new Princesses de Guermantes — or rather, centuries old, replaced from age to age by a series of different women, of different actresses playing the same part and then each in her turn sinking from sight beneath the unvarying and immemorial placidity of the name, one single Princesse de Guermantes, ignorant of death and indifferent to all that changes and wounds our mortal hearts" (6:389).

4. Plotinus, *The Enneads*, ed. John Dillon, trans. Stephen McKenna (London: Penguin, 1991), 266 (4.3.12).

5. Ibid., 277 (4.3.24).

6. Rodney Farnsworth, *Mediating Order and Chaos: The Water-Cycle in the Complex Adaptive Systems of Romantic Culture* (Amsterdam: Rodopi, 2001), 330.

7. [At this point, in the Seville text, in boldface, EKS prompts herself: "Include some over/under stuff from 'menwomen of sodom' re: weather/chaos—"]

8. René Girard, *Deceit, Desire, and the Novel: Self and Other in Literary Structure*, trans. Yvonne Freccero (Baltimore: Johns Hopkins University Press, 1965), writes with some justice: "Proust's laws are identical with the laws of triangular desire" (25).

9. As Pierre Hadot writes in *Plotinus, or The Simplicity of Vision*, trans. Michael Chase (Chicago: University of Chicago Press, 1993), "nothing can be found until it has been searched for; . . . the only way to build is to put various pieces together; and . . . it is only by using means that one can obtain an end. . . . [Reality], by contrast, . . . is able to find without searching, invents the whole before the parts, and is end and means at the same time" (41).

10. Leo Bersani (*The Culture of Redemption* [Cambridge: Harvard University Press, 1990]) and Julia Kristeva (*Proust: questions d'identité* [Oxford: European Humanities Research Centre, 1998]) are among the readers who have tried to use a different strand of psychoanalytic thought, organized around object relations, to do more justice to a Proustian reality that far exceeds Oedipal law, and some of my ambitions in this project are related to theirs.

11. Not to suggest that Plotinian and Buddhist-Hindu references are mutually exclusive. Plotinus himself, for example, joined the Roman army in middle age in order to travel, because "he became eager to investigate the Persian methods and the system adopted among the Indians" (Porphyry, quoted in Plotinus, *Enneads*, civ).

12. William Wordsworth, *The Major Works*, ed. Stephen Gill (Oxford: Oxford University Press, 2000), 299, "Ode," ll. 58–60.

13. Sleep and awakening is the context of Proust's only mention by name of Plotinus, along with his follower and amanuensis Porphyry (see V, 521).

14. Michael Balint, *The Basic Fault: Therapeutic Aspects of Regression*, foreword by Paul H. Ornstein (Evanston, Ill.: Northwestern University Press, 1992), 146.

15. See Girard, *Deceit, Desire, and the Novel*; Roland Barthes, *A Lover's Discourse*, trans. Richard Howard (New York: Hill and Wang, 1978).

16. Balint, *The Basic Fault*, 145.

17. Barbara Johnson, "Using People: Kant with Winnicott," in *The Turn to Ethics*, ed. Marjorie Garber, Beatrice Hanssen, and Rebecca L. Walkowitz (New York: Routledge, 2000), 57.

18. Balint, *The Basic Fault*, 136.

19. On this, see also my discussion of the relation of affect and drive in Silvan Tomkins in the introduction to my *Touching Feeling: Affect, Pedagogy, Performativity* (Durham: Duke University Press, 2003), 18.

20. Balint, *The Basic Fault*, 66.

21. See D. W. Winnicott, *The Maturational Processes and the Facilitating Environment* (Madison, Conn.: International University Presses, 1965).

22. Balint, *The Basic Fault*, 145. [In the English Institute version of this talk, a paragraph follows here. It reads: "As Barbara Johnson points out in her essay on Winnicott, there is no simple way to read this as a recipe for ethical intersubjectivity à la Levinas. *Used*—an inauspicious word in human relationships! I will be content at this point if we can agree that it describes an aspect of object relations that remains crucially important, both threatened and full of promise, throughout *A la recherche*."]

23. [At this point, in the Seville text, in boldface, EKS prompts herself: "insert more Charlus material here"; in the English Institute version, a note gestures to her *Epistemology of the Closet* (Berkeley: University of California Press, 1990), whose chapter on Proust, "Proust and the Spectacle of the Closet," does center on Charlus; EKS also gestures in the English Institute text to her *Coherence of Gothic Conventions* (New York: Arno, 1980), noting that her point about inside and outside is "especially true in De Quincy, who I'm convinced was an important influence on Proust."]

24. Balint, *The Basic Fault*, 136.

25. Plotinus, *Enneads*, 172 (3.4.6).

26. As Proclus articulates it, "Beyond all bodies is soul; beyond all souls the intellective principle; beyond all intellective substances, the One" (E. R. Dodds, ed., *Select Passages Illustrating Neoplatonism* [London: Macmillan, 1923] 28). Dodds emends the end of the first clause from "soul" to "the soul's essence" in his translation of proposition 20 of Proclus, *The Elements of Theology*, 2nd ed. (Oxford: Clarendon Press of Oxford University Press, 1963), 23.

27. "Every Kind must produce its next; it must unfold from some concentrated central principle as from a seed. . . . To this power we cannot impute any halt, any limit of jealous grudging; it must move for ever outward until the universe stands accomplished to the ultimate possibility. All, thus, is produced by an inexhaustible power giving its gift to the universe, no part of which it can endure to see without some share in its being. . . . There is . . . no principle that can prevent anything from partaking, to the extent of its own individual receptivity, in the nature of Good" (Plotinus, *Enneads*, 340–41 [4.8.6]).

28. Gregory Shaw, *Theurgy and the Soul: The Neoplatonism of Iamblichus* (University Park: Pennsylvania State University Press, 1995): "Anything that received the god and mediated its presence functioned as a sacred receptacle whether it was a stone, a plant, a smell, or a song" (50).

29. Jean Seznac, *The Survival of the Pagan Gods*, trans. Barbara F. Sessions (New York: Pantheon, 1953), 309, paraphrasing Paul Laumonier, *Ronsard, poète lyrique* (Paris: Hachette, 1909): "*aucune des croyances, aucune des cérémonies, de paganisme ne lui demeure étrangère. . . . Qu'elles vissent de l'Asie, de Delphes, de l'Egypte, de Rome; qu'elles fussent primitives, classiques ou décadentes, naives ou artificielles, peu lui importait*" (379). On pagan reference across Renaissance media including landscaping, see Joscelyn Godwin, *The Pagan Dream of the Renaissance* (Grand Rapids, Mich.: Phanes, 2002). On European interactions between monotheism and polytheism, especially in relation to gender, see Barbara Newman, *God and the Goddesses: Vision, Poetry, and Belief in the Middle Ages* (Philadelphia: University of Pennsylvania Press, 2003).

30. Plotinus, *Enneads*, 170 (3.4.5).

31. Meira Likierman, *Melanie Klein: Her Work in Context* (London: Continuum, 2002), 110.

32. See Robert Irwin, *Arabian Nights: A Companion* (London: Penguin, 1995), 280–81.

33. See Robert Mack, ed., *Arabian Nights' Entertainments* (Oxford: Oxford University Press, 1995), 927 n. 8.

34. Connecting genii to the Indian pantheon as well as the Koran, Irwin writes: "The notion that spirits could be controlled through correct manipulation of certain magical objects probably derives from a debased form of loosely Neoplatonic ideas popular in late antiquity" (*Arabian Nights*, 205).

35. *Il ritorno d'Ulisse in patria*, by Claudio Monteverdi, directed by William Kentridge, Lincoln Center, New York, March 2004.

36. Lee Breuer, program notes for *The Red Beads*, Mabou Mines Theater Company, created by Breuer and Basil Twist, directed by Breuer, composed by Ushio Torikai, New York University's Jack H. Skirball Center for the Performing Arts, September 2005.

37. [EKS prompts herself in a note here: "paragraph on master-slave dialectic vis-a-vis genie and Fr?"]

38. Balint, *The Basic Fault*, 145, 136.

39. Quoted from Tim Dirks, review of *Dark Victory*, directed by Edmund Goulding, Filmsite, http://www.filmsite.org/dark2.html (final emphasis added).

40. For example, "She would not allow herself . . . to be done out of her role in the ritual of these gala days" (3:437).

41. As when Françoise insists on doing her hair: "But when I came into the room I saw between the cruel hands of Françoise, as blissfully happy as though she were in the act of restoring my grandmother to health, beneath aged straggling tresses which scarcely had the strength to withstand the contact of the comb, a head which, incapable of maintaining the position into which it had been forced, was rolling about in a ceaseless whirl in which sheer debility alternated with spasms of pain" (3:454). "Françoise, with innocent brutality, brought her a mirror. I was glad for the moment that I had managed to snatch it from her in time, before my grandmother, whom we had carefully kept away from mirrors, caught even a stray glimpse of a face unlike anything she could have imagined. But alas, when, a moment later, I bent over her to kiss that beloved forehead which had been so harshly treated, she looked up at me with a puzzled, distrustful, shocked expression: she had not recognised me" (3:455). [EKS adds a note to herself in caps here—"ALSO, THE MEDUSA SCENE HERE"—and elaborates a bit: "Françoise makes HER the medusa; snakes (leeches) representing not castration, but the solar rays of recognition (including self-recognition) of which she is being shorn."]

42. Elisabeth Ladenson, *Proust's Lesbianism* (Ithaca: Cornell University Press, 2007), 116.

43. [EKS adds a note to herself here: "In expansion, stuff about vol. V, albertine/ weather/ ma/ Françoise/ vocation, omnipotence here."]

44. Edmund Wilson ("A Short View of Proust," *New Republic*, March 21, 1928, 140–48) writes that as Proust "is equipped, like many modern travelers, with moral passion but no religion, he will be compelled . . . to make a reli-

gion of art" (143). And M. H. Abrams, in *Natural Supernaturalism: Tradition and Revolution in Romantic Literature* (New York: Norton, 1971), offers Proust as the supreme modern instance of "conversion to the religion of art. . . . This vocation is to be an aesthetic evangelist" (81).

45. The question of whether, and how far, "mysticism" may be coextensive with "religion" has, of course, a dense and contentious history, in which I would be content not to meddle. That it was in the air as a question at the turn of the twentieth century, however, is attested by the 1902 publication date of William James's *Varieties of Religious Experience*. One also does not want to reify mysticism. Proust's closeness with Neoplatonism is patent, but he does not have, like Yeats, hermetic or esoteric interests; and the historical/epistemological question of whether his Plotinian sense of reality puts him in touch with a "perennial philosophy" obviously does not excite him.

46. One could add the transformational object described by Christopher Bollas, in *The Shadow of the Object* (New York: Columbia University Press, 1987), leading to his introduction—also very suggestive as applied to Proust—of the concept of genera in *Being a Character* (New York: Farrar Straus and Giroux, 1992).

47. Friedrich Nietzsche, "Ecce Homo," in *Basic Writings of Nietzsche*, trans. Walter Kaufmann (New York: Modern Library, 2000), 780.

48. Pierre Hadot, *Plotinus, or, The Simplicity of Vision*, 32; the next two citations from Hadot are drawn from pp. 34 and 35, respectively.

49. "I had very soon formed a mutual bond of friendship, as strong as it was pure, with these two young persons, Mlle Marie Gineste and Mme Céleste Albaret. Born at the foot of the high mountains in the centre of France, on the banks of rivulets and torrents (the water flowed actually under the family home, turning a millwheel, and the house had often been devastated by floods), they seemed to embody the spirit of those waters. Marie Gineste was more regularly rapid and staccato, Céleste Albaret softer and more languishing, spread out like a lake, but with terrible boiling rages in which her fury suggested the peril of spates and whirlwinds that sweep everything before them" (4:331–32).

"There, with his little cane, he's all furs and lace, such as not even a prince ever wore. But that's nothing compared with his tremendous majesty and his even more profound kindness" (4:334). "I remained silent; Céleste interpreted my silence as a further instance of guile: 'Ah! forehead that looks so pure and hides so many things, nice, cool cheeks like the inside of an almond, little hands all soft and satiny, nails like claws,' and so forth. 'There, Marie, look at him sipping his milk with a reverence that makes me want to say my prayers. What a serious air! Someone really ought to take a picture of him as he is just now. He's just like a child. Is it by drinking milk, like them, that you've kept that clear complexion? Ah, what youth! Ah, what lovely skin! You'll never grow old. You're lucky, you'll never need to raise your hand against anyone, for you have eyes that know how to impose their will. Look at him now, he's angry. He shoots up, straight as a gospel truth'" (4:334–35).

"Céleste would sometimes reproach her husband with his failure to understand her, and I myself was astonished that he could put up with her. For at certain moments, quivering, raging, destroying everything, she was detestable. It is said that the salt liquid which is our blood is only an internal survival of the primitive marine element. Similarly, I believe that Céleste, not only in her bursts of fury, but also in her hours of depression, preserved the rhythm of her native streams. When she was exhausted, it was after their fashion; she had literally run dry. Nothing could then have revitalised her. Then all of a sudden the circulation was restored in her tall, slender, magnificent body. The water flowed in the opaline transparence of her bluish skin. She smiled in the sun and became bluer still. At such moments she was truly celestial" (5:336–37).

Cavafy, Proust,
and the Queer Little Gods

I can't even remember when or how I started to read translations of C. P. Cavafy's poetry — probably thirty years ago or more. The invitation to participate in a conference on Cavafy offered something like a madeleine moment to me, one that I haven't yet figured out all the resonance of, but that seems to open up something like an *Arabian Nights'* treasure of suggestion. For a few years now I've been working on a book on Proust. Now, working on a book on Proust is a wonderful place in which to spend some years. If I'm going to be overly confiding, as apparently I am, I've placed a lot of trust in Proust's well-known antidepressant effect — especially nowadays in a global situation where dread, paralysis, and a newly intimate shame of citizenship seem to exert so much the opposite pressure.[1] And so far, *A la recherche du temps perdu* has worked well in this respect. My attention, in these rereadings of Proust, was attracted to a feature of his writing that is oddly easy not to notice, though I've come to think of it as integral to the buoyant sense of possibility that traverses even the bleakest or saddest of his meditations. That is, how populated the Proustian universe is with gods; how saturating and at the same time promiscuous his sense of divinity seems to be. These beings, drawn from various cultures and located at various points on the axis between the human and the transcendent, turn up sometimes in fabulous set pieces, but far more often in asides or even, all but subliminally, in the innumerable passages that they can make sound conventional, euphuistic, or just French. I'll have more to say about their various functions, but among the ontologically exceptional beings, besides plain vanilla gods and goddesses, that the divinity-field comprises in Proust giants, phantoms, sirens, devils, demigods, fairies, Nereids, Oceanides, witches, Norns, monsters, nymphs, peris, shawabti, sorceresses, Danaides, Furies, fire spirits, magicians, Arabian rocs, ghosts, genii and djinns, sphinxes, sibyls, dryads, household gods, river gods, druids, Pythian priestesses, Parcae, Brahmas, prophets, and angels — to name only a few.

So I had spent quite a long time teaching, writing, and puzzling about these Proustian "queer little gods" (as I thought of them) when I received a chance invitation to do some work on another writer, the early-twentieth-century, Greek-language, gay poet C. P. Cavafy. That the invitation was irresistible became (mystifyingly) clear long before I realized why: simply (I finally saw) because my sense of these odd beings in Proust, both the initial sense of their qualities but also the peculiar feelings of tenderness and intimacy with which I had always seemed to regard them, must have flowed directly from a wellspring of stored-up and half-remembered encounters with the lyrics of Cavafy.

I even found myself grappling to remember a particular, indicative poem, one that turned out, when found, to be "The Footsteps":

> Eagles of coral
> adorn the ebony bed
> where Nero lies fast asleep —
> callous, peaceful, happy,
> in the prime of his body's strength,
> in the fine vigor of youth.
>
> But in the alabaster hall that holds
> the ancient shrine of the Aenobarbi
> how restless the household gods —
> they tremble, the little Lares,
> and try to hide their insignificant bodies.
> They've heard a terrible sound,
> a deadly sound coming up the stairs,
> iron footsteps that shake the staircase,
> and now faint with fear, the miserable Lares
> scramble to the back of the shrine,
> shoving each other and stumbling,
> one little god falling over another,
> because they know what kind of sound that is,
> know by now the footsteps of the Furies.[2] (26)

What kind of poem was this to find lodged in one's mind under such circumstances? I think its combination of horror and funniness must have helped embed it in the walls of memory. Funniness, or I could even say cuteness, since it's easy to imagine a Disney cartoon of the trembling Lares "shoving each other and stumbling, / one little god falling over another" in their discombobulated race for the actually nonexistent door of the shrine. The poem underlines the physicality of all these gods, and also their respective scales: Lares, the protective domestic gods, as miniature representations of the human figure, Furies as projections of it so outsize they can only figure metonymically, by sound. In fact, the smallness of the Lares seems already internalized in their psychology, if the line "they . . . / . . . try to hide their insignificant bodies" more than borders on their hiding the insignificance *of* their bodies — as though the shame of being small had demoralized them even before fear itself did.

The one poem, then, dislodged and decondensed from memory, already begins to sketch the dimensions of a complex divinity-scape. It's a pagan environment that features not only more gods than one, but more than one level of god. And in fact to be a god means different things for Lares than for Furies, rather as being a fictional character is a different thing in Spenser from what it is in Charlotte Brontë: that is, the difference in ontology between them isn't that one is more or less real than the other. It's to be sought rather in their qualitatively different histories, the different representational strategies and needs that brought them into being, their incommensurable scales and idioms, the different kinds of use available to be made of them. Thus not only are the Lares local and vulnerable and the Furies scouringly invincible; but unlike the Furies, the Lares in Cavafy's poem display subjectivity. Lares can not just be vanquished but also can be placed, as here, in untenable or false positions — while the Furies, so closely aligned with an absolute ethical enjoinment, are only barely not an allegorical abstraction, and the more chilling for that. And the Lares' localness, while it attaches them to a particular historical house — the Aenobarbi — as well as to the physical house where Nero lies asleep, attaches them just as firmly to the intimate spatiality of the shrine: a little house within a house, but one oriented toward its missing fourth wall, like a dollhouse, a diorama, a hearth, or puppet theater.

As Cavafy's poem "The Footsteps" expanded in my mind, like the Japanese paper flowers unfolding in water in *Du coté de chez Swann*, ramifying around it the whole nimbus of its association with other images and moments in Cavafy, I was able to see in how many ways — and with what complexity — the religious ecology of each of these two writers' worlds seemed responsive to the other. Near-contemporaries in a protomodernist European moment, when the polarity between assertive skepticism on the one hand, and monotheistic Judeo-Christian belief on the other, might have seemed to dominate or even to constitute the landscape of relations to divinity, both Proust and Cavafy found forms of access to such relations where the entire issue of belief is subordinated to other issues of performativity and relationality.

For Proust, writing about the France of his own lifetime, the divinity-field, while it seems to have a basically Plotinian orientation, is a kind of ahistoric, free-floating, kaleidoscopic intertextuality that magically keeps all these ontologically intermediate kinds of beings in play at once. The landscape of divinity for Cavafy, on the other hand, is the precipitate of very distinctly imagined, dynamically historicized processes and events. In the eastern Mediterranean cultures of classical and late antiquity, and in the ebbs, flows, and especially the tide pools of the Roman imperium and the diasporic culture of Greece, Cavafy recognized a field of historical change and heterogeneity in which (and from which) a highly differential field of divine relation could be explored.

In fact, maybe it's doing no more than recapitulate a generic difference between the lyric and the *roman-fleuve* if we find ourselves moving between Proustian divinity and Cavafian divinity as if between a cloud and its precipitates. Clearly, as we'll see, in any literary circumstance a kind of Ovidian condensation is going to be built into the meaning and function of the pagan gods. And as in Proust, so in Cavafy, relation to these little gods is a way of figuring and mediating, together, both sexuality and vocation. But Cavafy's lyrics offer a series of close-ups on the workings of such divine condensation. In particular, Cavafy's in love with the way divine relations work through very specific performative utterances, such as invocation or prayer, set, like gemstones, in a more or less elaborated periperformative surround.

Let me start with a short discussion of the Proustian divinityscape. It's hard to convey through a few examples how this vast and eclectic field, the unsystematized proliferation of ontologically intermediate beings loosely attached—at once inside and outside—to places, persons, families, substances, ideas, music, buildings, machines, emotions, and natural elements, feels as one immerses oneself in reading Proust. Surprisingly pervasive, surprisingly easy to lose sight of, the divinity-field characterizes the vital atmosphere of Proust reading more than its landmark moments. Often very attaching, neither omniscient nor omnipotent, local rather than omnipresent, these beings lack the somber sublimity of monotheistic deity. Theirs is not the dimension of "laws" or "truths" or of truth or the Law, even though it is possible to read Proust as if those were his chief subjects.

Sometimes the invocation of these gods sounds like a kind of throwaway erudition, a sublimed version of the honking, mock-heroic cant that emanates from the narrator's friend Bloch. Sometimes it sounds like a fine French gallantry, where every woman is a goddess and most men too. Often it makes a shimmering play of capturing as if in motion the very processes of condensation and precipitation that animate any imaginative project of writing. As when

> I suddenly discerned at my feet, crouching among the rocks for protection against the heat, the marine goddesses, . . . the marvellous Shadows, sheltering furtively, nimble and silent, ready at the first glimmer of light to slip behind the stone, to hide in a cranny, and prompt, once the menacing ray had passed, to return to the rock or the seaweed over whose torpid slumbers they seemed to be keeping vigil, beneath the sun that crumbled the cliffs and the etiolated ocean, motionless lightfoot guardians darkening the water's surface with their viscous bodies and the attentive gaze of their deep blue eyes.[3] (2:689)

As almost unimaginably heterogeneous as Proust's divinities may be, a lot of them seem to cluster around the notion of what's called a *daimon* in Greek, *genius* in Latin, and the obviously but obscurely related *jinni* in Arabic. Over many centuries of transmission and displacement, these terms have come to indicate varied, even contradictory kinds of being — think of how *daimon* stands for both a malevolent demon, on the one hand, and on the other the tutelary spirit that repeatedly materializes to warn Socrates of hidden danger. The Neoplatonists, like Proust, have a special interest in such spirits, especially in their guardian or tutelary functions. Centrally, in Plotinus, building on Plato, each individual in each new incarnation, whatever its spiritual level, has an accompanying *daimon* or genius who represents the next higher spiritual level. "The *Timaeus*," Plotinus writes, "indicates the relation of this guiding spirit to ourselves: it is not entirely outside of ourselves; is not bound up with our nature; is not the agent of our action; it belongs to us as belonging to our Soul."[4]

In Proust the *daimon* is often designated by its Latin name as a *genius*. The Latin phrase *genius loci*, or spirit of the place, is the only form in which English speakers still hear "genius" used in this sense: a spiritual familiar, like the "guardian" shadows in the passage I just cited, who both animates from within and stands as somehow distinct from the place or person to whom it belongs. Often combining the guardian, very local function of the *lar* with the tutelary function of a *daimon*, these beings may manifest themselves only for the blink of an eye, or may develop a sustained and modulating presence. To psychologize, their ontology is thus somewhat like that of the internal object in Melanie Klein: in the description of one Kleinian, "a part of the world lodged within, which both becomes identity and yet differs from what the individual feels to be himself."[5] A few Proustian examples of the many: the wind that is the "tutelary genius" of Combray (1:204). The invisible familial "genie" who, in the face of the Duchesse de Guermantes's socialist beliefs, nonetheless "reminded the servants of this woman who did not believe in titles to address her as 'Madame la Duchesse'" (3:602). The "Venus Androgyne" (4:434) that, for the likes of M. de Charlus, "is always the spirit of a relative of the female sex, attendant like a goddess, or incarnate as a double, that undertakes to introduce him into a strange drawing-room" (4:414). There are even genii to explain the mystery of gaydar: "Each man's vice . . . accompanies him after the manner of the tutelary spirit who was invisible to men so long as they were unaware of his presence. . . . Ulysses himself did not recognise Athena at first. But the gods are immediately perceptible to one another, like as quickly to like, and so too had M. de Charlus been to Jupien" (4:18).

And if these familiars consent to such quotidian offices of courtship, it is no surprise that they also continually mediate the experience of art. As when, recognizing the *"petite phrase"* of Vinteuil's sonata, "Swann felt its presence like that of a protective goddess, a confidante of his love, who, in order to be able to come to him through the crowd and to draw him aside to speak to him, had disguised herself in this sweeping cloak of sound. And as she passed, light, soothing, murmurous as the perfume of a flower, telling him what she had to say, every word of which he closely scanned, regretful to see them fly away so fast, he made involuntarily with his lips the motion of kissing, as it went by him, the harmonious, fleeting form" (1:494). Characteristically, too, while the tutelary presence of the little phrase condenses outside of him, it affects his internal geography as well. "The little phrase, as soon as it struck his ear, had the power to liberate in him the space that was needed to contain it; the proportions of Swann's soul were altered; a margin was left for an enjoyment that corresponded no more than his

love for Odette to any external object and yet was not, like his enjoyment of that love, purely individual" (1:335).

Proust, of course, has long been valued for his remarkable powers
of demystification—of stripping away the glamors of atmosphere and
nostalgia, however lovingly they may have been evoked, to expose as
a bare skeleton the inexorable laws of envy and desire, the Oedipalizing
ones that govern both romance and society itself. It's hard to account
for the relation in Proust between his passionate projects of demystification, on the one hand, and what I'm describing here on the other
hand as an irrepressible mysticism—his mysticism that, like Cavafy's,
and unlike, say, that of Yeats, owes nothing to the esoteric or occult.

What I seem by now strongly to see in Proust—though I can't trace
the points of such a recognition in this chapter—is a psyche whose via-
bility is equally threatened by the conjoined fantasies of annihilation
on the one hand, omnipotence on the other. And of the two, the fantasy of omnipotence is probably more dangerous. From the child who
can't stop thinking it's in his power to force a goodnight kiss from his
mother; to the adult whose life is dominated by his absolute ownership
of Albertine; to the writer whose understanding of mastery is inseparable from the demand to defy death. In short, one of the casualties
of the orientation toward omnipotence is an evacuation of the middle
ranges of agency.

But those inexorable, demystifying Laws, whose revelation makes
A la recherche such a trophy text for Freudian and Lacanian critics,
actually seem to partake of the same logic of omnipotence and annihilation—a logic that, through a Kleinian lens, comes to look frighteningly rigid and friable. The logic of the almost subliminal divinity-field,
on the other hand, is a very different thing. Maybe surprisingly, what
those gods and genii offer Proust's narrator seems to be not an access
to any superpowers, but an elastic, pervasive, very cathectible network
of versions of nonomnipotent power. What is the goddess of the "little
phrase" really doing as she makes herself musically available to Swann?
She relieves him deeply, but not for instance by offering herself to him.
Instead his consolation seems to accompany the knowledge, for the
first time his own, realized knowledge, that it is thinkable that Odette
just may not love him—no matter what he does. It is because he can let
go of the paranoid hypervigilance of omnipotent fantasy that the internal proportions of his soul are altered. And again, the profusion of
such ontologically unplaceable beings seems to represent a flowering
of Proust's Neoplatonic mysticism—a Neoplatonism that compasses

the possibility of nondualistic relations of many important kinds: between law and contingency, the eternal and the ephemeral, the universal soul and that of the individual.

That Cavafy, like Proust, could conceive the gods in terms of internal objects is perhaps clearest in a poem that doesn't even mention divinity:

The Souls of Old Men

Inside their worn, tattered bodies
dwell the souls of old men.
How unhappy the poor things are
and how bored by the pathetic life they live.
How they tremble for fear of losing that life, and how much
they love it, those befuddled and contradictory souls,
sitting — half comic and half tragic —
inside their old, threadbare skins. (11)

It's hard to read this poem as other than disenchanted, but it's also hard not to read it through that earlier image of the minor guardian gods — the trembling, miserable, but oddly appealing *lares* — from "The Footsteps." In fact, those wretched *lares* seem to function for Cavafy as a kind of seed image of demoralization, of what happens when one makes a claim on internal resource, on one's nous, only to find it shrunken and itself in need of rescue. The panicky image occurs again in "Trojans":

. . . when the great crisis comes,
our boldness and resolution vanish;
our spirit falters, paralyzed,
and we scurry around the walls
trying to save ourselves by running away.

Yet we're sure to fail. . . . (22)

Like the befuddled souls trembling inside the threadbare bodies of the old men, in "Trojans" our paralyzed, faltering spirit seems distinctly internal to "us" but at the same time *is* us, to judge by the tragicomic scurrying of our own half-paralyzed motility. We both contain and also *are* these soul-genies — they rattle around inside us but also constitute us.

So it would be an understatement to say that omnipotence isn't an issue that engages Cavafy's psychic fears and energies. He has lyrics, like the ones I've quoted, that are very interested in diminution and *im*potence, starting with that seed image of the impotence of the little gods. But I don't see any evidence that the axis between that and omnipotence is at all a magnetic one for him. For him, as for Proust, the gods' modesty — their lack of the grandiose tone, of monotheistic sublimity — is a highly prized value; but for Cavafy it's not contrasted to some opposing psychological or philosophical absolute.

Instead, in Cavafy the pagan gods' mediation of both writing and desire tends to be direct, and also, especially in the poems that bear most clearly on his vocation, to be on the same scale as the human body. In fact, the beautiful gods and beautiful young mortals readily exchange functions and even turn into one another. One way this happens is through the time-honored mediation of Eros — most ontologically insinuating and tropologically suggestive of the little gods:

> . . . .
> He's completely devoted to books —
> but he's twenty-three, and very good-looking;
> and this afternoon Eros entered
> his ideal flesh, his lips.
> An erotic warmth entered
> his completely lovely flesh —
> . . . .

("He Had Come There to Read," 129)

If a tutelary goddess represents Proust's most characteristic pagan invocation, Cavafy's would certainly be a muse, this young male muse. Notoriously, Eros is the most slippery of queer little gods, always switching back and forth between being an embodied pagan deity and a psychological abstraction. It is impossible to say, for instance, in what century this poem may be set — or even what millennium. In this poem, too, it's ambiguous whether Eros has really entered more into the flesh of the twenty-three-year-old boy, or the watching eyes of the poet; or has slipped from one to the other; or if boy and poet might be the same person at different ages. The same set of questions is peculiarly characteristic of Cavafy's way of framing Eros throughout his poetry. Several times, though, he makes it more explicit that the invocation of Eros, of "erotic warmth," in the shape of the beautiful young man who may or may not be his own younger self, is not only an erotic ritual (seemingly a ritual attached to masturbation), but also central to his creation of poetry. His Eros, then, is also his muse; and performatively speaking, the candidly autoerotic *in*vocation of this god, alchemized by memory, also more or less simply constitutes Cavafy's account of poetic *vocation*.

> . . .
> Delight of flesh between
> those half-opened clothes;
> quick baring of flesh — the vision of it
> that has crossed twenty-six years
> and comes to rest now in this poetry.
> ("Comes to Rest," 97)

If we ask what it means when reading Proust to say a divinity is invoked, we'll find places where the god or goddess is mentioned by name; or is alluded to; or brought into the reader's presence by some descriptive tour de force. But invocation in Cavafy often means just this kind of potent, performative ritual invocation, with its murmurous repetitions that bring autoerotic and poetic reverie to the same point.

Come Back

> Come back often and take hold of me,
> sensation that I love come back and take hold of me —
> when the body's memory awakens
> and an old longing again moves into the blood,
> when lips and skin remember
> and hands feel as though they touch again.
>
> Come back often, take hold of me in the night
> when lips and skin remember . . . (43)

To Call Up the Shades

> One candle is enough. Its gentle light
> will be more suitable, will be more gracious
> when the Shades arrive, the Shades of Love.
>
> One candle is enough. Tonight the room
> should not have too much light. In deep reverie,
> all receptiveness, and with the gentle light —
> in this deep reverie I will form visions
> to call up the Shades, the Shades of Love. (106)

Now that's more like what I call invocation. Or at least what J. L. Austin would, if invocation is included, as it ought to be, among the limited number of speech acts he referred to as explicit performative utterances. Famously, Austin's explicit performative is exemplified in a cluster of sentences in the first person singular present indicative active, about which, as he says, "it seems clear that to utter the sentence (in, of course, the appropriate circumstances) is not to *describe* my doing [a thing] . . . or to state that I am doing it: it is to do it" (6).[6] Examples of the "Austinian" or explicit performative include I promise, I bequeath, I apologize, I sentence, I dedicate, I beg, I invoke, I pray, and so forth — anything that, before you've uttered those particular words, hasn't happened, but after your utterance, it definitely has. And while neither of these two poems includes the phrase "I invoke" — although they plausibly might have — it's clear that by the end of each poem, some specific ritual has been enacted that, at the beginning, had not yet been.

In a recent article in the European journal *Arcadia*, Maria Boletsi broaches our present topic under the title "How to Do Things with Poems: Performativity in the Poetry of C. P. Cavafy."[7] She points out not only how unusually frequent these explicit performative utterances are in Cavafy — itself a notable fact — but also how frequently the explicit performatives turn out to be, according to her understanding of Austin's categories, infelicitous or unhappy. Which is to say, for one reason or another, these utterances often don't, in their performative function, *work*: the promises aren't kept, the prayers aren't granted (not what Austin meant by unhappy, actually). The next move Boletsi makes is therefore to broaden out from "examin[ing] speech acts that appear *within* a number of Cavafy's poems (promises, threats, warnings, etc.)" to "ask[ing] how some poems function as performatives themselves, considered in their totality" (398). In moving from the unit of the explicit performative utterance to that of the poem as a whole, now understood to be itself a performative utterance, she expands the notion of performativity from making a particular, named thing happen (a promise or, say, an invocation) to making *something* happen — anything at all.

In working as it were outward from the edges of Austin's explicit performative utterance, still under the name of performativity, Boletsi places herself in sterling company among those thinking about the topic. Austin himself made clear that it is impossible to draw a firm line between performative and non-performative utterances, or indeed between "explicit" performative utterances and those that have a more generally performative effect. Since then, both deconstruction and gender theory have been interested in extending Austin's performative ever further from its localized dwelling in a few exemplary utterances or kinds of utterance. If Jacques Derrida used the performative to unpack the contradictory features of language as a whole, Judith Butler, even more influentially, has argued that discourse may be most performative of all when it isn't even verbal.

Even in the more restrictive sense of the term, Cavafy does have some poems, like the two I've just quoted, that seem entirely constituted by and as an explicit performative utterance. What's far more characteristic, though, as Boletsi intimates, are those in which the explicit performative is only one, albeit central, element in the poem, or even (I would add) where it hovers off to the side — poems about preparing a proclamation of welcome, say, or what someone wears for a coronation or abdication. Or how an immortalization ritual comes to be interrupted — since given the importance of the gods' mediation in Cavafy's historical and psychological microcosms, prophecies, prayers, ceremonies, and supplications loom as large as divine invocations. Epitaphs, especially — though I don't think Austin would entirely concur in calling them explicit performatives — seem to fill this lapidary function for Cavafy. By "lapidary" I mean to instance not only the sense of these utterances as being condensed and powerful, but the sense that as much happens around them as actually in them: their preparation, their circulation, their reception, their changing market value, in short their *setting* are as much Cavafy's preoccupation as the intrinsic quality of the stone. Or more accurately I guess, the interplay of meaning (or kinds of meaning) between the gemlike explicit performative on the one hand, with its density compacted by long eras of iterative pressure, and on the other hand the ductility, the modernity, the contingency of its setting.

So while there's a lot of point in a critical trajectory that would extend the aegis of performativity directly out from the edges of the explicit performative, I find Cavafy among the writers who most makes one wish for better ways to register the crucial differentials, as well. In *Touching Feeling*, in the essay called "Around the Performative," I start trying to do that.[8] In that essay I call these surrounding utterances periperformative and define them in the following way: while not themselves explicit performatives in the Austinian sense, they explicitly refer to those Austinian performatives. Thus they are directly around or about the explicit performatives (hence the Greek prefix *peri*).

As I've said, periperformative utterances specifically are not, and probably by definition cannot be, also explicit performative utterances, even though they refer to them. In fact, it's because they refer to explicit performatives, as much as because they sometimes negate them, that they do not themselves fall into that category. My copybook example is Abraham Lincoln's powerful periperformative in the Gettysburg Address: "But, in a larger sense, we can not dedicate—we can not consecrate—we can not hallow, this ground." Now, it's not because of being a negation that "we cannot dedicate this ground" is a periperformative rather than a performative utterance. The affirmative periperformatives "we enjoyed dedicating this ground" or "we probably *do* have authority to consecrate it" are similarly not Austinian performatives—they don't themselves get the dedication accomplished—even though (or, I am saying, exactly because) they explicitly *refer to* such utterances. Those last two examples will also serve to illustrate that while the periperformative is a mode in which many eloquent and/or interesting things can get said, periperformative utterances can also be perfectly banal, and are no less periperformative for being so.

A more contemporary example of a periperformative smackdown comes from the end of the summer of 2007. I hope some of you won't have forgotten the story of Senator Larry Craig, aka Larry "wide stance" Craig, Larry "I am not gay and I never have been gay" Craig, a corrupt and homophobic Republican, from Idaho, who pled guilty to trying to initiate gay sex in a men's room police sting at a Minnesota airport. As soon as this news became public (and I mean instantly) there ensued a tornado of the most brutal denunciations and repudiations of Craig—not from the Democrats, as one might think, but from his fellow Republicans. It was they who, almost without exception, demanded that he resign from the Senate on the spot, fearful that the stigma of his offense might homosexually contaminate the image of the entire party.

Larry Craig held out against this phobic onslaught for four long days, and then made a public announcement in which, to the loud relief of Republicans and the quizzical interest, if not regret, of many other folks, he held a news conference in which he formally announced, "It is my intent to resign from the US Senate effective Sept. 30." From what might be called a Wittgensteinian point of view, this simply *was* a resignation: at least when I go to Google (that ultimate repository of Wittgensteinian wisdom) and type in "Craig resigns," I find, literally, no fewer than seventy-two thousand newspaper, magazine, and blog headlines dated September 1, 2007, that contain the exact words: "Craig resigns."

It wasn't till another three or four days had passed that this classic Austinian performative act of resigning began to exhibit some periperformative cracks, and the difference between "I resign," with its absolute performative efficacy, on the one hand, and "I *intend* to resign" on the other, which after all does no more than describe a state of mind with respect to a performative act, turned out to be, from an Austinian point of view, consequential. And even as I write today, as a result, over two months after his supposed resignation date of September 30, Larry Craig, unbowed and *un*resigned, is still serving in the US Senate.

Suppose we agree, then, that one feature of periperformative utterances is specifically *not* to have the performative force of the Austinian utterances to which they refer. Then of what use or interest are they? Obviously, if rather bathetically, it is only the periperformative mode in which any discussion of explicit performatives can proceed: one use of periperformatives is to explore and exhibit the structure and force of the Austinian performative. In the essay of mine that I mentioned earlier, for instance, I tried to show how the periperformatives' definitional dependence on reference itself can be used to undermine the pretense, in the explicit performative, of depending only upon self-reference. The periperformative can similarly undermine the understanding that an explicit performative involves only a single illocutionary act, the one named in the utterance itself. Furthermore, while explicit performatives, formulaic as they generally are and sanctified by iteration, can often be seen to do the work of Althusserian interpellation, the periperformative is the more characteristic mode of attempted disinterpellation. Suppose (to imagine a different legal situation) a judge demands that I plead guilty or not guilty, in a case where either of those pleas would be a legitimate performative act; but either of them would equally reinscribe the law's legitimacy in regulating, shall we say, my private religious or sexual or drug-related behavior. I *could* also respond explicitly that in such functions I am not properly a subject of the law, and hence can't be either guilty *or* innocent of "the crime," which I don't acknowledge to be one. But such an utterance, like any other expression of opinions or feelings, such as "I'm angry that you could even ask me that," or "I'm not overly fond of green beans," would have exactly zero proper performative force, which is to say in this context, legal force. Its gravity from that point of view would be confined to the periperformative realm.

How language can resist performative interpellation was surely a matter of great interest for Cavafy; I see him exploring some of the same performative issues as, shall we say, Thoreau. It seems clear for example in "Walls," one of the very earliest poems in his canon, and one whose youthfully melodramatic tone would seem to have made it ripe for later repudiation.

Walls

> With no consideration, no pity, no shame,
> they have built walls around me, thick and high.
> And now I sit here feeling hopeless.
> I can't think of anything else: this fate gnaws my mind —
> because I had so much to do outside.
> When they were building the walls, how could I not have
>   noticed!
> But I never heard the builders, not a sound.
> Imperceptibly they have closed me off from the outside
>   world. (3)

Yet I think Cavafy continued to be motivated by this understanding of how processes like interpellation work — with regard to, for example, the closet. The "I" in this poem seems suddenly to realize that he has been in a position where even his ongoing silence was turned into a speech act of consent. That's how the closet works: it can be constructed of nothing more active than a series of silences, and the surrounding world of presumptions does the rest of the work.

Another of the very early poems that Cavafy allowed to remain in his canon — and hence, I infer, one that had some kind of foundational importance for him — took its title from Dante, "Che fece . . . il gran rifiuto" ("He who made . . . the great refusal," 12). Refusal, especially with regard to the world's presumptions, appears to have been and remained a numinous, identifying implicating kind of speech act for him. A related poem:

Growing in Spirit

> He who hopes to grow in spirit
> will have to transcend obedience and respect.
> He will hold to some laws
> but he will mostly violate
> both law and custom, and go beyond
> the established, inadequate norm.
> Sensual pleasures will have much to teach him.
> He will not be afraid of the destructive act:
> half the house will have to come down.
> This way he will grow virtuously into wisdom. (188)

But "refusal" really names a question for Cavafy, a subject for the most delicate exploration, rather than an answer. One option, refusal by way of polemic, seems never to have been so much as a possibility for him as a writer — whether because polemical refusal would be bound to prove damagingly symmetrical, and hence legitimating, to "the established, inadequate norm"; or because, like the non-plea legal plea in my last example, it would be performatively invisible to it. Instead, his restrained irony and ascetic approach to lyricism represent the order of periperformtive refusal that seemed most meaningful to him. The poem "Myris: Alexandria, A. D. 340," about a Christian youth, remembered after his early death, who's been part of a group of young pagan aristocrats, seems to suggest the minimalist aesthetic that Cavafy found among the most suitable — though still not, in his opinion, exactly hopeful — for acts of disinterpellation:

> . . . .
> We'd known, of course, that Myris was a Christian,
> known it from the very start,
> when he first joined our group the year before last.
> . . .
> He never spoke about his religion.
> And once we even told him
> that we'd take him with us to the Serapeion.
> But — I remember now —
> he didn't seem to like this joke of ours.
> And yes, now I recall two other incidents.
> When we made libations to Poseidon,
> he drew himself back from our circle and looked elsewhere.
> And when one of us in his fervor said:
> "May all of us be favored and protected
> by the great, the sublime Apollo" —
> Myris, unheard by the others, whispered: "not counting me."
> (163)

One final aspect of the potential interest of periperformatives: their relation to affect. As we've seen, the articulation of emotion has no place in the efficacy of Austinian performative utterances. To say you're enraged at having to choose between an innocent and a guilty plea is to say, in the eyes of the law, exactly nothing. In fact, one of the things Austin most wanted to clarify with his discussion of explicit performatives is that they can entirely bracket off the question of subjectivity or affect from that of efficacy. If I've willed my vast estate to a cat hospital, it won't do you any good to argue in court that I was actually rather ambivalent about cats. By the light of explicit performative utterance, what I *feel* or even *intend* is conclusively subordinated to what, performatively, I *do*. The periperformative, by contrast, is the grammar in which affect and subjectivity can be explicitly brought into relation with issues of performative force.

The feature of periperformative utterances, that by definition they can't be performatively efficacious, suggests that Austin would class or diagnose them under what he calls "the doctrine of the *etiolations* of language." He explains further about "the etiolations": "A performative utterance will . . . be *in a peculiar way* hollow or void if said by an actor on the stage, or if introduced in a poem, or spoken in a soliloquy. . . . All this we are *excluding* from consideration [among the performatives]" (22, emphasis in the original). Thus, inclusion in a poem is supposed to have the same "etiolating" effect on direct performative force as, I've been arguing, inclusion in a periperformative utterance has. But by the same token, such a poem can itself become a periperformative utterance in the richest sense—that is, one that opens out for meditation the very grounds of performative force, including the unexpected ways in which histories and subjectivities, however occluded, continue to be woven into its efficacy.

Cavafy had a particular, *avant la lettre* fascination with Austinian performatives; whether quoted or referred to, they are a central presence in many of his lyrics. While put out of performative action *by* their inclusion in a poem, the magnetic presence of these performatives has a way of suffusing the space of such poems with their periperformative implication. It's a mode that Cavafy can never get enough of; no wonder the life of Cavafy's performative world tends to take place around the performative utterance, more than in it. For example, there is the prayer—an archetypal explicit performative—after which this early lyric of Cavafy's is named:

Prayer

The sea engulfed a sailor in its depths.
Unaware, his mother goes and lights
a tall candle before the ikon of our Lady,
praying for him to come back quickly, for the weather to
 be good—
her ear cocked always to the wind.
While she prays and supplicates,

the ikon listens, solemn, sad,
knowing the son she waits for never will come back. (6)

On performative grounds, one might well raise the question of whom or what the mother is supplicating here — whether the material icon, the Virgin herself, the Son, or the Father — if anyone at all; if she doesn't just have a need to be in the space of prayer. What seems more immediate is that the supplicated being, however defined, may be omniscient about the son's fate, but it is not, at least in this performative context, omnipotent. Nor abstract and disembodied. Instead, the Christianity that makes the defining framework for this particular, dislocated performative seems to be part of a universe in which divine power not only can be represented through a numinous, anthropomorphic object, but is palpably circumscribed. In short, this is a universe, or maybe a region or historical moment, or simply a poetic, that is understood to embrace monotheism within the same gestalt as paganism.

This scene of prayer, like the subject of the maternal, is itself very characteristic of Cavafy's poetry. This poem could be set at any time from late antiquity, when icons of the Virgin became part of Christian worship, up to the present. Nonetheless, while the subjects of a sailor's danger or a mother's fearful prayer carry no date, it would be exactly wrong to generalize from this poem that Cavafy directed his work toward a universality that could be divorced from history. Rather, within the signifying chain of his poetry this scene raises very indicative questions about the performative meaning of a specific act of prayer. What is the force of praying for something bad not to happen, when it has already happened? Austin might classify such a performative as "unhappy" or void, in the same way and on the same grounds that he classifies making a bet after the race is over (14). But more likely the prayer isn't infelicitous at all, since it *has* effectively gotten prayed, even if its supplication cannot be granted by the being to whom it was uttered.

Yet even supposing the prayer to be "happy," the poem is steeped in the unhappiness of its performative situation. Most striking is the way "the ikon listens, solemn, sad," trapped in the temporal dislocation that afflicts this particular act of prayer. The icon is also immobilized, presumably, in the facial sadness or solemnity that is a long-standing feature of Orthodox iconography. Then, it may be sad because it *is* an icon, two-dimensional and powerless to move or speak. It may be immobilized in the projective gaze of the mother, who can read its solemnity only as a sadness prophetic of her own future. It may also be immobilized by the force of its own identification, as a grieving mother, with the future devastation of the mother who is praying in front of it.

How very characteristic of Cavafy's poetry is the location of "Prayer." Born in 1863 to a family of Greek merchants that had settled in Alexandria, Egypt, Cavafy arrived at his full vocation as a poet rather late in life, around age forty, largely through the gradual crystallization of his complex understanding of Alexandria itself. In scores of specifically historical lyrics, which comprise the majority of his slender *Collected Poems*, Cavafy reconstructs or (more often) invents scenes that he locates in classical or late antiquity around the Mediterranean basin. Greek and Roman culture, along with the advent of Christianity, are the axes of his vision. But the poems are rarely set in Rome itself, never in Athens. Mostly instead his vision scans the parabolic outposts of Alexander's empire: cities in Ionia, Cappadocia, Syria, Persia, Judaea, Mesopotamia, Libya, as well as Egypt—cities where a cosmopolitan Hellenistic culture, transmitted through a resisted Roman rule, is more than a superficial overlay in relation to the rooted regional traditions; while, in poems with a later setting, the eventual supervention of Christianity remains spotty and incomplete.

In this field of diasporic culture, as well as sometimes anticolonial and sometimes postimperial formulations of identity and religion, it's not surprising that the speech act of prayer would prove a specially indicative one. The issues around the performativity of prayer extend far beyond yes-or-no questions about its rhetorical efficacy; they extend, as we have already seen, to historically sensitive questions about the subjectivity of the gods themselves. In another of Cavafy's poems about prayer, for instance, in the Alexandria of late antiquity, the life of another son is at risk:

Kleitos' Illness

Kleitos, a likeable young man,
about twenty-three years old—
with an excellent upbringing, a rare knowledge of Greek—
is seriously ill. He caught the fever
that reaped a harvest this year in Alexandria.

The fever found him already worn out morally
by the pain of knowing that his friend, a young actor,
had stopped loving and wanting him.

He's seriously ill, and his parents are terribly worried.

An old servant who brought him up
is also full of fear for Kleitos' life;
and in her terrible anxiety
she remembers an idol she used to worship
when she was young, before she came there as a maid,
to the house of distinguished Christians, and turned Christian
  herself.
She secretly brings some votive cake, some wine and honey,
and places them before the idol. She chants whatever phrases
she remembers from old prayers: odds and ends. The ninny
doesn't realize that the black demon couldn't care less
whether a Christian gets well or not. (138)

The explicit performative utterance here is unhappy, not this time because the pagan idol is impotent, but because it's so partial—it's anything but a universal god. But the ecology of this act of prayer comprises not only a "distinguished," universalizing Christianity on the
one hand, and a jealously fragmented, apparently indigenous peasant
idolatry, with its "odds and ends" of "old prayers," on the other. Kleitos's "excellent upbringing" is signalized by his "rare knowledge of
Greek," an item of prestige in this Roman colony—suggestive, at least
in other Cavafy poems, of a suavely internationalist Neoplatonic learning, at the feet of often itinerant sophists—and equally resonant with
the young man's sexual predilection. In a poem called "The Photograph," for instance, and in an image that's frequent in his poetry,
Cavafy writes of a "dream-like face, the figure / shaped for and dedi-
cated to the Greek kind of sensual pleasure" (198); in another poem,
he writes of "the elegant and severe cult of Hellenism, / with its over-
riding devotion/ to perfectly shaped, corruptible white limbs" ("Of the
Jews (A. D. 50)," 98). In "Kleitos' Illness," the young man's susceptibility to infection is associated with his being "worn out morally" by
his lover's rejection. The poem makes one wonder whether the array of
responses to his danger, among his parents, the servant who brought
him up, and the idol to whom she is trying to pray, may not also be in-
flected by the sense of his sexuality, with its associations here of cultural privilege and also, if I may put it this way, of etiolation; bringing credit to his upwardly mobile family and evoking their tenderness,
but also, decisively alienated from the chthonic idol, endangering the
grounds of the family's perpetuation.

But while the epithet "Greek" generally carries at least some homosexual implication—and often far more than that—the full redolence

of Greekness in this diasporic cultural and demographic setting is much harder to pin down. In this next poem, whose expressive title is "Going Back Home from Greece," the nature of "being Greek" is a topic for the two colonials on shipboard—both participants, once again, in the global market in philosophy.

Going Back Home from Greece

Well, we're nearly there, Hermippos.
Day after tomorrow, it seems—that's what the captain said.
At least we're sailing our seas,
the waters of Cyprus, Syria, and Egypt,
the beloved waters of our home countries.
Why so silent? Ask your heart:
didn't you too feel happier
the farther we got from Greece?
What's the point of fooling ourselves?
That would hardly be properly Greek.

It's time we admitted the truth:
we are Greeks also—what else are we?—
but with Asiatic affections and feelings,
affections and feelings
sometimes alien to Hellenism.

It isn't right, Hermippos, for us philosophers
to be like some of our petty kings
(remember how we laughed at them
when they used to come to our lectures?)
who through their showy Hellenified exteriors,
Macedonian exteriors (naturally),
let a bit of Arabia peep out now and then,
a bit of Media they can't keep back.
And to what laughable lengths the fools went
trying to cover it up!

No, that's not at all right for us.
For Greeks like us that kind of pettiness won't do.
We must not be ashamed
of the Syrian and Egyptian blood in our veins;
we should really honor it, take pride in it. (199)

In this poem the most explicit and central periperformative gesture— "It's time we admitted the truth"—actually seems to define the privileged Greekness itself: not, as it emerges, in terms of nationality or blood, but to define it *as* a speech act, that of "admitting the truth." In fact it may be a speech act that an imperial subject is best situated to instantiate; a version of colonial overlearning whose taste is quite other than servility or abjection.

While I'd argue that the kind periperformative structuration we've seen in these poems is at work in a great many of Cavafy's lyrics, his operative sense of what counts as an explicit or "Austinian" performative utterance seems to extend further than Austin's own in a couple of important ways. First, as I noted earlier, I don't think Austin would include the epitaph among his classic examples of the performative: the epitaph isn't reliably in the first person or present tense, for example, and more tellingly, there isn't a single, formulaic verb that names the illocution it accomplishes, never mind a verb that is characteristically used within the utterance itself (as in "I welcome my guests," "I beseech you," or "I invoke the goddess Athena"). In his dozen or so poems that explicitly cite epitaphs, Cavafy unfolds their crystallized implications by writing about and "around" them in a way that's exactly analogous to what he does elsewhere with prayers, declarations, guarantees, coronations, and prophecies.

In trying to get the feel of Cavafian periperformativity, it's worth looking back at the *Greek Anthology*, one of his most fertile sources, to see the kinds of energy that he did and did not borrow from it. A collection of Greek and Hellenic inscriptions and pseudo-inscriptions, which is also to say, of things that were or might have been chiseled into stone, the *Greek Anthology* is, among other things, a distillation of the performative utterances that are addressed by human beings to the gods. As such, it is peculiarly rich in (what Austin would come to call) explicit performatives: prayers, curses, invocations, the dedication of votive gifts, and (by the same classification Cavafy was to make) many, many epitaphs. Here's an early example, an actual votary inscription, by Perses, probably from the late fourth century B.C.: it comprises 100 percent full-strength concentrated explicit performative utterance.

> Artemis,
> This Zone, this Breastband & girlish frock
> Take, votive, from her whom you delivered,
> In her tenth month, of a most harsh childing,
> Timaessa.[9] (trans. Peter Whigham, 55)

If you wonder what it would sound like to elaborate a poem *as* and *within* the performative, rather than *around* it, here's an example from the first century A.D. It has just the same structure as the previous example, and performs just the same act, though it is literary in the sense of not being an actual inscription.

> A yellow-coated pomegranate, figs like lizards' necks,
>   a handful of half-rosy part-ripe grapes,
> a quince all delicate-downed and fragrant-fleeced,
>   a walnut winking out from its green shell,
> a cucumber with the bloom on it pouting from its leaf-bed,
>   and a ripe gold-coated olive — dedicated
> to Priapus friend of travellers, by Lamon the gardener,
>   begging strength for his limbs and for his trees.
> (Philip [of Thessalonika], ca. 40 A. D., trans. Edwin Morgan,
>   217)

Yet this way of making a poem, by elaborating the performative act proper by attaching richer figures of speech, more suggestive metaphors, to the functional elements of the basic speech act, is extremely distant from Cavafy's practice. Instead, reading through the barest of the inscriptions in the *Greek Anthology*, and especially the epitaphs, I kept thinking that what it would take to make any one of them a plausible, indeed an eloquent, Cavafy poem would be only the most minimal act. Say, the addition of a title and a date: "Tomb of Ion, 200 B. C." "Tomb of Demetrius, Alexandria, 31 A. D." The addition might thus consist only of a name, maybe a place, a number — information that might already, for that matter, have been contained within the original inscription without changing the inscription's performative force. No, the minimal but crucial difference made by the title, in our imaginary Cavafy composition, is like the difference made by a frame surrounding something on the wall. It generates a telling distance, a space in which resonance can happen — a distance that also becomes internal to the work it frames. Cavafy's presence, Cavafy's choice, Cavafy's periperformative act indeed vitiates (as Austin would put it) the direct performative force of the supposed original act — even the direct relation to the gods. What it brings instead, something of which Cavafy was endlessly and gratefully mindful, is a shareable and meditative middle distance of relation, a space in which the unforeseen becomes possible.

The "Cavafian" thought experiment we've just performed involves the most minimal periperformative intervention in a purely performative utterance. More typical, as we've seen, are poems that give a fairly elaborate periperformative staging to explicit performatives that may be quoted briefly or even just offstage. Going further, in a very few poems, but among the most haunting, a simple phrase in quotation marks—not even a performative, but maybe a phrase described as "sublime"—is accorded this exemplary, structuring status. One final example:

Anna Dalassini

In the royal decree that Alexios Komninos
put out especially to honor his mother—
the very intelligent Lady Anna Dalassini,
noteworthy in both her works and her manners—
much is said in praise of her.
Here let me offer one phrase only,
a phrase that is beautiful, sublime:
"She never uttered those cold words 'mine' or 'yours.'" (145)

The periperformative relations of this lucid poem are rather subtle. It begins by referring to a properly performative imperial decree, one that (as Savidis tells us) in the year 1081, designated Anna Dalassini as regent of the Byzantine emperor, in anticipation of her son's temporary absence at war. But, periperformatively, the poem's speaker tones down the performative force of that decree, emphasizing instead its more purely descriptive and affective content of praise. And indeed the phrase that is the kernel of the poem—"She never uttered those cold words 'mine' or 'yours'"—while it elegantly uses a grammatical point to make an emotional one, is entirely constative rather than performative. No, the only explicit performative in this lyric (and one whose force, Austin to the contrary, actually isn't etiolated even by the fact that it appears in a poem) is "*Here let me offer* one phrase only." I take that to be an only slightly understated and modest version of, shall we say, "I hereby offer"—which couldn't be more purely Austinian, as it quietly slips the poet's performative agency into the already downplayed position of the emperor's. Furthermore, the speech act of choosing, appreciating, citing—across the evoked space of nine centuries—adds value to the emperor's phrase: the kind of added value that is neither mine nor yours.

I've mentioned that one very pregnant aspect of the periperformative is to offer a field in which multiple motives and directionalities, in fact multiple forces of illocution, can be brought to bear on understanding a single, performative speech act. It's probably inevitable, then, that I would be stuck with wanting too many things from this meta-periperformative discussion. To begin with, I've long puzzled over the status of the idea of periperformative utterance. Given that there logically has to be such a thing, as long as there is a class (however uncircumscribable) of explicit performative utterance — given that, does the new classification have any more than nominal substance; is it of any *use*? Encouragement has come mainly from realizing over time how many of the moments in writing that speak most irreducibly to me seem to display this structure: as who should say, if the nose contains a receptor for it, then there must actually be such a smell.

As I finish, I'd like to hark back to an image from the beginning of this chapter, in which I evoked one version of the spatiality of the gods: the shrine of the *lares* from Cavafy's poem "The Footsteps," with its resonances of a stage, a hearth, a diorama, a dollhouse, a puppet theater. I hope it will make more sense now if I generalize this image a little. It reflects, I think, some of the power of one kind of modern relation to the gods that is no longer exactly pagan, but neither is it a relation of disbelief. It is a relation that values the gods for their finiteness, their plurality, their condensation of the stuff of intense feeling, need, dependency, and creation. This small, concentrated, theatrical space also maximally invests the relations of selection and quotation — as when Cavafy lets us watch him pick out, shall we say, his Kaiserion puppet for today's play, watch him dress Kaiserion up for coronation. There are many, many moments in Cavafy where the artist who comes most to mind is Joseph Cornell, the collage artist and "dollhouse" maker, with his own relation to the heavenly inhabitants.

My particular range of reading being what it is — or indeed probably for a more substantive reason — such moments of art have seemed to me to cluster around recognizably queer authors and cultural venues. Queer, I might even say, verging on camp. But that's supposing we managed to think of camp, as I believe we need to, not in terms of parody or even wit, but with more of an eye for its visceral, operatic power: the startling outcrops of overinvested erudition; the prodigal production of alternative histories; the "over"-attachment to fragmentary, marginal, waste, lost, or leftover cultural products; the richness of affective variety; and the irrepressible, cathartic fascination with ventriloquist forms of relation. Beyond that, I've obviously had the motive of instilling in you something like the specific sense of a Cavafian voice — whether or not its specificity really is, as I'm imagining, a distillation of the periperformative. It's felt to me as a poet, as I think it did also to W. H. Auden, James Merrill, Randall Jarrell, Louise Gluck, and many others, that this calm voice, so contagious and easy to internalize, was unexpectedly also like a new mental faculty in which new things could happen. So why not keep spreading it around? Cavafy's divinity, like Proust's divinity, offers to explore a wealth of such relation.

And finally I'll admit to wanting to get further—much further than I could in this chapter—with the issue of plural gods and little gods, divinities on different scales, the periperformative setting in motion of a whole ecology of these ontologically intermediate beings, and what the effects of their explicitation might be. Cavafy clearly shares this fascination. Accordingly I'll end with a poem called "The God Abandons Antony," one of several about Marc Antony's loss of the battle of Actium in 31 B.C. The central, explicit performative utterance in the poem is that of saying goodbye, a repeated instruction to Antony to say goodbye—and the clearest thing about that speech act here is its pure gratuitousness; there is nothing it will make happen. Yet it makes the space in which a series of almost subliminal slippages can take place: to begin with, among Antony's protector god Dionysos, the city of Alexandria, and an erotically charged woman (Cleopatra?); between abandoning and being abandoned, leaving and being left; between losing a city, having the gods leave a city, having a city leave its own place; between all of these and an inexplicable music, and the listening to it.

The God Abandons Antony

When suddenly, at midnight, you hear
an invisible procession going by
with exquisite music, voices,
don't mourn your luck that's failing now,
work gone wrong, your plans
all proving deceptive—don't mourn them uselessly.
As one long prepared, and graced with courage,
say goodbye to her, the Alexandria that is leaving.
Above all, don't fool yourself, don't say
it was a dream, your ears deceived you:
don't degrade yourself with empty hopes like these.
As one long prepared, and graced with courage,
as is right for you who proved worthy of this kind of city,
go firmly to the window
and listen with deep emotion, but not
with the whining, the pleas of a coward;

listen—your final delectation—to the voices,
to the exquisite music of that strange procession,
and say goodbye to her, to the Alexandria you are losing. (33)

NOTES

In the spring of 2007, EKS was invited by Panagiotos Roilos to participate in a conference at Harvard, "In Fantasy and Logos: Desire, Intertext, and Fragmentation in C. P. Cavafy." In the paper she delivered on December 7, 2007, she thanks Roilos "for having conceived and organized this timely and genuinely fascinating conference" along with Theresa Wu "for their care in putting the logistical bits together so thoughtfully." A version of the conference paper, "Cavafy, Proust, and the Queer Little Gods," appears in the conference proceedings (Panagiotos Roilos, ed., *Imagination and Logos* [Cambridge: Harvard University Press, 2010]) and is the basis for the chapter in this volume, which also draws upon "C. P. Cavafy and Periperformative Lyric Space," delivered at the London School of Economics on November 3, 2007, and "The Performative in Reserve: How Not to Do Things with Words," delivered at Le Centre de Recherche Climas de l'Université Michel de Montaigne Bordeaux III, June 7, 2008. Several pages in this chapter on Proust contain material that also appears in chapter 1.

1. "Antidepressant poetics" is a rubric I heard from Jonathan Flatley (personal communication), and from there it's gone on to a long, productive career in my head.

2. All citations from C. P. Cavafy are to *Collected Poems*, rev. ed., trans. Edmund Keeley and Philip Sherrard, ed. George Savidis (Princeton: Princeton University Press, 1992).

3. All citations from Marcel Proust are to book and page number in the six-volume *In Search of Lost Time*, trans. C. K. Scott Moncrieff and Terence Kilmartin, rev. D. J. Enright (New York: Modern Library, 2003).

4. Plotinus, *The Enneads*, ed. John Dillon, trans. Stephen McKenna (London: Penguin, 1991), 170 (3.4.5.).

5. Meira Likierman, *Melanie Klein: Her Work in Context* (London: Continuum, 2002), 110.

6. All citations from J. L. Austin are to *How to Do Things with Words*, 2nd ed., ed. J. O. Urmson and M. Sbisà (Cambridge: Harvard University Press, 1975).

7. I quote from Maria Boletsi, "How to Do Things with Poems: Performativity in the Poetry of C. P. Cavafy," *Arcadia* 41, no. 2 (2006): 396–418.

8. See Eve Kosofsky Sedgwick, "Around the Performative: Periperformative Vicinities in Nineteenth-Century Narrative," *Touching Feeling: Affect, Pedagogy, Performativity* (Durham: Duke University Press, 2003), 67–91.

9. All page citations from *The Greek Anthology* are to Peter Jay, ed., *The Greek Anthology and Other Ancient Epigrams* (London: Penguin, 1981).

Making Things,
Practicing Emptiness

When I was invited to speak about "The Construction of an Identity in Artistic Practice," I was excited by the topic and by the possibility of applying it to my own practice as a visual and tactile artist: excited, but in a somewhat perverse way. For me, the slow and late-in-life emergence of a distinct artistic practice involving textiles has not mostly involved the construction of an identity, nor a change of identity, nor even the deconstruction of one, but something very different: a meditative practice of possibilities of emptiness and even of nonbeing.[1] In fact, it seems likely to me that this is true of many or most artists and craftspeople, but it's of the essence of such possibilities that they have so little aptitude for being put into words. Which is why I'm going to speak only of my own practice, framing it in narrative and thematic terms, even at the risk of somewhat betraying its own, quite strenuous resistance to being translated into verbal propositions.

When I began my practice as a visual and textile artist, almost a dozen years ago, I already had an identity—and quite a public one: as a literary critic and poet, but mostly as one of the founders of the new discipline of queer theory. My two decades of thinking, lecturing, and writing in that area had been almost recklessly generative in terms of a public identity, in fact. This was mostly because issues of homosexuality were suddenly becoming such a salient, openly contested area of public discourse; and I'd managed to make myself available, to a certain extent, to offer a face and voice and a particular style to a theory movement, within a much larger emerging gay lesbian queer and transgender movement, that embodied some of the deepest-rooted energies of a great many cultural producers both within and outside of the academy. To be able to fill this role for a while, and substantially affect the shape of some antihomophobic approaches, was a tremendous privilege.

And while I was and remain happy about the writing and teaching I did under those rubrics — and, in fact, continue to do — I've gotten into the habit of thinking of the textile art work in quite different ways from that. The language for this latter work, to the degree that I have language for it, tends to come from Buddhism, through a series of connections — which I don't know whether to see more as overdetermined and almost inevitable or underdetermined and all but accidental. It all goes back to the time, about eleven years ago, when these two motives, the textiles, the Buddhism, came bounding into my life almost together. I think back on that moment a lot because it also bears so much the stamp of mortality, my mortality: it was the time when I learned that the breast cancer for which I'd been treated several years earlier had silently metastasized to my spine, and hence had become incurable.

Now at the time I received this diagnosis in 1996, the median survival time for people with metastatic breast cancer was less than three years — and to be honest, the median is not much longer now; although there are more and more people, like me, whose cancers turn out to be what the doctors call "indolent," and whose survival can be nursed along, by good doctoring and good chemotherapies, for surprisingly many years with quite a viable quality of life. (And may I remark how fond I've become of that word "indolent," and how fully I identify with it?) But in 1996, it seemed unlikely I would even be alive into the new century; and the imperative to try and wrap my mind around the reality of death, what it might mean both in itself and for how I'd live whatever long or short time remained of my life, became suddenly very material and pressing, in a way I don't think it tends to be for healthy people in their forties. That sense of urgent and even exciting intimacy with nonbeing, intimacy with the kind of questions it asks of life, built itself more and more into the center of my understanding, and particularly my practice of art. By now it has come to feel much less like dread or excitement or relief or any kind of a claim on pathos — indeed less like any other, particular emotion — than like a kind of law of perspective, a strangely spacious framework of impermanence in which ideas, emotions, selves, and other phenomena can arise in new relations.

Actually it was just before this diagnosis that I was finding I had fallen suddenly, intrusively, and passionately in love with doing textile work. That is, before the *diagnosis*, but I think it may have happened after I'd started having the neck pains that were misdiagnosed for several months before they turned out to represent the cancer recurrence. I can't exactly remember the order in which things happened, actually. I just found myself cutting up fabrics, especially old kimonos, which I've always been fond of, to make into other fabrics—appliqués, collages (fig. 1), and an odd kind of weaving that used scraps of already-woven cloth as its weft material (in fig. 2 and fig. 3 [detail], the warp on the scarf is silk yarn, and the weft is kimono scraps and other materials).

But really I've always loved textiles. I used to sew my own clothes (though ineptly), back in college when I had time for it and no money, and the feel of any kind of fiber between my thumb and fingers—in a gesture I probably got from my grandmother, who also taught me to crochet and embroider—just is the rub of reality, for me. It's funny that the same brushing-three-fingers gesture is mostly understood to whisper of money, the feel of the coin, as a bottom-line guarantee of reality. I've learned that this gesture is also called "the weaver's handshake," because of the way a fabric person will skip the interpersonal formalities when you're introduced and move directly to a tactile interrogation of what you're wearing.

So I've always loved textiles, without doing much about it, but something different was happening right around then, something that kept kidnapping me from my teaching and writing tasks and pinning me to my kitchen table with a mushrooming array of "arts and crafts" projects and supplies. Why? Here's one thing that was different: I think I was finally giving up the pretext of self-ornamentation, to which my love of textiles had always clung before. For instance I had all these gorgeous silk clothes I'd bought or made but never ever wore. It's funny that it wouldn't happen before age forty-six, or that it could happen then, but somehow I think I finally got it, that to tie my very acute sense of beauty to the project of making myself look beautiful was definitely a mug's game. Apparently the notion of a visual or tactile beauty that might be impersonal, dislinked from the need to present a first-person self to the world, came as news to me—late, late news. But exciting!

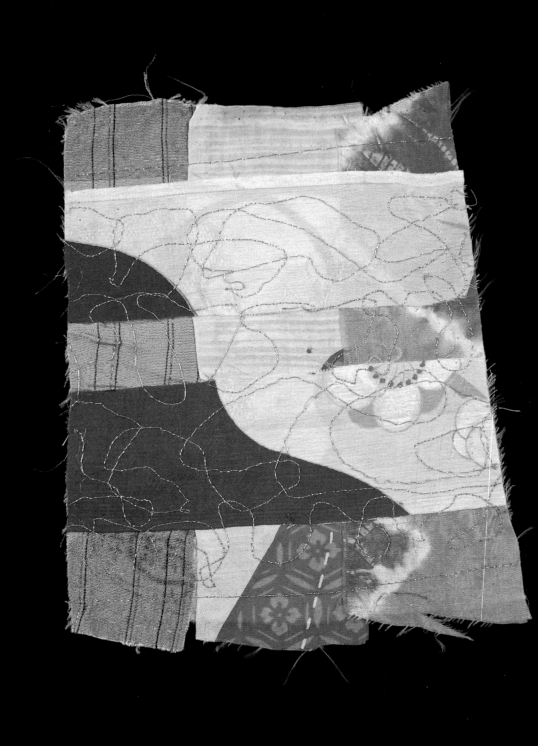

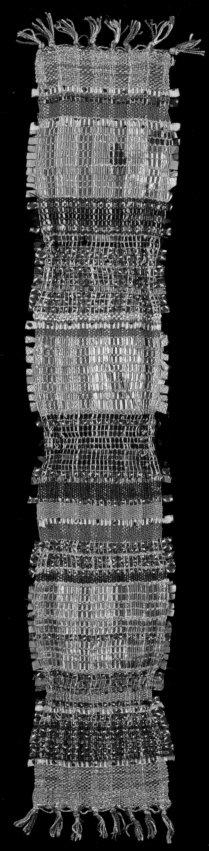

2

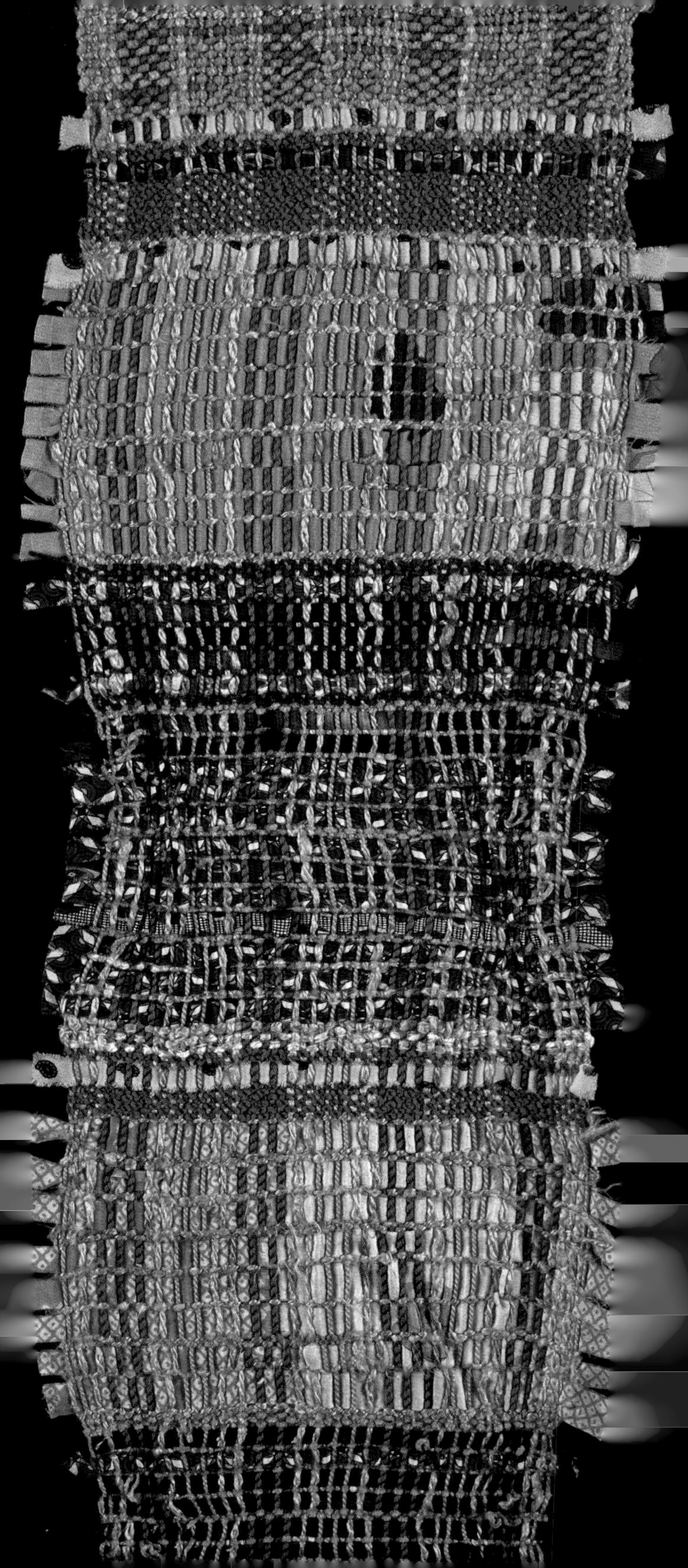

My fingers were very hungry to be handling a reality, a beauty, that wasn't myself, wasn't any self, and didn't want to be.

It was also, oddly, before the diagnosis, though also I think after the pain started, that I found myself reading about Tibetan Buddhism. Not hard to see why it appealed to me from first introduction: for one thing, the emphasis that Buddhist mysticism places on nondualism, which some people struggle hard to get the feel of, seemed almost funnily *haimish* to me. In the words of the Heart Sutra, perhaps the central text of East Asian Buddhism:

> Form does not differ from emptiness, emptiness
>   does not differ from form.
> Form is emptiness, emptiness is form.
> . . .
> No appearing, no disappearing.
> No taint, no purity.[2]

Such nondualism was very congenial to what seems a native tendency of my mind, for one thing; but for another, my literary education was steeped in the early days of American deconstruction, a theoretical movement that was premised on the attempt to identify and unpack the many tacit dualisms that structure Western thought and writing. My shorthand for this relation at the time was "Deconstruction is the theory, Buddhism is the practice."

The piece in figure 4, from just a couple of years later, is sewn together from mulberry paper and silk — it's based on photographs of an eighteenth-century site in Thailand, where there are a lot of images of meditating Buddhas that have been mutilated by trophy hunters, as in this second piece (fig. 5), which shows many of them with just their heads lopped off (figs. 6 and 7 are a couple of details of that second piece). Returning to the first piece (fig. 4), you see that some of them have been so vandalized over the centuries that only their knees remain. Even with those Buddha images, though, their silence and the sense of their seated presence is so powerful that you can almost feel the column of their spines and nerve centers rising up between their knees, even in the literal absence of most of their bodies. It's one of the most palpable images I know, of how it can be that — in the words of the Heart Sutra — form does not differ from emptiness nor emptiness from form. It gives a sense of how dynamic and living a thing empti-

A good
meditation,
Osho says,
i m a g i n e
yourself as
not having a
head

A good meditation, Osho says: imagine yourself as not having a head.

ness is in Buddhist thought—the attributes that make the Dalai Lama compare emptiness to the space inside a bell.[3] Also, thematically speaking, one of the attractions these images held for me at that time was that my own spine was in bad trouble. The rather ghostly image, just above the small iteration of the Buddha's knees in figure 8, is from a bone scan from that period (fig. 9 is a close-up of the scan).

Much more generally, the fact that, like the practice of making things, so much of Buddhist art and practice is nonverbal has made it especially available to crystallize one of the most severe discomforts I'd been feeling in my vocation as a writer and theorist: that the very propositional nature of verbal utterance has so many central and misconceived dualisms built into it. One of those dualisms is the way the sentence structure of many languages, including English, both depends on and reinforces a strict dichotomy between the active and the passive voice. Any verb, aside from the verb "to be," generates a doer and a done-to. And by this simple, built-in grammatical feature it thus makes it almost impossible for any language user to maintain a steady sense of the crucial middle ranges of agency: the field in which most of consciousness, perception, and relationality really happen.[4]

Unsurprisingly, one of the many other dualisms that doesn't do much for me is the supposed opposition between craft and art. Also no doubt unsurprising is a certain, informal or "wabi-sabi" aesthetic that prefers funky craft to finely done craft. But the craft aspect of art making—or, more simply put, of thing making—does seem (doesn't it?) to be an exceptionally fruitful place for exploring those middle ranges of agency. Or maybe my sense of craft comes from the contrast with my peculiar relation to writing, where (at least according to a no doubt very eccentric idea of perfection) I'm an insane perfectionist—to a degree that amounts to endless self-punishment—and am fueled by a neurotic demand for mastery even in this area that, intellectually, I know so well puts mastery altogether out of the question. But really I think anyone who's verbally quick at all—verbally and conceptually—is liable to develop such grandiose illusions of magical omnipotence in relation to language—exactly because, unlike making things, speech and writing and conceptual thought impose no material obstacles to a fantasy of instant, limitless efficacy. Nor for that matter is there anything to slow down the sudden, utter spoiling of such fantasy, as soon as it occurs to one that the instant persuasion, radical conversion, or irresistible en-

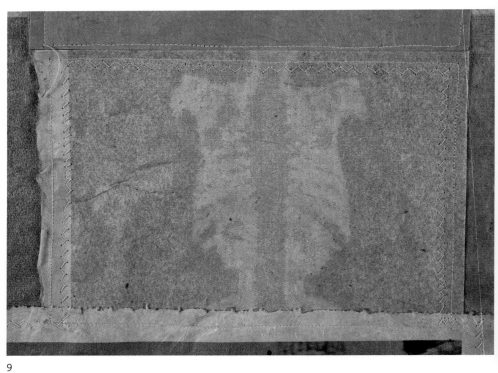

9

lightenment of one's listeners has not exactly been the universal result of one's latest speech act. Theoretical writing in particular has a tendency to overdramatize the oscillations between the feelings of being omnipotent on the one hand, mortifyingly powerless on the other.

Yet how different it is to set to work with physical materials — especially for somebody, like me, who isn't overendowed with either natural facility or acquired skills for fashioning images and objects. Melanie Klein argues that it can be a relief and relaxation, rather than a big tragedy the way it is in Freud, when one manages to get disabused of the fantasy of omnipotence, together with the reflex fantasy of utter impotence. One has at last the reassuring sense of a grounding in reality. I feel this wonderfully in my material practice, with the ways that paper, fabric, thread, and other supplies press back so reliably, so palpably, against my efforts to shape them according to models I've conceived. In these circumstances perfectionism, for me, would make no sense at all, and the disturbing fantasy of omnipotence has no opportunity to arise. Instead, there are second-by-second negotiations with the material properties of whatever I'm working on, and the questions "What will it let me do?" and "What does it want to do?" are in constant, three-way conversation with "What is it that I want to do?" So in my art there's no shortage of instances where mastery of the material world is pretty inconceivable, and traces of negotiations with the middle ranges of agency are visible to a marked extent. It feels wonderful to exist and to be active in that space of suspended agency. But it's also true that the techniques I'm attracted to are the ones where, even when they're done competently, or even most beautifully, the will of the artist is only one determinant of the art that emerges — and often not the most important determinant.

The marbling technique in figure 10, for example, called *suminagashi*, originated in Japan of the twelfth century, a period of very influential Buddhist penetration. Like European paper marbling, suminagashi is done by floating ink on water. European marbling is all about keeping these liquid elements under the artist's control, for instance by making the water viscous with carageenan, or by combing through the ink in regular patterns with toothed implements.[5] Suminagashi has the alternative emphasis. Playing on the immemorial Taoist and Zen fascination with the potent but unwilled behaviors of water, it uses chemicals not to thicken the water, but actually to make it even more liquid. (Of course even European-style marbling, with the thickened water, can be used in a suminagashi way).

In figure 10, and in several more to follow, I'm using a text from Proust; this one reads "For beauty is a series of hypotheses"[6] (2:399). Figure 11 also says "For beauty is a series of hypotheses." It's an accordion book (figs. 12, 13 [detail]). As you can see, the individual letters are marbled separately. I used a resist to cover the shape of each letter—some of the resists didn't work too well, so I also outlined the letters, in pencil. I wanted reading it to involve a series of hypotheses.

But actual Japanese suminagashi is really the most meditative of arts: you use successive drops of ink to make a lot of concentric circles, anywhere from four or five to hundreds of them, and then you sit back and watch as the complex drama of competing surface tensions keeps the water surface breathing, shifting, expanding and self-enfolding. (In fig. 14 the charcoal pattern at the top is suminagashi.) If you want to influence the design on this evolving surface at all, you can do so with a soft breath, or by brushing it lightly with a feather. And then at some moment when you like what you see happening, you gently drop onto it your paper or your cloth. What results is a snapshot of a living spatial dynamic—one that, like the infinitely receding, self-similar bifurcations of roots, branches, and capillaries in a tree, or of rivulets in a delta, is a veritable badge of chaos—or rather the deep intimacy of chaos with order that disrupts the schematics of both dimension and scale.

I've written quite a lot elsewhere about texture, the base-line attraction of any textile art, and how the very fact of texture seems to confound any understanding of perception in terms of passive as opposed to active.[7] "To perceive texture is always, immediately, and de facto to be immersed in a field of active narrative hypothesizing, testing, and re-understanding of how physical properties act and are acted upon over time. To perceive texture is never only to ask or know What is it like? nor even just How does *it* impinge on *me?* Textural perception always explores two other questions as well: How did it get that way? and What could I do with it? . . . I haven't perceived a texture until I've instantaneously hypothesized whether the object I'm perceiving was sedimented, extruded, laminated, granulated, polished, distressed, felted, or fluffed up. Similarly, to perceive texture is to know or hypothesize whether a thing will be easy or hard, safe or dangerous to

FOR BEAUTY IS A SERIES OF HYPOTHESES

11

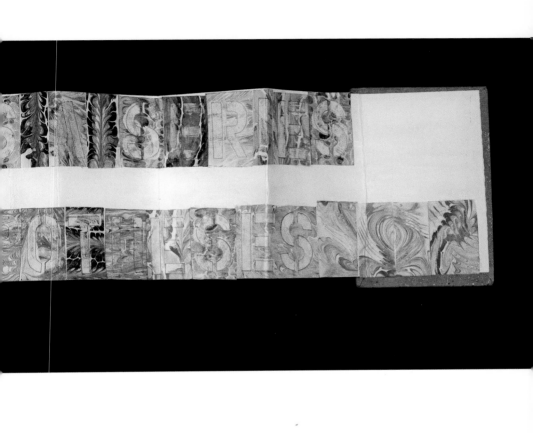

12

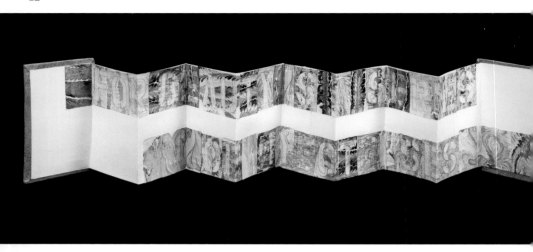

13

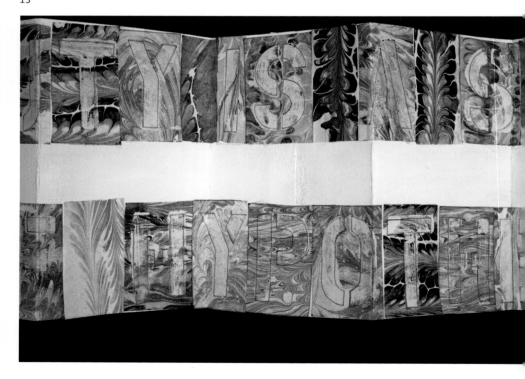

grasp, to stack, to fold, to shred, to climb on, to stretch, to slide, to soak. Even more immediately than other perceptual systems, it seems, the sense of touch makes nonsense out of any dualistic understanding of agency and passivity; to touch is always already to reach out, to fondle, to heft, to tap or enfold, and always also to understand other people or natural forces as having effectually done so before oneself, if only in the making of the textured object." This partly explains why that gesture of the "weaver's handshake" seems to epitomize not only a mode of perception, but a contact with the nub of reality itself.

The pieces I'm going to be discussing from here onward are taken from my two most recent shows, the first one called "Bodhisattva Fractal World" (fig. 15) and the second called "Works in Fiber, Paper, and Proust" (fig. 16).[8] Very obviously, hands and handiwork, and the deep, inherent relationality of touch and texture, are among the strongest motives in this work. Perhaps more surprising is the term "fractal." Yet fractals are nothing fancier than a way of talking about fractional dimensions, between-dimensions: that is, the ways that everything in the whole world has of refusing the classical geometric definitions where the dot occupies zero dimensions, the line one, the plane two, and volume three — with maybe a fourth dimension, that of time, thrown in for good measure. As F. David Peat writes,

> What is the dimension of a ball of string? Seen from a great distance, it appears as a dot, a zero-dimensional figure. As we approach, we realize that this dot is a three-dimensional sphere. Closer still, we notice that the ball is composed of a single thread — a twisted line, a one-dimensional figure. Look even closer and the thread becomes a long cylinder, a three-dimensional figure. Under a magnifying glass the cylinder is seen to be made up of individual fibers, tiny twisting lines. So what is the dimensionality of string?[9]

The fractal, the fractionally dimensional, seems like, among other things, a language invented exactly to talk about texture. In pictorial terms, a fractured dimensionality might be a way of describing the struggle staged in perspectival realism, between the receding space of illusion and the frontal space of the picture plane. But even aside from any ambition of realist illusion, the reality of texture itself, be it only the texture of paint on canvas or that of canvas (or any other textile)

BODHISATTVA FRACTAL WORLD

16

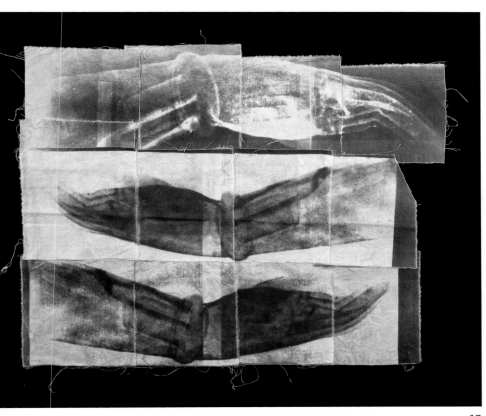

pure and simple, leads one just as feelingly along the defile of fractal dimension.

To a considerable extent, then, I've been thinking in these fractal terms about the surface design techniques I've practiced in my recent work. Figure 17 x-rays the hands of a wooden Guanyin statue. The main approach to actual figuration in this work is through cyanotype, an extremely primitive photo-printing technique, like blueprint, in which these tenth- to twelfth-century bodhisattva statues are reproduced (figs. 18 and 19).[10] Cyanotype is satisfying because it's easy and funky, and because the rather sluttish printed surface, with its abrupt smears of over- and underexposure, and all the hypervisible shadow accidents of Scotch tape, creases, and dangling bits of thread, does interfere in such a magnetic way with the illusionary three-dimensional space of

18

AS IN THE CLASSIC-
AL LANDSCAPES
WHERE IN THE
PLACE OF A VAN-
ISHED NYMPH THERE
IS AN INANIMATE
SPRING, A
DISCERNIBLE AND
CONCRETE INTEN-
TION HAD BEEN
TRANSFORMED INTO
A CERTAIN LIMPIDITY
OF TONE, STRANGE,
APPROPRIATE, AND
COLD.

19

the sculptures. It makes me think of the texture of Victorian interior space that Walter Benjamin described, in particular the velvet insides of the cases in which spectacles, pocket watches, thermometers, and cutlery were kept, "tending [their] traces as nature tends dead fauna embedded in granite."[11] Especially it evokes, to me, the excitingly amateurish surface textures generated by the great domestic photographers of the nineteenth century, such as Julia Margaret Cameron and Clementina Lady Hawarden.[12]

Now I'm going to confuse things by bringing in another Japanese set of techniques beginning with an S. By contrast with suminagashi or Japanese marbling, the multicolored textile surfaces in these two shows — they're called *shibori* — don't look like illustrations from a contemporary book on fractals. (I'll return to fig. 20 later; just note now that the left panel is made with a shibori technique.) But in my mind, the relation of shibori to fractional dimension is even more resonant than that of suminagashi. Shibori is the Japanese name for a class of techniques that are done all over the world, but most prominently in Japan, Africa, and South Asia. Of course, sometimes they do look like textbook illustrations of fractals. The twentieth-century American version of shibori was called tie-dye. Shibori is cloth that is bound into a three-dimensional shape and then dyed, while the cord or other binding that keeps it in the new shape also functions as a resist, preventing that part of the fabric from being suffused with the dye. As Yoshiko Wada writes,

> After the cloth is returned to its two-dimensional form, the design that emerges is the result of the three-dimensional shape of the cloth, the type of resist, and the amount of pressure exerted by the thread or clamp that secured the shape during the cloth's exposure to the dye. The cloth sensitively records both the shape and the pressure; it is the "memory" of the shape that remains imprinted in the cloth.[13]

A lot of shibori is left in a kind of springy, elastic state that dramatizes its dimensional betweenness. But even when the cloth that has been subjected to these transitions is pressed flat, it displays the memory of dimensional process on its surface. The trace of time as it crosses with dimension is so graphic that Wada, who revived this craft in contemporary Japan, was able to teach herself to decipher the history of the making of the most complex shibori patterns from as long ago as

THIS FINAL SCENE I'LL NOT SEE

TO THE END - MY DREAM

IS FRAYING

20

the sixth century, and present them to modern-day craftspeople in a sequential narrative of instruction.

Figure 21 shows two rolled-up bundles of silk and paper that are about to be dyed in indigo, from a shibori class that I took from Wada at Haystack. The next two images (figs. 22 and 23) are pieces that emerged from these two sausages. They're extremely different, and most of the differences have to do with how the material was folded before I wrapped it up with thread and dyed it (fig. 22 is paper; fig. 23 is silk). In all these examples, the connection between the folded and unfolded, or so-called "three-" and "two"-dimensional states of the shibori, is very intimate, but the connection is not one of similarity — the folded and unfolded states don't look even remotely alike.

I'm sure you've had the experience of seeing the same image in three and then two dimensions — say, in life and then in a video of the live event — but these images don't have at all that relationship to each other. The very distinguished twentieth-century theoretical physicist,

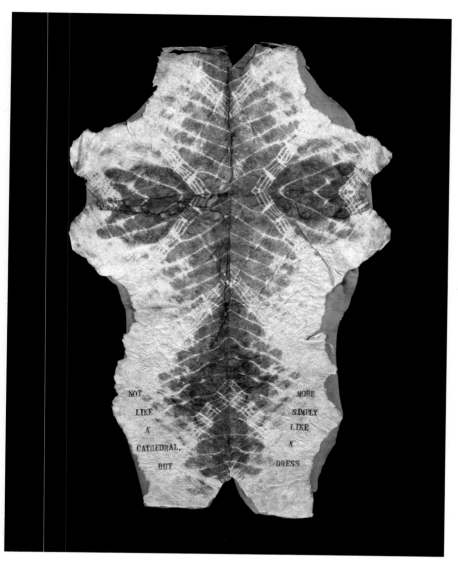

22

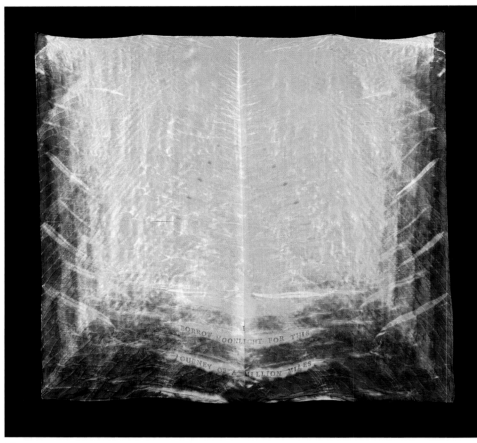

23

David Bohm, liked to use the topos of cutting snowflakes or chains of paper dolls to describe the difference:

> Everybody has seen an image of enfoldment: You fold up a sheet of paper, turn it into a small packet, make cuts in it, and then unfold it into a pattern. The parts that were close in the cuts unfold to be far away.[14]

A single cut or point will also multiply in the unfolded version to become twenty cuts or points; and their angles of orientation to each other, like their distance and their number, will turn out very different in the unfolded from the folded version. Here the mark of the scissor works as the marks of dye and resist do in shibori: they gain a kind of material purchase, in one moment and dimensionality, that persists, albeit transformed and even unrecognizable, into a changed one. And neither folded nor unfolded state can be called realer than the other.

David Bohm (1917–92) is quite an involving figure for me, to the degree that I've so far been able to understand his thinking. A communist in his early years, and always politically engaged, he grew increasingly interested in the ways his rigorous, unorthodox physics seemed cut from the same cloth as a not-quite-articulable holism that resonated with both Hindu and Buddhist traditions. Bohm didn't, as far as I know, have a fascination with textiles, but along with the motion of fluids, he found the dimensional play of folding and unfolding to be peculiarly congruent with his way of understanding ontology and consciousness. For him, what he called the "holomovement" of the universe served the function that's served, in Buddhism, by emptiness or nonbeing: the reservoir of potential out of which all dharmas (that is, things) spontaneously arise and into which they disappear. In the 1987 interview from which I just quoted, for example, Bohm said, in a description that might as easily have been of emptiness itself, the emptiness that isn't other than form:

> I propose something like this: Imagine an infinite sea of energy filling empty space, with waves moving around in there, occasionally coming together and producing an intense pulse. . . . Everything emerges by unfoldment from the holomovement, then enfolds back into the implicate order. I call the enfolding process "implicating," and the unfolding "explicating." The implicate and explicate together are a flowing, undivided wholeness.

Thus, as in shibori or paper cutting, a structure that's very complex, repetitive, or disorienting in the lower-dimensional, explicate order could also emerge as very simple in the higher-dimension implicate — or vice versa. In that interview, conducted late in his life, Bohm asked:

> Is there anything that will exist beyond death? That is the question everybody has always asked. It doesn't make sense to say something goes on in time. Rather I would say everything sinks into the implicate order, where there is no time. But suppose we say that right now, when I'm alive, the same thing is happening. The implicate order is unfolding to be me again and again each moment. And the past me is gone. ["Snatched back into the implicate order," the interviewer interjects.] That's right. Anything I know about "me" is in the past. The present

"me" is the unknown. We say there is only one implicate order, only one present. But it projects itself as a whole series of moments.

I'm very responsive to this folding/unfolding, complexifying/simplifying account of the ontological status of the individual. It's also very like the way East Asian Buddhism describes the "identity" of the bodhisattva, any bodhisattva—a figure who exists, among many other things, as a singular aspect or emanation of the Buddha, as a future or past Buddha, as an aiming toward enlightenment, as an already enlightened being who has vowed to forgo Nirvana until all sentient beings have become enlightened, and as an idea whose instantiation arises on earth and in all other universes with the commonplace, near-imperceptible ubiquity of grains of sand.

In "Bodhisattva Fractal World," the figure who occupies this fractal space is Guanyin, the Chinese version of the bodhisattva of compassion. As bodhisattvas go, Guanyin is compact with indications of the fractal and the tactile. Just at the thematic level, the emphasis on the hand is clear in the iconography of the particular statues that I'm obsessing about in these pieces, statues that emerged from the late T'ang and Song, around the turn of the last millennium. There are a lot of positions and embodiments in which the bodhisattva of compassion appears, across the historical Buddhist world. Some important ones feature, for instance, eleven heads, or a green face, or a halo made of the moon, or a baby companion, or a thousand hands, sometimes with an eye in the middle of each hand.

The particular, seated position of many of these unhaloed, two-armed, Chinese Guanyin statues, with one knee up and the corresponding arm or hand draped so expressively across the knee, is called the "royal ease" position, and it always indicates this particular bodhisattva, Guanyin (fig. 24). In Indian Buddhist art, it seems to have been the *regal* connotations of the "royal ease" position that were emphasized. In the iconography of China, though, which took Guanyin to its heart more than any other bodhisattva and arguably even more than the Buddha himself, "royal ease" became a position in which Guanyin communicated a reserve and dignity whose ground tone was nonetheless an even more profound accessibility.

Even leaving the characteristic hand gesture aside, I want you to see how open those Guanyin bodies are, how different from that of the Buddha in his fully absorbing, rock-steady and inextricable full-lotus

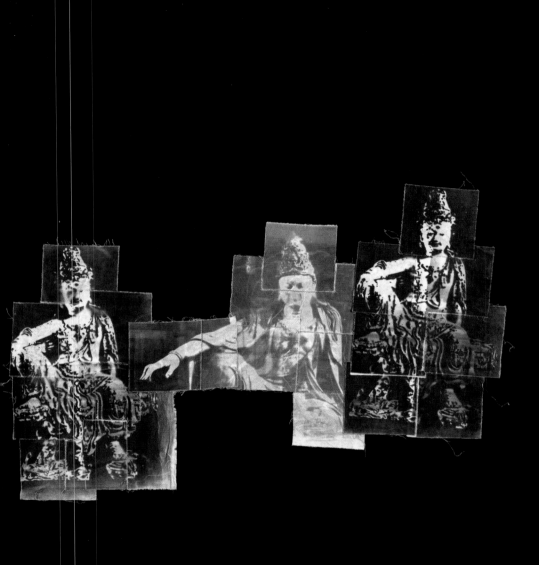

25

leg twist, even in the most mutilated example, as in figure 25, another one of those beat-up Buddha statues from Thailand. In "royal ease" the feet are separated, flexed, and ready to move, even as they dramatize relaxation. In many statues, the left leg steps or dangles downward, as though the bodhisattva were ready to descend from the pedestal. In this position Guanyin offers a radically open pelvis, and frequently an open armpit as well—if the statue were a person, you'd know their smell as well as their look. And yet for the most part, these Guanyins, relational perhaps but not interpersonal, no more open a space of seduction than of abjection, transport, or resentment. To borrow a Buddhist formulation, the fractal dimension of compassion is that of not self, not other, not both self and other, and not neither self nor other.

And "similar" seems to me to characterize their relation to gender. Up to about the eighth century, the bodhisattva was usually portrayed as a man, while after about the twelfth century, Guanyin in China was generally seen and known in female form. The Guanyins of the inter-vening centuries are often much harder to classify in terms of gender. My own thought and hope is that, even in the expression of a strong sensuality, many of these regal and loved divinities may not have been shaped or perceived through the eyes of gender at all—not male, not female, not both male and female, and not neither male nor female.[15]

Perhaps the most notable of the dualisms built into language is the simple dualism between the subject and the object of utterance. I'm not referring this time to the grammatical distinction between the subject and the object of a sentence—instead, to the much broader, inbuilt dis-tinction between the writer or speaker on the one hand, and the reader or listener on the other.

Now I've always used the first person singular freely in my writing, which clearly intensifies the visibility of this built-in, subject/object bipolarity. But attempts to make writing more impersonal or anony-mous sounding, for instance by banishing the first person singular al-together, using an inclusive sounding "we" or anonymous "one," only seem to inscribe the dualism even more deeply in the effort to make it invisible. It's interesting, for example, that the Heart Sutra itself, a key text of East Asian Buddhism, only begins in the form of a sutra, that is, a teaching—a propositional exposition, however enigmatic, of the truth of non-propositionality. For instance the lines I've quoted, like virtually all sutra language, are addressed unidirectionally from one named being to another named being, bodhisattva to disciple, in a specifically pedagogical framework. The Heart Sutra ends, however, not in the form of a sutra proper but with a mantra in Sanskrit: "*Gaté, gaté, paragaté, parasamgaté, bodhi svaha!*" Unlike sutras, mantras are traditionally not translated; this one translates, to the degree that it is translatable, as something like "Gone, gone, gone beyond, gone utterly beyond, enlightenment, svaha!" Like any mantra it is fully performa-tive, an a-grammatical and thus non-propositional and unaddressed "charm," whose utterance *is* a truth or realization rather than express-ing one. As one practitioner writes, "A mantra is not like a prayer to a divine being. Rather, the mantra . . . *is* the deity, is enlightenment, im-mediately manifest."[16]

There's a rather mysterious photograph that seems related to this issue (fig. 26). Taken in 1926 on the China-Tibet border, it shows, as its caption explains, "A [Buddhist] monk on the banks of the upper Yellow River [who] repeatedly raises and lowers a[n engraved] board on the surface of the water, each time 'printing' the river with images of Buddhist deities which are carried away downstream."[17] Of course, the varieties of Buddhist culture contain lots of analogues to this practice: prayer flags, like these on a mountain pass in Tibet (fig. 27), these around a stupa in Nepal (fig. 28). Every time the wind blows, the air of Asia gets "imprinted" by the texts and images on chains of prayer flags. When small hand-held prayer wheels get rotated by the flick of a wrist from a lone pilgrim, or large stationary prayer wheels by the gentle push of monks or pilgrims circumambulating a stupa, the wheel of dharma is itself turned (fig. 29). (Dharma is the sanskrit word for "path," but it also means "things," phenomena in general, reality and realities.) And the so-called "prayers" on these prayer flags and wheels are pictures, sutras, and mantras, rather than requests or even praise addressed to a powerful being from a powerless one; so what happens here again is a promulgation of something—something that simply exists—by no one, to no one, in a kind of unanswerable impersonality. No one sends the message, concomitantly no one seems to receive it, and yet it—what?—it messages, messages itself on the wind and water, always beside the splitting "point" of directional address, in a way that's somehow efficacious; if only through its promiscuous refusal to generate the rhetorical dyad of subject and object, or agent and acted-upon.

So I loved the way these Buddhist mantras had of not merely challenging but undoing a whole series of dualisms that normally seem inextricable from language itself: not only the dualisms of active/passive, subject/object, and speaker/hearer, but also signifier versus signified, reference versus performativity, the presumed divorce between language and "reality," between the linguistic and the material worlds. A wish to either deny or instantiate the real materiality of language has long been an animating motive in both the philosophical literature and the art of the West; and the latter of these wishes, the wish to instantiate that materiality, has obviously animated a lot of my work as well. So the complete exclusion of language from my art was never in the cards. That exclusion would have consolidated the dualism between language and "real" materiality, in a clearly unsatisfying way. And yet, for a variety of reasons, the Buddhist mantras aren't available for these

27

purposes to me in the same way they are to people really steeped in Buddhist traditions. For me to produce versions of traditional prayer flags would allude to a particular, Buddhist relation to language, but it wouldn't, in the same sense, *work*.

So in "Bodhisattva Fractal World," the first of these two recent bodies of work, I took as my main source of texts a recently published book called *Japanese Death Poems*.[18] These poems are English translations of haikus traditionally written, in proximity to death, by monks and other Zen practitioners from the seventeenth century to the early twentieth. (You'll recognize the process being used in fig. 30 as shibori; the text reads, "I have always known that I would take this path, but yesterday I did not know that it would be today."[19]) I liked these particular utterances because while they often have a first person, it isn't my first person—and furthermore, it's a first person at the very edge of its decomposition. Then in addition, these haiku respond so directly to a sense of urgency I continue to have: so *this* is what it feels like to die. (The text in fig. 31 reads, "Reality is flowerlike: cold clouds sinking through the dusk.") Or at least: this is a way it *can* feel to die, if you've got your mind properly wrapped around the reality of the process. Or this is *a* way that dying can feel, or the way *a* dying can feel, or sound.

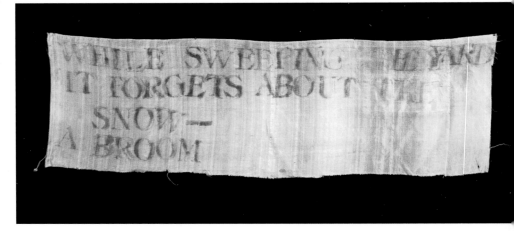

32

33

—Figure 32: "While sweeping the yard it forgets about the snow—a broom."[20]

—Figure 20: "This final scene I'll not see to the end—my dream is fraying" (of course I loved the textileness of "my dream is fraying," something about this anomalous Guanyin, too).[21]

—Figure 33: "I borrow moonlight for this journey of a million miles."[22]

—Figure 34: "The most exclusive love for a person is always a love for someone else" (Proust 2:563).

Besides *Japanese Death Poems*, as I've mentioned, the other source for the language in these pieces was the writing of the twentieth-century French novelist Marcel Proust. I don't have time here to go on about Proust in the way I'd dearly love to do, but I will say that I've been deeply immersed in Proust for much longer than I have been in Buddhism; that they feel *very* closely related to me, and function as touchstones to my sense of reality in very similar ways; and furthermore that I've learned to look in Buddhism for something I now realize I've always found in Proust: a mysticism that, unlike many uses of Buddhism, is made up out of dailiness; a mysticism that doesn't depend on so-called mystical experiences; that doesn't rely on the esoteric or occult, but rather on simple, material metamorphoses as they are emulsified with language and meaning. Which is why the title of this most recent body of work is "Works in Fiber, Paper, and Proust"—not works "on," but works "*in*," reflecting my interest in using Proust's language and thought as a medium, one with a texture and materiality comparable to other artistic media, that can be manipulated through various processes to show new aspects.

The final work I want to show you, from that group, is in an invented form that I think of as a "loom book" (fig. 35; figs. 36 and 37 [details]). It goes back to the shared prehistory of fabric looms and stringed musical instruments, as technologies for exploring what the one-dimensionality of string can generate when it is placed under tension. And in the case of the loom book, the weft (and indeed the supplementary warp) that crisscross the loom in the making of the piece are actual phrases and clauses, though not ones that can quite be strung together in a temporally clear linear alignment. The phrases from Proust that are woven into the loom book, meanwhile, make me think so much of the alternate dimensional forms of the "explicate" and "implicate," in

34

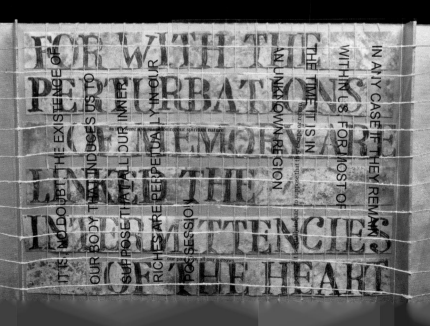

FOR WITH THE PERTURBATIONS OF MEMORY ARE LINKED THE INTERMITTENCIES OF THE HEART

IT IS, NO DOUBT, THE EXISTENCE OF OUR BODY THAT INDUCES US TO SUPPOSE THAT ALL OUR INNER RICHES ARE PERPETUALLY IN OUR POSSESSION

as if it were a vase oft losing our spiritual nature

our past, all our sorrows

IN ANY CASE IF THEY REMAIN WITHIN US, FOR MOST OF THE TIME IT IS IN AN UNKNOWN REGION

it is irrational that to suppose that they began to our regions

David Bohm's folding and unfolding model of individual identity in the universe: in the universe, that is, or in the cradle of emptiness itself.

From Proust:

— It is, no doubt, the existence of our body that induces us to suppose that our inner riches are perpetually in our possession.

— Our passions, all our sorrows.

— Perhaps it is equally inexact to suppose that they escape or return.

— As if it were a vase enclosing our spiritual nature.

— For with the perturbations of memory are linked the intermittences of the heart.[23]

NOTES

Michael Petry invited EKS to speak on "The Construction of an Identity in Artistic Practice." This talk was given first at Goldsmith's College, London, on July 4, 2007, and subsequently at the University of York, on November 1, 2007, hosted by Jason Edwards. As indicated in the notes, "Making Things, Practicing Emptiness" draws occasionally on "Come as You Are," a talk delivered at the State University of New York at Stony Brook on June 28, 1999, in conjunction with "Floating Columns / In the Bardo," a show of EKS's work also displayed at the City University of New York's Graduate Center.

1. [EKS elaborates on this point in "Come as You Are." Picking up on an analogy between an amnesiac patient and the realization of nonself in Soygal Rinpoche, *The Tibetan Book of Living and Dying* (ed. Patrick Gaffney and Andrew Harvey [New York: Harper Collins, 1992]), she writes as follows (the concluding paragraph here also can be found in *Touching Feeling: Affect, Pedagogy, Performativity* [Durham: Duke University Press, 2003], 24):

It's not that I resonated so much with the notion of a true identity hovering somewhere behind the false ones, but it did seem so plausible that one would respond in exactly that way if one somehow did forget just who one was. All the dreams in which I'm sitting on somebody's thesis defense, but can't remember ever seeing them before much less reading their dissertation; feel desperate to cover this gap in my cognitive continuity; and in the event prove able to *do just fine* with it, generating ornery objections, judicious praise, and endlessly articulated opinions with the best of them. Whew! Leaving me to wonder, by the way, in these dreams, whether everybody on the committee might be as clueless as myself. The compulsive way we "argue" by showing each other's opinions to be mutually contradictory — as if we could best conceal the pathetic, makeshift patchiness of our own ego by exposing that of someone else.

Generating opinions, in fact, came to feel like a key to this desperate ego-retro-improvisation, and strikingly so in my academic world—opinions as a way of laboriously, noisily, endlessly treading water rather than risking submersion in the salty depths of one's amnesia. One of the reasons I found I loved making *things*, weavings and collages, rather than texts: *things* neither hold nor are opinions, and, ideally, cannot be mistaken for them.

What's with the amnesia thing, though? Why identify so strongly with that? I have some ideas though I'm not quite sure. For one thing, though I didn't exactly find myself in a hospital with no memory of my name, I did suddenly find myself wearing an outer-space-looking neck brace, getting lots of attention from very grave-looking doctors, getting my body "imaged" with a minute intensiveness that descended to the level of cells and molecules, and being gently told to think in terms of maybe two or six more years of life instead of maybe thirty or fifty. I'd already learned from the initial cancer diagnosis that a common response to catastrophic news, at any rate one that I seem prone to, is a quite violent pulverizing of the attention span. It's probably a great defense mechanism, a kind of enforced "one day at a time": sufficient unto this particular second is the disaster thereof, so don't make any connections with the last second or the next. It's an effect that can take a long time to recede—that is, if it ever does. Not so surprising, then, that at that juncture I felt closer to the amnesia than to the project of patching together a current story to conceal it.

What may have been adding to that sense of amnesia is the accumulating cognitive effect of the various cancer therapies I underwent. Most of the (little) research on so-called "chemobrain" focuses on high-dose adjuvant chemotherapy, which I didn't have, but it often seems to me that I do feel the accumulated cognitive effects of some combination of the original chemo I took, and the subsequent years of radical hormone suppression. I wouldn't say I feel stupider now than before—but I'm encountering a whole lot more verbal blockages, some of them quite dramatic, and as for numbers, the only appropriate phrase is "Forget it." In fact, before I learned about the phenomenon of chemobrain, I often wondered whether I might have suffered one or more small, unremarked strokes.

But then it also seems, and I don't know what the ontological status of this observation can be—but it also seems as though the whole baby boomer generation, or maybe just *everybody* in our culture, is suddenly losing our memory together, or at least becoming obsessed with the specter of such cognitive loss. Don't you think so? It's as though all the amnesiacs in that hospital ward were suddenly trembling on the verge of just not bothering to come up with cover stories at all.

Barbara Herrnstein Smith is fond of the notion of the "senile sublime," as she calls it, and I've always been attracted to it, too. She uses it to describe various more or less intelligible performances by old brilliant people, whether artists, scientists, or intellectuals, where the bare, cold bones of a creative structure seem finally to emerge from what had been the obscuring puppy fat of personableness, timeliness, or sometimes even of coherent sense. Who wouldn't find it magnetic, the idea of emerging into this senile sublime?]

2. Seung Sahn, *The Compass of Zen* (Boston: Shambhala, 1997), 130, the source as well for the later citation from the Heart Sutra.

3. [EKS heard the Dalai Lama say this at a teaching that took place on May 25–27, 1997, in the Great Buddha Hall at the Chuang-Yen Monastery in Carmel, New York. In "Come as You Are," written at that time, she says: "Teachings on this sutra emphasize that 'emptiness' here—or indeed emptiness anywhere—should be thought of as like the empty space on the inside of a bell—emptiness not blank but vibrant and gravid with subtle energy, potential, and arising. But maybe we can also think of the experimentally fantasied 'emptiness' of a child's voided insides, as the child learns to link that to the power of material formation, of the formal and of what is not herself." The latter point picks up from a discussion just before the citation from the Heart Sutra that compares dying and toilet training: "Suppose that getting toilet trained is about learning, forcibly, to change the process of one's person into a residual product—into something that instead exemplifies the *im*personal in its lumpishly ultimate and taboo form. Isn't this one of the tasks of dying, as well? Suppose the many, stubborn, transformational negotiations with chosen cloth objects at that period are a medium for experimenting with the dimensions and new possibilities of this unwelcome imperative. Another such imperative is the letting go of the infantile cutaneous touch of the person you love, who also loves you. These are also among the tasks of dying."]

4. [EKS has a tantalizingly fragmentary note here: "Example of 'thinking'—Nietzsche? Bion. Or fucking?"]

5. Anne Chambers, *Suminagashi: The Japanese Art of Marbling, A Practical Guide* (London: Thames and Hudson, 1991) shows a good example on p. 24 and gives a sketch of how this is achieved on p. 9.

6. All citations from Marcel Proust are to book and page number in the six-volume *In Search of Lost Time*, trans. C. K. Scott Moncrieff and Terence Kilmartin, rev. D. J. Enright (New York: Modern Library, 2003). I'll talk more later about the choice of texts on these pieces.

7. See Sedgwick, *Touching Feeling*, 13–25; passages from 13–14 are cited in the sentences that follow.

8. ["Bodhisattva Fractal World" was displayed at Dartmouth College and the Johns Hopkins University in 2002–3; "Works in Fiber, Paper, and Proust" was seen at Harvard University in 2005 and at the University of York in 2007. EKS quotes below from the description she offered of the latter show: "The pieces in this show emerge from a decades-long engagement with Marcel Proust's novel, *A la recherche du temps perdu*, but they are not meant either to illustrate the book or to evoke its time, place, or atmospheres. The show's title reflects my interest in using Proust's language and thought as a medium, one with texture and ma-

teriality comparable to other artistic media, that can be manipulated through various processes to show new aspects. But if these are works 'in' Proust in the same sense that they're 'in' fiber or paper, they also reflect the transformative potential of a prolonged immersion in someone else's mental world, a way of being 'in Proust.' I am especially interested in the dailiness of a mysticism that doesn't rely on the esoteric or occult, but on simple material metamorphoses as they are emulsified with language and meaning."]

9. Ian Marshall, Danah Zohar, and F. David Peat, *Who's Afraid of Schrodinger's Cat?* (New York: William Morrow, 1997), 154–55.

10. The text in figure 19 quotes Proust (3:55).

11. Walter Benjamin, *Charles Baudelaire: A Lyric Poet in the Era of High Capitalism*, trans. Harry Zohn (New York: Verso, 1983), 46.

12. On these photographers, see Carol Mavor, *Pleasures Taken* (Durham: Duke University Press, 1995) and *Becoming: The Photographs of Clementina, Viscountess Hawarden* (Durham: Duke University Press, 1999).

13. Yoshiko Wada, Mary Kellogg Rice, and Jane Barton, *Shibori: The Inventive Art of Japanese Shaped Resist Dyeing; Tradition, Techniques, Innovation* (Tokyo: Kodansha International, 1983), 54. For illustrations of technique, see p. 69; on historical patterns and for a diagram of how they are made, see pp. 78–79.

14. F. David Peat and John Briggs, "Interview with David Bohm," www.fdavidpeat.com/interviews/bohm.htm.

15. On these histories and iconographies, and for pertinent illustrations, see *inter alia*: John Blofeld, *Bodhisattva of Compassion* (Boston: Shambhala, 1977); Tove E. Neville, *Eleven-Headed Avalokitesvara: Chenresigs, Kuan-yin or Kannon Bodhisattva; Its Origin and Iconography* (New Delhi: Munshiram Manoharlal, 1999); Diana Y. Paul, *Women in Buddhism: Images of the Feminine in the Mahāyāna Tradition*, 2nd ed. (Berkeley: University of California Press, 1985); Chün-fang Yü, *Kuan-yin: The Chinese Transformation of Avalokitesvara* (New York: Columbia University Press, 2000); the Chinese language book by Li Yinhao translated as *The Guanyin Treasures* (Taipei: Art Taipei, 1993); and Robert E. Fisher, *Buddhist Art and Architecture* (London: Thames and Hudson, 1993).

16. Lorne Ladner, *Wheel of Great Compassion* (Somerville, Mass.: Wisdom, 2000), 9.

17. Michael Aris, *Lamas, Princes, and Brigands: Joseph Rock's Photographs of the Tibetan Borderlands of China* (New York: China House Gallery, China Institute of America, 1992), 86.

18. Yoel Hoffman, *Japanese Death Poems* (Rutland, Vt.: Charles E. Tuttle, 1986). The text for figure 32 is from this book (154).

19. This is a version of lines by Ariwara no Narihira, the supposed author of *Tales of Ise* (trans. Henry Harris [Rutland Vt.: Charles E. Tuttle, 1972]), where it appears as *dan* #125 (158). It is also in the *Kokinshū* (the first imperial collection, ca. 905), where it is #861, the second-to-last in the section on grief. It is

translated in *Kokinshū: A Collection of Poems Ancient and Modern* (trans. Laurel Rasplica Rodd with Mary Catherine Henkenius [Princeton: Princeton University Press, 1984]) as follows: "although I've heard / there is a road we all must / travel never did / I think I might set out on / it yesterday or today" (296).

20. *Bashō and His Interpreters: Selected Hokku with Commentary*, compiled, translated, and with an introduction by Makoto Ueda (Stanford: Stanford University Press, 1992), 346.

21. Hoffman, *Japanese Death Poems*, 287.

22. Ibid., 275.

23. [EKS cites phrases used in her loom book that come from Proust 3:211–12: "For with the perturbations of memory are linked the intermittencies of the heart. It is, no doubt, the existence of our body, which we may compare to a vase enclosing our spiritual nature, that induces us to suppose that all our inner wealth, our past joys, all our sorrows, are perpetually in our possession. Perhaps it is equally inexact to suppose that they escape or return. In any case if they remain within us, for most of the time it is in an unknown region. . . . But if the context of sensations in which they are preserved is recaptured, they acquire in turn the same power of expelling everything that is incompatible with them, of installing alone in us the self that originally lived them."]

Melanie Klein and
the Difference Affect Makes

Sometimes I think the books that affect us most are fantasy books. I don't mean books in the fantasy genre; I don't even mean the books we fantasize about writing but don't write. What I'm thinking of here are the books we know about — from their titles, from reading reviews, or hearing people talk about them — but haven't, over a period of time, actually read. Books that can therefore have a presence, or exert a pressure in our lives and thinking, that may have much or little to do with what's actually inside them.

Again, I don't mean here the books that, rightly or wrongly, we minimize and dismiss without having read them — whether from competitive anxiety or anticipatory boredom. No. Instead, at least for me — and you can tell that over the years I've developed a commendably rich and varied spiritual practice of failing to read books — there are a few special titles that persist as objects of speculation, of accumulated reverie. Far from minimizing I seem to enhance and enrich them over time, investing them with my own obsessions and the fruits of my varying thought and self-relation. Except of course it's not "them" I invest in this way, but their titles or their authors' names as valued, phantasmatic objects internal to myself.

If this sounds like part of a Melanie-Kleinian kind of dynamic of projection and introjection, it is exactly that, and in some ways it especially characterizes my difficult relation over time to the work of Melanie Klein. One odd feature of this history is that I can't remember when, in this decades-long process, I did start actually reading Klein rather than just brooding over her. I don't know what it says about her writing or my reading process, either, that it hasn't been so much the actual experience of rereading Klein that has kept dramatically punctuating the great attractions I've repeatedly found in her work. Instead it's been encounters with other writers' persuasive paraphrase of her, notably those of R. D. Hinshelwood and, more recently, Meira Likierman.[1]

Here's another, less sunny story from my personal history that I also, for some reason, think of as very Kleinian.

For this one, picture me around age three, in Dayton, Ohio, where my grandmother has come from New York to visit our family. Today's outing: we're going to Rike's, the local department store, where my six-year-old sister will get to pick out a new doll. I, in turn, am the recipient of her current doll, an eight-inch or so plastic doll representing a girl of about her age. And at Rike's, too, I'm supposed to pick out a new blanket for my "new" doll.

Except that I absolutely don't want my sister's doll. Characteristically, I have a well-reasoned account of what's wrong with it: it's not big enough for me. I need — and somehow feel emboldened to demand — a doll that is bigger, baby- or toddler-shaped, and new. A doll on the smaller and grown-up scale of the one I've been given, I'd simply lose. (And it's true, small-muscle coordination is about the least precocious thing about me, if you don't count emotional maturity.) I can remember offering this explanation to my parents with the calm confidence of someone quoting a well-known adult dictum: younger children need larger-scale toys. An argument that apparently didn't persuade, since the next thing to happen seems to be my descent into the awful whirlpool of tantrum mode. What I remember better, though, is the aftermath: me later abject, flattened by the ordeal of my rage, trailing through the innards of the department store in a state of apparent social death. Also the numb shock of finding, before the end of our afternoon there, that the smaller, inappropriate doll I was carrying has indeed disappeared.

I could go on for ages about this story — which, while it's remained accessible in my memory for a long time, is the kind that nonetheless re-arrives on the scene with a fairly ferocious new vitality when I'm really engaged with Melanie Klein. Along with the sense of access to vivid insight, these periodic reengagements with Klein are accompanied by painful dreams and painfully crabby days. Also by series of uncontrolled flashes in which many aspects of my life, including those I'm especially fond or proud of (call them Buddhist ones), appear in the light of fragile, exhausting, sometimes impoverishing, and barely successful defenses against being devoured by my own cycles of greed, envy, rage, and, in particular, overwhelming anxiety. There isn't even the comfort of self-pity, since Klein makes so very palpable the exacerbated grain of psychic lives that are much less tolerable than one's own. And even though for me everything in Klein resonates with issues about vocation, thought, reading, and especially writing, I also don't have the Romantic consolation that these upsets are the extremities of genius. Rather they're testimony to the almost grotesquely unintelligent design of every human psyche.

I've always taken to heart Thoreau's guess that quiet desperation characterizes the majority of lives. The question of whether or not mine is part of that majority—though I have plenty of questions about the question itself, including who's asking it—that question nonetheless still feels crucial to me and many times frighteningly unsettled. Klein is one of the people who most upsets me by unsettling it—vastly more than Freud or Lacan does, for example, and even more than the Marxist or anticolonial perspectives from which my preoccupations are so effectively made to feel marginal, even to me.

I keep remembering that there's nothing so special about the incident with the doll, but the clanging emotional and intellectual vibration it evokes, when I'm deep into Klein, effortlessly traverses not only the different *areas* of my life, but the whole range of scales on which the life is lived, from its micro-irritants to love and work to abstruse theoretical activity to investments in death or even enlightenment. In fact that's why I started out telling the story: I think I meant it as a fairly simple story about scale. Just to say how the right scale of doll for my older sister was the wrong scale for me, how I needed something chunkier. I needed, or thought I did, something with decent-scale, plastic, resiliently articulated parts that I could manipulate freely and safely (safely for *it* as well as me): this seemed to be the condition for my loving or identifying with the creature, even just not abandoning it.

And, I was going on to say, as an adult that's the way I now am about ideas. I like them pretty chunky. Not dramatic or caricatural, certainly not dualistic (never dualistic), but big, big and palpable; big enough so there's no swallowing risk, and also so I won't forget them, which hasn't become any less of a danger as I've gotten older. I'm happy with ideas where you can do a lot of different things with them and be in many relations to them, but they'll push back against you—and where the individual moving parts aren't too complex or delicate for active daily use.

In some ways Melanie Klein is perfect in offering ideas on just this scale. Her work has a reassuring groundedness, a sense of reality. I realize that remark may sound implausible to anyone unwilling to sail through sentences about the cannibalistic defense of the good partial breast against the devouring invasion of the feces. But as someone whose education has proceeded through Straussian and deconstructive, as well as psychoanalytic, itineraries where vast chains of interpretive inference may be precariously balanced on the tiniest of details or differentials, I feel enabled by the way that even abstruse Kleinian work remains so susceptible to a gut check. It may not be grounded in commonsense, but it is phenomenologically grounded to a remarkable degree. A lot of this quality is owing to the fact that Klein's psychoanalysis, in contrast to Freud's, is based in affect and offers a compelling account of the developments and transformations of affective life. Likierman helpfully uses the word "qualitative" to distinguish Klein's approaches, and I think "qualitative" in this context translates neatly as "affect-based." Likierman writes, for instance, that in contrast to Freud's undifferentiated notion of primary narcissism, in Klein "the infant is . . . equipped from birth to apprehend a qualitative essence in different kinds of life experiences."[2]

About Klein's theoretical formulations, Likierman also identifies her "tendency to use a term both to describe the subject's internal experience and, simultaneously, to offer a technical psychoanalytic designation of a phenomenon . . . while Freud's thinking distinguished between theoretical definitions and subjective descriptions."[3] This tendency of Klein's, again, while reflecting a sort of Ferenczian refusal to conceptually privilege the supposed objectivity of the psychoanalyst over the patient's subjectivity, also seems to reflect a difference between the kind of distance involved in theorizing about drive versus theorizing about affect.

But the invitingly chunky affordances of Klein's thought probably have most to do with a thematic aspect of her view of psychology: it's she who put the objects in object relations. In her concept of phantasy-with-a-*ph*, human mental life becomes populated, not with ideas, representations, knowledges, urges, and repressions, but with *things*, things with physical properties, including people and hacked-off bits of people.

If this almost literal-minded animism makes Kleinian psychic life sound like a Warner Bros. cartoon, you might think it would be far too coarse-grained, too unmediated to deal with adult creativity in ambitious intellectual or artistic modes. Even Freud, after all, who, unlike Klein, invested so much of his best thought in issues of representation, had to either interpret actual creative work in diagnostic terms or bundle it away under the flattening, strangely incurious rubric of sublimation. Paradoxically, though, this is one of the areas of Klein's greatest appeal: she makes it possible to be respectful of intellectual work without setting it essentially apart from other human projects. That our work is motivated—psychologically, affectively motivated—and perhaps most so when it is good work or when it is true: with Klein this is an extremely interesting fact, much more so than an ignominious or discrediting one. If anything, Klein presents the course of very ordinary psychological development in terms that will be especially recognizable to ambitious or innovative thinkers. An example is Klein's focus on projection and introjection. Resorting again to Likierman's paraphrase:

> In Klein's understanding, early Oedipal experience is a particular mythology, created by the phantasy transposition of oral and anal events from the primitive life of the body to an infantile narrative about images and their relationships. . . . In this process, adults are felt to be the stuff of myths—strange supernatural creatures or powerful and fearful deities who use their bodies to exchange magical substances and bring forth new life.
>
> . . . Klein began to portray mental life as creative in essence. Her descriptions conjure up all the key features of human creative activity, including the forging of new images to reflect life experience, the use of these in internal narratives, the creation of symbols as a central mental activity, and the mental creation of a subjective, personal mythology, an inner world inhabited by "phantastic" beings and dominated by their adventures and relationships. Just as Klein's accounts were earlier suggestive of a link between the creation of weapons and pre-genital aggression, they now invoked links between the developing ego and a work of art.[4]

This becomes especially true in her writing after 1935, where Klein gives a detailed account of what she calls the depressive position, involving the vicissitudes of relation to a "good internal object": a relation that is conceived as virtually intersubjective, profoundly ambivalent, and a locus of anybody's special inventiveness. I see now that the good internal object is what I was writing about in 1992 in this untitled, sonnet-like little poem that I included in my collection, *Fat Art, Thin Art*. The poem talks about how an internal, anthropomorphized figure makes a relational space for me, however troubled, in which an orientation toward futurity and creation becomes possible.

> What I would be when I grew up,
> I never wondered that (maybe I knew that);
> I wondered other things: if I'd be
> sane. Loved.
>   But I did
> bend to divine one thing,
> the fate of — "my talent." Shyly
> as a big sister I would yearn
> to trace its avocations, its vocations,
> what *it* would want to be when *it*
> grew up; what it would need the world to be.
> Say I've abused, betrayed it a thousand times:
> still I am grateful
> there was even that bad way to care for the child.[5]

If anything, in fact, as I suggested earlier, Klein's account of internal object relations resonates *so* fully with the structure and phenomenology of intellectual work that it makes a problem for some of the very kinds of thinking that it also stimulates. I think this is why Klein isn't used more explicitly in critical theory, even though so many theorists, queer and otherwise, have drawn important energies and ideas from her. There is a kind of clangor or overload from the intense way these resonances flash out at the reader at so many microlevels and metalevels at once. Engaging closely with Klein often feels like getting stoned, in the sense that the unchecked proliferation of the reader's sense of recognition, endlessly recursive and relentlessly architectonic, quickly turns into a kind of fractal ineffability, resistant to the linear formulations of ordinary exposition. But when deconstructive or Lacanian insight, for example, proliferates at different levels in a similar way, an effect of fine-spun abstraction or even sublimity results; while with Klein, the additional, unmediated charge of all that thematized bad affect — anxiety in particular — can be genuinely disabling to cognitive function. At least I've often found it so.

That's a lot of the reason why secondary studies of her work, like Likierman's monograph and Hinshelwood's dictionary, are peculiarly indispensable in trying to actually use Klein. Both of those books do for readers a lot of the work of abstraction, of absorbing the trans-ferential near-chaos that can be generated in learning from Klein's work; both books could be described as being, in a good sense, "well-analyzed," a term that one wouldn't apply to Klein herself or to how the reader feels in encountering her. But much more, productive work can be done on Klein at this mediating level. And while that process goes directly against many of my own close-reading, literary impulses, it does hold out the promise of a good new handful of chunky tools and the affordances for using them.

For me, as well, there has been a lot of help, in approaching Klein, from having two other sets of ideas concurrently in mind. One is an understanding of Buddhist psychological thought, especially in the Tibetan tradition, that often diverges sharply from Klein but at other times comes close enough to clarify it startlingly, or vice versa. The other, in which I've been involved almost as long, is the work of Silvan Tomkins (1911–91), an American psychologist who pioneered in the understanding of affect.[6] Though he was interested in psychoanaly-sis, Tomkins was most influenced by early work in cybernetics and systems theory. His sophisticated understanding of feedback mecha-nisms—such as the transferential and recursive ones set in motion so disruptively in the process of encountering Klein—seems to give him an invigorating theoretical purchase on the workings of affect, one that permits him the rare achievement of doing full justice to the qualita-tive differences among the affects without triggering disruptive affect spirals in his reader.

Tomkins's systems-theory framework, which Klein was born half a generation too early to be at home with, offers another way of be-ginning with chunky ideas and using them to get to a lot of different places; and also like Klein's work, does so without the shortcut of a structuring dualism. And from a feminist and queer perspective I find it helpful to have a second, binocular angle of vision that begins fur-ther outside of psychoanalysis than Klein, that is more programmati-cally resistant to some of the damaging assumptions that have shaped psychoanalysis in (what I think of as) its Oedipal mode: the defining centrality of dualistic gender difference; the primacy of genital mor-phology and desire; the determinative nature of childhood experience and the linear teleology toward a sharply distinct state of maturity; and especially the logic of zero-sum games and the excluded middle term, where passive is the opposite of active and desire is the opposite of identification; and where one person's getting more love means a priori that another is getting less.

Here's one example of the importance of the excluded middle term: a crucial dynamic of omnipotence and powerlessness that emerges from the work of Melanie Klein. In Freud's view, notoriously, our relation to omnipotence is pretty simple: bring it on. According to Freud's work, we want as much power as we can get and indeed start out with the assumption that we are omnipotent; everything after that is the big, disillusioning letdown called reality. Yet in a sense, Freudian analytic theory, especially in its structuralist or Lacanian aspects, never does let go of an implicit view that power of any sort or degree can only mean omnipotence. What changes with maturity and Oedipalization is the view of whom or what you have power over, rather than the understanding of power per se *as* omnipotence. One must give up the infantile fantasy of owning Mother, this formulation says, but as one matures and masters an economy of substitution, one can achieve both ownership of other women and an ownership (however displaced and distributed) of the means of production of meaning itself.

For the Kleinian subject, however, unlike the Freudian one, omnipotence is a fear at least as much as it is a wish. It is true here, as in Freud, that the infant's self and its constituent parts, like others and their parts, can only be experienced as all or nothing, either helpless or omnipotent. The problem is that the infant's desires are passionately experienced but intrinsically self-contradictory. The Kleinian infant experiences a greed — her own — whose aggressive and envious component is perceived as posing a mortal threat both to her loved and needed objects and to herself. Thus the perception of oneself as omnipotent is hardly less frightening than the perception of one's parent as being so.

In fact, this all-or-nothing understanding of agency is toxic enough that it is a relief and relaxation for the child eventually to discover a different reality. The sense that power is a form of relationality that deals in, for example, negotiations (including win-win negotiations), the exchange of affect, and other small differentials, the middle ranges of agency — the notion that you can be relatively empowered or disempowered without annihilating someone else or being annihilated, or even castrating or being castrated — is a great mitigation of that endogenous anxiety, although it is also a fragile achievement that requires to be discovered over and over.

Clearly, one of the main cruxes for such issues is the status of repression. For Freud, "the theory of repression is the corner-stone on which the whole structure of psycho-analysis rests"; and of course its importance extends far beyond psychoanalytic thought.[7] To offer a reductive paraphrase, Freudian repression is an internal defense mechanism—the prototype of defense mechanisms in general, as Laplanche and Pontalis note—that is modeled on and in fact originates with external prohibition.[8] Civilization, in the Freudian view, cannot coexist with the individual's uncorrected sense of omnipotence, with the untrammeled satisfaction of the individual's inherently insatiable desire, or with its uncensored expression or even self-experience. To internalize societal prohibition in an effective but not paralyzing way is, for Freudian psychoanalysis, *the* maturational task of the individual. While different kinds of psychoanalytic politics may be more or less invested in the repressive needs of civilization as opposed to the countervailing claims of individual desire, such arguments have the almost uniform effect of reinforcing a single structuring assumption: that psychic activity is ultimately, definitionally constituted by the struggle between intrinsic desire and imposed or internalized prohibition. Other defining concepts, such as the unconscious itself with its inaccessible topography and distinctive hermeneutic imperatives, are founded on the absolute primacy of repression. In Freudian psychoanalysis, repression is both entirely necessary and largely sufficient as a determinant of the nature of psychic life.

Melanie Klein, like Silvan Tomkins, works not so much against the concept of repression as around it. Without contesting either the existence or force of repressive mechanisms—both external and internalized—Klein views them in the context of other, earlier, and more violent conflicts and dangers that, by contrast, result directly from the internal dynamics of the emerging psyche in what Klein came to call the paranoid/schizoid position. The whole Freudian dialectic between desire and prohibition is only a secondary development for Klein, and one among several such. Moreover, the structure and importance of repression as a secondary defense mechanism vary according to how the individual has already dealt with such primary defense mechanisms as splitting, omnipotence, and violent projection and introjection.

What defines the paranoid/schizoid position into which we are born, in all its terrible fragility, are five violent things. The first is the inability of the self to comprehend or tolerate ambivalence—the insistence on all-or-nothing. The second is its consequent, "schizoid" strategy of splitting both its objects and itself into very concretely imagined part-objects that can be only seen as exclusively, magically good or bad—where those are not in the first place ethical designations but qualitative judgments perceived as involving life or death. Third, as we've mentioned, is that, in the paranoid/schizoid position, the sense of agency, too, occupies only two extreme positions. The self and its constituent parts, like others and their parts, can only be experienced as either powerless or omnipotent. Fourth is a kind of greed for "good" things that is figured in terms of ingesting them and holding them inside, where they are liable to remain distinct and magically alive, doing battle with "bad" contents and vulnerable to being devoured or fatally contaminated by them. And fifth is the mechanism of projection, classically that of attributing to other people the unacceptable parts of oneself, but given, as we'll see, a new immediacy in the work of Klein.

⁊ Overall, perhaps the crucial difference from Freud is that in Klein, what these primary defense mechanisms have to defend *against* is not prohibitive external impingement, as in Freud, but instead the devastating force of a largely endogenous anxiety. By analogy, in Tomkins, the conflict of substantive affects *with other substantive affects* is at least as basic and consequential as any conflict with outside forces, however intimately internalized.[9] It is not mainly "civilization" that needs the individual to be different from the way she spontaneously is. The individual herself needs to be different, insofar as her intrinsic impulses conflict with one another even more drastically than they conflict with the claims of her environment. Instead of the undifferentiatedly blind, pleasure-seeking drives of the Freudian infant, which encounter no check but the originally external ones of prohibition or lack, the Kleinian infant experiences a greed whose aggressive and envious component is already perceived as posing a terrible threat both to her desired objects and to herself. The resulting primary anxiety is an affect so toxic that it probably ought to be called not anxiety, but dread. It is against this endogenous dread that the primary defense mechanisms are first mobilized—the splitting, the omnipotence, the violent projection and introjection.

These defenses in turn, which may be mitigated but never go away, can impress their shape on the internal experience of repression as well as the social experience of suffering from, enforcing, or resisting repression. The complex developments that later characterize the depressive position will also have an impact on the shapes ultimately taken by repression. It remains true, however, that endogenous primary dread, whose corrosive force varies from person to person for essentially constitutional as well as environmental reasons, takes the central place in Kleinian thought that desire and repression occupy in Freudian psychoanalysis.

Of course this issue of repression is not a question of interest only within psychoanalysis. The primacy of repression structures a near-universal, dualistic Western view of politics and, for example, religion as rigorously as it does a Freudian view of the psyche. Foucault demonstrates as much in volume 1 of his *History of Sexuality*, in his justly famous, though ultimately circular analysis of what he calls the repressive hypothesis. According to the repressive hypothesis that Foucault attempts to disassemble here, which is entirely of a piece with Freud's own repressive hypothesis, the history of sexuality could only be that of the "negative relation" between power and sex, of "the insistence of the rule," of "the cycle of prohibition," of "the logic of censorship," and of "the uniformity of the apparatus" of scarcity and prohibition: "Whether one attributes it to the form of the prince who formulates rights, of the father who forbids, of the censor who enforces silence, or of the master who states the law," — or, we might add, that of the internalized superego — "in any case one schematizes power in a juridical form, and one defines its effects as obedience."[10] In other words, Foucault describes the whole range of Western liberatory discourses — those of class politics, identity politics, Enlightenment values, and the projects of sexual liberation including psychoanalysis — as being congruent and continuous with one another precisely in their dependence on the centrality of external and/or internal repression.

More disturbingly, Foucault demonstrates a devastating performative continuity between the diagnostics of these projects, the way they analyze the central problematic of Western culture (repression), on the one hand, and on the other hand their therapeutics, the ways in which they propose to rectify it. For if there is some problem with the repressive hypothesis itself, if in important ways repression is a misleading or even damaging way to understand the conditions of societies and individuals, then the main performative effect of these centuries-long anti-repressive projects may be the way they function as near-irresistible propaganda for the repressive hypothesis itself.

Perhaps inevitably, Foucault in turn seems to me to be far more persuasive in analyzing this massive intellectual blockage than in finding ways to obviate it. The moves demonstrated in volume 1 of *The History of Sexuality*, at any rate, like much of Foucault's work before that book, might instead be described as propagating the repressive hypothesis ever more broadly by means of its displacement, multiplication, and/ or hypostatization.

The structure of this kind of conceptual impasse or short circuit is all too familiar: where it is possible to recognize the mechanism of a problem, but trying to remedy it, or even in fact articulate it, simply adds propulsive energy to that very mechanism. For one example: in Buddhist psychology samsara, the treadmill going-nowhere of death and rebirth to which lives are bound within history, is driven ever harder and thus made ever more exhausting, not only by striving for personal advantage or even progress in altruistic pursuits, but by spiritual striving as well. Such vicious circles work like Nietzsche's analysis of *ressentiment*, which he diagnoses as a self-propagating, near-universal psychology compounded of injury, rancor, envy, and self-righteous vindictiveness, fermented by a sense of disempowerment. Nietzschean *ressentiment* is not only epistemologically self-reinforcing but also contagious at a pragmatic level. Its intrinsic relationality is spontaneously generative of powerful systems. What is the most defining act, the conclusively diagnostic act of *ressentiment*? It is *accurately* accusing *someone else* of being motivated by it. Where then to find a position from which to interrupt its baleful circuit?

If I've correctly identified an important, damagingly circular dynamic of Foucault's influential volume, then I also understand better the source of an inveterate impatience I've felt with critical work conducted—as it seems to me, rather blindly—under the aegis of the "Foucauldian." By now there seems to be a near-ineradicable Foucauldian common sense structuring the routines of work in the fields of cultural studies, literature, history, and others. But arguably, the formative queer theory work of the 1980s, some of my own very much included, has generated a disciplinary space called queer, where those circular Foucauldian energies inhere with a strikingly distinctive intimacy.

꒐ Characteristically, Klein's resource in such a situation is neither to minimize the importance of this circular mechanism nor to attack it frontally. Instead she contextualizes it newly—just as she had reshaped the view of repression by framing it as a defense mechanism among others rather than the master key to mental functioning. Klein in fact is fearfully attuned to human relations that are driven by the uncontrollable engines of *ressentiment*: *tu quoque*, it takes one to know one, or in technical terms, "I know you are but what am I?" which have been so fecund for queer thought. She sees this dynamic in terms of the "primitive" defenses that characterize the paranoid/schizoid position: the prophylactic need to split good from bad, and the aggressive expulsion of intolerable parts of oneself onto — or, in Klein's more graphic locution, *into* — the person who is taken as an object. Klein writes that these projected "bad parts of the self are meant not only to injure but also to control and to take possession of the object"; she calls this mechanism "projective identification." [11]

Projective identification is not only a form of magical thinking found in infants, but virtually coextensive with Nietzschean *ressentiment* in adults. It is a good way of understanding, for example, the terrifying contagion of paranoid modes of thought — and it certainly seems indispensable in understanding political dynamics as well as many a small-group interaction, including those in the classroom. For instance, a professor who's unable to tolerate or contain the anxieties of competition may run a classroom in which everyone finds themselves unusually anxious about power or disempowerment. A professor's disavowed issues about originality can turn into a maelstrom of plagiarism anxieties that circulate in all directions. Or a professor who is unable to provide a home for her own discomforts about sexuality can accumulate a group of students whose learning process is clogged with manipulative or resentful scenes of seduction. All this is not even to mention the projective identifications that originate with our students, who can be just as self-ignorant or as disruptively charismatic as ourselves, if not more so. Again both in and beyond the classroom many of us, I think, are familiar with situations where our own or other people's preemptive need to disown feelings of racism, misogyny, anti-Semitism, and so forth — feelings that almost inevitably arise but are experienced as intolerable — is liable to propel circuits of interpersonal accusation that are explosive with the very forms of hatred that are under internal erasure. Projective identification is related to Freudian projection but more uncannily intrusive: for Freud, when I've projected my hostility on to you, I believe that *you* dislike *me*; for Klein, additionally, when I've projected my hostility *into* you, you *will* dislike me.

Thus for Klein's infant or adult, the paranoid/schizoid position — marked by insatiability, hatred, envy, and anxiety — is a position of terrible alertness to the dangers posed by the hateful and envious part-objects that one defensively projects into the world around one, and vice versa. The depressive position, by contrast, is an anxiety-mitigating achievement that the infant or adult only sometimes, and often only briefly, succeeds in inhabiting. And it becomes increasingly unclear in Klein's writing after 1940 whether she envisioned a further space beyond the depressive position.

Not that she saw people as doomed to, at best, a permanent state of depression per se. Rather, the depressive position becomes, in Klein's latter writing, a uniquely spacious rubric. Despite its name it comes to encompass, for example, both the preconditions of severe depression and also quite a varied range of resources for surviving, repairing, and moving beyond that depression. It is the site for Klein's explorations of intellectual creativity; it is also the space in which challenges to a normalizing universality can develop.

What makes the depressive position "depressive"? The threshold to the depressive position is the simple, foundational, authentically very difficult understanding that good and bad tend to be inseparable at every level. "The infant," as Hinshelwood summarizes this argument, "at some stage is physically and emotionally mature enough to integrate his or her fragmented perceptions, bringing together the separately good and bad versions. *When such part-objects are brought together as a whole they threaten to form a contaminated, damaged, or dead whole object*," whether internal, external, or both—what I take to be a description of the experience of depression per se.[12]

"Depressive anxiety," Hinshelwood continues, "is the crucial element of mature relationships, the source of generous and altruistic feelings that are devoted to the well-being of the object."[13] Only from this position, then, can one begin using one's own resources to assemble or "repair" the part-objects into something like a whole, albeit a compromised one. It is worth emphasizing that Klein's rhetoric of reparation does not assume that the "repaired" object will resemble a preexisting object—there is nothing intrinsically conservative about the impulse of reparation. Once assembled, these more realistic, durable, and satisfying internal objects are available to be identified with, to offer one and to be offered nourishment and comfort in turn. Yet the pressures of that founding, depressive realization can also continually impel the psyche back toward depression, toward manic escapism, or toward the violently projective defenses of the paranoid/schizoid position. We feel these depressive pressures in the forms of remorse, shame, the buzzing confusion that makes thought impossible, depression itself, mourning for the lost ideal, and—often most relevant—a paralyzing apprehension of the inexorable laws of unintended consequences.

My own uncomfortable sense is that, for me at any rate, activist politics takes place—even at best—just at this difficult nexus between the paranoid/schizoid and the depressive positions. Suppose the paranoid/schizoid, entirely caught up in splitting and projection, to be always saying, like Nietzsche or Harold Bloom, "Those others are all about *ressentiment*." Or you can translate it into Republicanese: "*Those others* are all about partisan rancor." Suppose the depressive to be able to say at least intermittently, "We, like those others, are subject to the imperious projective dynamics of *ressentiment*; what next? By what means might the dynamics themselves become different?" As I understand my own political history, it has often happened that the propulsive energy of activist justification, of being or feeling joined with others in an urgent cause, tends to be structured very much in a paranoid/schizoid fashion: driven by attributed motives, fearful contempt of opponents, collective fantasies of powerlessness and/or omnipotence, scapegoating, purism, and schism. Paranoid/schizoid, in short, even as the motives that underlie political commitment may have much more to do with the complex, mature ethical dimension of the depressive position.

In an earlier essay, "Paranoid Reading and Reparative Reading," I speculated about why queer theory in general seems to display, if anything, a distinctive surplus or overdetermination in its elaboration of paranoid energies and forms of thought.[14] That tendency is fully visible in *Epistemology of the Closet*, for one example, whose rhetorical and polemical energy are so dependent on the projective symmetries of "It takes one to know one"—even as the analysis of those symmetries, in all their tricky performative pragmatics, is also the constative project of the book.[15] "Paranoid Reading and Reparative Reading" also takes up the marked centrality of paranoia in other founding texts of queer theory and activism. But in those speculations I overlooked the crudest, most contingent, and probably also most important reason why paranoia seems so built into queer theory as such. To quite get that, I think one has to have experienced gay life in the 1980s and early 1990s, when queer theory was still a tentative, emergent itinerary. That was also the moment when AIDS was a new and nearly untreatable disease—bringing a sudden, worse than Euripidean horror into the lives of urban gay men and their friends. It was not an uncommon experience then to be in a room of vibrant young people, conscious that within a year or two, all but a few of them would have sickened and died.

What's equally hard to reconstruct now is the not knowing what kind of response to AIDS might crystallize from the state and the public sphere. This was the time when, despite the hecatombs of dead, the word "AIDS" didn't cross the lips of the US president for the first six years of the epidemic, while prominent legislators and complacent pundits busied themselves with fake-judicious, fake-practical, prurient schemes for testing, classifying, rounding up, tattooing, quarantining, and otherwise demeaning and killing men and women with AIDS. Now we live in a world in which most of these things haven't happened, at least in relation to AIDS. But they were staples of public discourse at the time, and there was no visible brake on their implementation from any sanctioned, nonhomophobic argument in the public sphere. The congruence of such fantasies — fantasies that never understood themselves to be such — with Foucauldian understandings of how panoptic power gets embodied through the disciplines of bureaucracy, law, psychiatry, science, and public health was inescapable to those who awaited or fought to prevent their implementation.

Dread, intense dread, both focused and diffuse, is a good name for the dominant tonality of those years for queer people, at least for those who survived. The punishing stress of such dread, and the need of mobilizing powerful resources of resistance in the face of it, did imprint a paranoid structuration onto the theory and activism of that period, and no wonder. The wonder, at least to me, is at the resoundingly vigorous resource of thought and action that many people were able to mine from that otherwise impoverishing, and humiliating, enforced resort to the paranoid position.

In the mid-1990s, developments both public and private came together, for me, to eventuate in some changed relations to paranoid thinking and writing. A nodal point was the summer of 1996, when news from the Eleventh International AIDS Conference in Vancouver indicated for the first time that for many, HIV could plausibly be treated as a chronic disease through the use of cocktails of newly developed drugs. The brutally abbreviated temporality of the lives of many women and men with HIV seemed suddenly, radically extended if not normalized. Along with many, many others, I was trying over that summer to assimilate an unaccustomed palette of feelings among which relief, hope, expansiveness, and surprise set the tone. But the end of that summer was also the time that, in a strange chiasmus, I learned that my breast cancer, diagnosed in 1991, had spread and become incurable. So my own temporality and mortality came into an unexpected kind of focus — informed by my immersion in the AIDS emergency, but experienced, as it also happened, through a very different set of affective frameworks.

I've often wondered why my relation to my own disease hasn't involved the emotions of anger, disbelief, or even dread to anything like the degree that I felt them in relation to the AIDS experiences of people I cared about. Surely it has something to do with the differences between a new disease and an old one; a highly stigmatized disease and one that, even then, was much less so; and more generally, vicarious as opposed to direct experiences of pain and debility. But I'd also invoke my lifelong depressiveness. Among its other effects, it had endeared to me the idea of nonbeing, as well as made me perhaps oversensitive to the psychic expense extorted by the paranoid defenses. Without necessarily being secure in my depressive position, I knew for sure that the paranoid/schizoid was no place I could afford to dwell as I dealt with the exigencies of my disease. This was also the moment when a lot of Buddhist reading helped me find (or construct) an articulated psychological framework that promised to sustain some of the antinomies of my situation.

At any rate, for reasons both private and public, I found myself at this point increasingly discontented with the predominance of the self-perpetuating kinds of thought that I increasingly seemed to be recognizing under the rubric of paranoia. Other first-generation queer thinkers seem to have felt a similar need and moved in different directions with it; while I see my own work since then as a series of experiments aimed at instantiating, and making somehow available to readers, some alternative forms of argument and utterance. Twenty-first-century mainstream gay and lesbian culture and politics, meanwhile, have resolutely pushed the whole AIDS experience behind them with an all but programmatic disavowal of trauma and dread — but with the expensive result that those venues have become affectively hollowed out, brittle, and banalized. I also see that a lot of more recent queer theory has retained the paranoid structure of the earlier AIDS years, but done so increasingly outside of a context where it had reflected a certain, palpable purchase on daily reality.

Sometimes I think of the shape of my present life in terms of a flight from that dangerous-feeling, activist proximity of paranoid/schizoid energies — a flight into depression, occasionally, but on a more reliable basis and more productively and pleasurably, a flight from depression into pedagogy ("pedagogy" not referring, for me, to the academic institution so much as to a mode of relationality — not only in the classroom, but equally around it and, especially, as a writer). Last year at a meeting of my department's graduate admissions committee, one colleague was complaining about a particular applicant whose personal statement focused on being diagnosed with depression in the middle of college. "I hate it when they use depression as an excuse," this colleague said. To which another one responded, "Depression is no excuse! Excuse, hell — it's a prerequisite."

I don't know whether it's true that intellectuals and teachers, especially in the humanities, are more prone to depression than other people; but I strongly believe that, as Klein would have predicted, for the many of us who are prone to it, this tendency is woven as densely into our abilities as into our disabilities, our quite individual creativity as much as our sometimes stereotypical forms of blockage.

When I connect pedagogy in particular to the issue of depression, I have in mind the reflections of Silvan Tomkins on the depressive *personality* in the educator as well as Klein's notion of the depressive position. Tomkins discusses depressiveness, or the depressive personality or script, as a durable feature of many people's way of being, a dynamically constitutive feature of their best aptitudes as well as disabilities, regardless of whether or not, at a given moment in life, they are experiencing depression. At some places in Tomkins, this depressiveness seems like a widespread and rather generalized state; at others, Tomkins gives it a minoritizing slant that has more than a whiff of the autobiographical. For Tomkins, the most notable feature of the depressive, on emerging from childhood, is that he or she has a passion for relations of mimetic communion — ideally, two-way or mutual mimesis, based on the sweetness and anxiety for the child of imitating and being imitated by an adult, albeit one who is only intermittently attentive. This mimetic passion is combined, however, with an intense susceptibility to shame when such relations fail. This is a recipe both for overachievement in general and for pedagogical intensity in particular. Tomkins writes:

> The depressive, like his parent before him, is not altogether a comfortable person for others with whom he interacts. As a friend or parent or lover or educator he is somewhat labile between his affirmations of intimacy and his controlling, judging, and censuring of the other. His warmth and genuine concern for the welfare of others seduces them into an easy intimacy which may then be painfully ruptured when the depressive . . . finds fault with the other. The other is now too deeply committed and too impressed with the depressive's sincerity to disregard the disappointment and censure from the other and is thereby seduced

further into attempting to make restitution, to atone, and to please the other. When this is successful, the relationship is now deepened, and future ruptures will become increasingly painful—both to tolerate and to disregard. So is forged the depressive dyad in which there is great reward punctuated by severe depression. The depressive creates other depressives by repeating the relationship which created his own character. The depressive exerts a great influence on the lives of all he touches because he combines great reward with punishment, which ultimately heightens the intensity of the affective rewards he offers others. . . . The depressive is concerned not only with impressing, with pleasing and exciting others through his own excellence, but also that others should impress him, should please him, and should excite him through their excellence.[16]

Tomkins makes explicit, moreover, that in these depressive dramas our students are likely to oscillate between two roles. On the one hand they can function for us as "substitute *parents* who are to be impressed [and] excited" but whose "boredom, . . . censure, and . . . turning away constitute an enduring threat and challenge." On the other hand, as they stand in for *ourselves as children*, we in the role of their parent will "censure [our] beloved children for their ignorance" and "love and respect them for their efforts to meet [our] highest expectations."[17] Or to recast the teaching situation in terms of a psychoanalytic encounter: sometimes I feel like my students' analyst; other times, floundering all too visibly in my helplessness to evoke language from my seminar, I feel like a patient being held out on by twenty psychoanalysts at once.

Among these and many similar dynamics, there's sometimes an unexpected psychological leverage from invoking another Buddhist idea: it's about karma. Not karma as a system of reward and punishment, in which, to be honest, I could not be less interested, but karma as plain causality, exemplified by the inexorable Rube Goldberg physics of those uncontrollable, paranoid/schizoid chains of projective identification; the ways in which what one already is puts its inevitable spin on what one says, does, and perceives—and vice versa. For *ressentiment*, then, read karma—the big, sloppy psychic hurricane footprint, the interactive histories that make someone difficult to be with or difficult to be. I'm imagining something like this, that the paranoid/schizoid position involves bad karma, lots of it—it emerges from bad karma and, through projective identification, sends more bad karma careening out into the world. And the depressive position involves the endless, heroic but discouraging attempt to turn bad karma into good karma.

In every religious tradition I know of, though, there is at least one stream of mystical thought that is heading somewhere different from this. In Buddhism you could paraphrase it like this: it's better to have good karma than bad karma; but the best thing of all, the most liberating and skillful thing, is to have no karma.

I should probably add that, at least in mystical Buddhism, no karma doesn't mean no action. Instead, it's the figure without karma, the bodhisattva, the ultimate teacher, who is able to perceive and be perceived clearly enough that the things they do are efficacious — and no more than efficacious.

It seems inevitable for us karmic individuals, trapped in the rounds of samsara, that even the invocation of nonkarmic possibility will be karmically overdetermined. It will have all too many uses, too many causes, and too many effects. Clearly it can function as evasion, as the notion of the aesthetic is now commonly seen as functioning. You might even see it as overdetermined by our depressiveness itself and by our pedagogical neediness. At any rate, that these elements can be closely proximate is clear. To me, though, apparently a vision of nonkarmic possibility, however subject to abuse, also illuminates some possibilities of opening out new relations to the depressive position.

NOTES

EKS lectured on Melanie Klein in 2005 and 2006 at Columbia and Harvard Universities. On the basis of these talks, she prepared a version of "Melanie Klein and the Difference Affect Makes" for the *South Atlantic Quarterly* issue "After Sex? On Writing since Queer Theory," ed. Janet Halley and Andrew Parker (*South Atlantic Quarterly* 106, no. 3 [Summer 2007]). The version printed there considerably expands the essay as originally offered, but it also cuts several passages. This version of the essay restores the cut passages to the previously published version; EKS borrows phrases and sentences from this essay in the first chapter of this book.

1. R. D. Hinshelwood, *A Dictionary of Kleinian Thought* (London: Free Association, 1998); and Meira Likierman, *Melanie Klein: Her Work in Context* (London: Continuum, 2002).

2. Likierman, *Melanie Klein*, 55.

3. Ibid., 108–9.

4. Ibid., 79.

5. Eve Kosofsky Sedgwick, *Fat Art, Thin Art* (Durham: Duke University Press, 1994), 19.

6. Eve Kosofsky Sedgwick and Adam Frank, eds., *Shame and Its Sisters: A Silvan Tomkins Reader* (Durham: Duke University Press, 1995).

7. Sigmund Freud, *The Standard Edition of the Complete Psychological Works of Sigmund Freud*, trans. under the general editorship of James Strachey (London: Hogarth, 1957), 14: 16.

8. Jean Laplanche and J.-B. Pontalis, *The Language of Psycho-Analysis*, trans. Donald Nicholson-Smith (New York: W. W. Norton, 1973), 392.

9. Adam Frank pointed this out to me.

10. Michel Foucault, *The History of Sexuality*, vol. 1, *An Introduction*, trans. Robert Hurley (New York: Pantheon, 1978), 82–85.

11. Melanie Klein, "Notes on Some Schizoid Mechanisms," 1946, in *The Writings of Melanie Klein*, ed. R. E. Money-Kyrle et al. (London: Hogarth, 1984), 3:8.

12. Hinshelwood, *A Dictionary of Kleinian Thought*, 138 (emphasis added).

13. Ibid.

14. Eve Kosofsky Sedgwick, "Paranoid Reading and Reparative Reading, or, You're So Paranoid, You Probably Think This Essay Is about You," in *Touching Feeling: Affect, Pedagogy, Performativity* (Durham: Duke University Press, 2003), 123–51.

15. Eve Kosofsky Sedgwick, *Epistemology of the Closet* (Berkeley: University of California Press, 1990).

16. Eve Kosofsky Sedgwick and Adam Frank, eds., *Shame and Its Sisters*, 225.

17. Ibid., 228–29 (emphasis added).

Affect Theory and Theory of Mind

Why did Silvan Tomkins's understanding of affect theory first seem so germinative to me on encountering it in 1991? Thinking even further back, I attach that sense of discovery to the very first of the axioms that began *Epistemology of the Closet*, published in the preceding year. The introductory axioms to *Epistemology*, those fussy final touches to the manuscript, tried to detail the most basic assumptions that weren't themselves explained in the chapters, but that I thought readers would need articulated in order to make any sense of the arguments the book contained. I realized the necessity for them in reverse order: "Oh, but even before *that* I need to have said . . ." So the book's Axiom 1, "People are different from each other," was the very last one I wrote, the final leftover—the *most* basic, but hence also the one about which I most didn't know if it was a suffocating commonplace, or a truth that retained its "power to galvanize and divide." I expanded on it there in the following terms:

Axiom 1: People are different from each other.
   It is astonishing how few respectable conceptual tools we have for dealing with this self-evident fact. A tiny number of inconceivably coarse axes of categorization have been painstakingly inscribed in current critical and political thought: gender, race, class, nationality, sexual orientation, are pretty much the available distinctions. They, with the associated demonstrations of the mechanisms by which they are constructed and reproduced, are indispensable, and they may indeed override all or some other forms of difference and similarity. But the sister or brother, the best friend, the classmate, the parent or child, the lover,

the ex: our families, loves, and enmities alike, not to mention the strange relations of our work, play, and activism, prove that even people who share all or most of our own positionings along these crude axes may still be different enough from us, and from each other, to seem like all but different species.[1]

So it's little wonder that when I came upon it the next year, Tomkins's work seemed to pulse with possibility. He made a case for affect as the system that uniquely mediates between the imperceptibly fugitive, almost impersonal nuance of a feeling, at one extreme, and at the other the most inveterate bent of a lifetime's motive and style of being, thinking, and relating. It was also exciting how firmly and flexibly, at once, Tomkins rooted such processes in the body and brain—at that time a profoundly unfashionable move in critical-theory discourse, though now the opposite.

It's not clear, however, despite Tomkins's example, and judging from the recent vogue for Darwinian neuroscience in both popular and theoretical discourses, that a synaptic vision per se is enough to support any understanding of truly diverse developmental possibility. That people are different from each other—I still wonder why and how that can remain so difficult to know; how best to marshal theoretical resources for its realization. In this chapter, as the title indicates, I am interested in putting into relief two relevant kinds of theory. Also two usages of the term "theory" that seem to intertwine in potentially productive ways: affect theory, theory of mind. An especially haunting volume of Proust, along with some emerging conversations on autism and neurodiversity, are also parts of this discussion.

Theory of Mind, to begin with, is an idea that has emerged over the past thirty years from the fields of animal behavior, child development, and cognitive neuroscience. Interestingly, though, the phrase "Theory of Mind" does not name any of these areas of study. It refers to something much more specific than, say, Philosophy of Mind. It names one, purportedly delineated and unitary cognitive ability that is said to develop in some few animals, and also in most people by around the age of four. Theory of Mind, something one purportedly either has or has not, is the stable understanding that, to put it crudely, people are different from each other. Specifically, as one writer puts it, Theory of Mind is "the realizing that others (and ourselves) have their own thoughts, feeling, perception, beliefs, and so forth—as opposed to thinking one's own 'mental' experience [is] identical to objective reality."[2] Theory of Mind refers to the ability to attribute to other people as well as oneself mental states like "pretending, thinking, knowing, believing, imagining, dreaming, guessing, and deceiving."[3]

By those who use the term, development of a Theory of Mind is understood as an access to sociality, leading of course to important ethical possibilities—it covers some of the same ground as the venerable philosophical problem of "other minds." Indeed, whether or not one understands that other people see things differently can represent both a minimal developmental standard and a very high ethical one. And in terms of human cognition, it has become common over the last decade—although, as we'll see, controversial—to define Theory of Mind in an exact negative relation to autism: Theory of Mind is the thing that autistic individuals don't have, and autism is the thing that people who don't have a Theory of Mind have.[4] In fact, many of the defining moves for Theory of Mind have come from autism researchers like Uta Frith and Simon Baron-Cohen, and the popularization of this negative equation is one of the things that have consolidated understandings of both Theory of Mind and autism as actually existing, unitary, and neurobiologically grounded things in the world.

What first attracted me to the notion of Theory of Mind—aside from its seeming connection with the urgency of Axiom 1—were some apparent complementarities to my Tomkinsian understanding of affect. First and maybe most idiosyncratic, I was interested in the attribution of theoretical activity to lay persons—including lay toddlers and even some lay primates. (I've learned since then that both some philosophers and some brain scientists argue that Theory of Mind is not, in their respective technical senses, a theory.[5]) But one of the things I value most in Tomkins, in his exposition of "affect theories" and some associated ideas, is the sense of irreducible continuity between what people with affects do, on the one hand, and on the other, what experts—people like Tomkins—do when they think about affects.[6] This sense of the continuity of theorizing activity seems to have several determinants in Tomkins's thought. It would be impossible without his understanding that affect and cognition—feeling and thinking, or one might also say motivation and thinking—are not just complexly interfused, but in human beings essentially inextricable (Tomkins 4:1–10). Tomkins's crucial move in identifying *interest* as an affect—one that's on a spectrum with excitement, and that has a distinctive role to play in (for instance) organizing perception as well as motivating exploration—draws an especially tight linkage between the systems of affect and cognition.[7] More generally, emerging as it does from early systems theory, Tomkins's work foregrounds the delicate mechanisms of feedback in human processes ranging from perception to very complex thought — and along with feedback, the concomitant importance of error making. Compared to the very wide spectrum of processes and subsystems along which he traces such congruence, the distance between lay psychologizing and a consciously applied scientific method is hardly impressive. And Tomkins is careful, when he characteristically includes lists of examples to illustrate affective-theory mechanisms, to suggest that his own work, however abstruse, does not take place at a different, metalevel from the folk theorizing of which he writes, but is closer to representing a further instance of it.

Tomkins introduces his concept of affect theory this way:

> When any stimulus is perceived . . . it may activate amplifying affect on an innate basis by virtue of the . . . neurological stimulation of the stimulus. . . . It may also recruit from memory further information concerning past affects experienced when the same or similar stimuli were encountered before, which in turn may activate further affect.[8]
>
> What will be thus recruited depends upon prior theory. After much cumulative experience, information about affects may become organized into what we term "theories," in much the same way that theories are constructed to account for uniformities in science or in cognition in general. An affect theory is a simplified and powerful summary of a larger set of affect experiences. (*Tomkins Reader*, 164–65)

Like scientific theories, too, affect theories are subject to constant revisions both large and small, based both on prediction and on retrospective resampling and reanalysis. "Early experience is continually being transformed by the experience which follows it, just as much as later experience may be transformed in terms of the memory schema of earlier experience" (*Tomkins Reader*, 121).

> The young human being is a relatively open system, because each new experience plays a vital role in the interpretation of the growing cumulative images of past experience. Indeed, human development might properly be defined as that phase of experience in which the analysis of past experience and future possibilities is conducted in the light of present experience. Development ceases when the contribution of present information becomes primarily illustrative, as a special case of past generalization.
>
> It is not unlike the relationship within any science, between what is established and its frontier. Those congealed bits of information called

"laws" can be incorporated into testing instruments so that precise values of any particular situation can be simply established, as for example by a voltometer. The growing edge of that science, however, is where the theorist puts questions to nature with great uncertainty and fear and trembling, and where the results of observation and experiment are truly new information which will inform the science and the scientist how he should choose between plausible alternatives and what he should believe. Theories within science also ultimately become senile and cease to struggle with genuine uncertainty. Development, in short, is characterized by a state of information processing in which there is a ratio of pronounced retro-action over pro-action, and senility is that state of information where pro-action dominates retro-action. (*Tomkins Reader*, 122)

Unlike Theory of Mind, that is — which once acquired is supposed to be quite a stable element of the psyche — affect theory, as Tomkins posits it, continues over the individual lifespan to behave *as* theory: that is, to a greater or lesser extent it remains subject to revision, reorganization, or even revolutionary disruption, though such internal events may become decreasingly probable.

Also in contrast to Theory of Mind, the breadth as well as the strength and specificity, of a given affect theory is one of the dimensions that is subject to change. An affect theory, Tomkins writes, "may be about affect in general, or about a particular affect." Using the affect of shame as an example, he continues:

Shame theory is . . . [a] source of great power and generality in activating shame, in alerting the individual to the possibility or imminence of shame and in providing standardized strategies for minimizing shame. Although shame theory provides avoidance techniques, it is also one of the major sources of the experience of shame, since it provides a shame interpretation of a large number of situations, which if there had been a powerful distress theory might have aroused distress, given a fear theory of equal generality and power might have aroused fear rather than shame, and given a monopolistic enjoyment theory might have altogether attenuated the negative aspects of the situation. . . . The existence of a shame theory guarantees that the shame-relevant aspects of any situation will become figural in competition with other affect-relevant aspects of the same situations. (*Tomkins Reader*, 165)

And Tomkins's mention of competition brings us to perhaps the most important difference between affect theory and Theory of Mind. We are given to understand, about Theory of Mind, that there is only one of them—shared by, well, almost everybody. In contrast to what we are told about Theory of Mind, in Tomkins's understanding of affect theory, though it's similar in being a form of lay theory, there can be and are very different affect theories. There can even be—in fact there are bound to be—different ones, on different scales of breadth and exclusivity, in operation (and in a dynamic relation to one another) in the same psyche at the same time.

I'd like to switch gears now and move to the question of literary relevance. As many of you know, cognitive neuroscience has begun to accrue a certain prestige in humanities departments over the past few years, but the full terms of its potential interest there have really yet to emerge. A popularizing 2006 book by Lisa Zunshine, titled *Why We Read Fiction: Theory of Mind and the Novel*, has offered the fullest suggestions yet of literary implications of Theory of Mind. Zunshine is interested in Theory of Mind mainly as it raises the question of narrative reliability; so it makes sense that the novel, with its historically shifting ground of point of view, its free-floating possibilities for irony, and its variations on free indirect discourse would be the focus of her attention.

From the term's very inception, the presence of Theory of Mind has been tested by whether or not the subject understands that somebody else could make an inference that the subject knew to be mistaken. Probably the best-known test for Theory of Mind is the so-called Sally-Anne test. As one researcher explains, "In this test, the child gets to see two dolls, Sally and Anne. Sally puts a marble into a basket and then leaves the room. Anne enters the room, takes the marble out of the basket and puts it into a box. The child then gets asked where Sally would look for the marble when she comes back to the room. It is seen as a sign of ToM [Theory of Mind] if the child understands that Sally doesn't know what Anne knows, and therefore answers that Sally will look in the basket where she put the marble herself." [9] Accordingly, for the reader whom Zunshine imagines, the knowledge that others have minds of their own primarily means the knowledge that they are capable of ignorance, concealment, or misrepresentation, or of being stupid, crazy, or methodically vicious. This lack of transparency of mind to mind is seen as the main engine of fiction, as mystery novels, novels of manners, and other psychological works are propelled by the characters' and/or the reader's growing ability to distinguish and classify the otherness of others' communications.

The main difficulties in doing so, Zunshine argues, are two. The first occurs where the novel's main narrator or primary point-of-view character turns out to be systematically unreliable—for instance, as in her long discussion of *Lolita*, where he may be a sordidly self-deluding pedophile. The second difficulty can lie in the sheer number of layers of nontransparency with which readers are presented. She quotes, for instance, a densely ironic paragraph from *Mrs. Dalloway* that presents the "cognitive challenge" of "processing fifth- or sixth-level intentionality," as also do Agatha Christie–type whodunits (where, for instance, A imagines that B believes that C perceives that D is lying about whether E supposes that F etc.). "We have to work hard," Zunshine writes, "for sifting through all those levels of embedded intentionality tends to push the boundaries of our mind-reading ability to its furthest limits."[10]

Zunshine calls one section of her book "Why Is Reading a Detective Story a Lot Like Lifting Weights at the Gym?," and indeed the athleticism of these wrestles with Theory of Mind is central to her sense of their appeal—which also means, to her, their link to human evolutionary fitness. And even though I take Zunshine's point that a workout with five or six layers of narrative irony can be an exhilarating thing, I'm dismayed by how much the bulk of her readings have to depend on that rackety warhorse of high-school English classes, the Unreliable Narrator. She suggests that by mastering Theory of Mind, with the attendant disciplines of neurobiology and human evolution, we can learn to ponder mysteries like "How do we know Henry James's governess isn't a delusional head case?" or "What if that erudite Professor Kinbote is just an evil queen?" But I don't want to attack Zunshine for being philistine or writing a popularizing book. However exquisite or abstruse she wanted to get, the problem is that her readings really do *have to* cleave to the most reductive version of the Unreliable Narrator problematic. The constraint lies in Theory of Mind itself.

After all, the reason one's heart sinks when students reach for the Unreliable Narrator is that that heuristic persists in addressing even the most complex narrative with a single, all too flattening, yes-or-no question: reliable or not reliable? As though a narrator or character who's not certifiable, vicious, or systematically mendacious is thereby reliable. But then as though "reliable" itself is a single thing to be, a single kind of normative transparency or relationality. But if that is assumed, it would essentially undo the space for individual difference that's supposed to be secured by achieving Theory of Mind in the first place.

Feeling the need for more usable theoretical accounts of mind, I keep circling back to a volume that comes late in Proust, one that presents extreme difficulties to me and, I think, to many other readers fascinated by *A la recherche du temps perdu*. The volume is most marked, perhaps, by the narrator's reckless articulation of different affect theories and his proliferating accounts of Theory of Mind. For me at least, the fascination of Proust's novel as a whole — Lisa Zunshine to the contrary — isn't much like going to the gym, but it is rather like a psychoanalytic transference: comparable in intensity, that is, but also in the unaccustomed, transformative kinds of relationality that it manages to keep in play over a very long experiential duration. When I teach a yearlong Proust seminar, I have to start out trying to open my students to the wide range of their likely feelings about the narrator and, indeed, the author: condescension, dependence, disgust, fury, indulgence, for instance, along with the more anxious and ethical forms of respect that seem proper to their graduate-student status. The adventure of Proust, after all, like the adventure of an analysis, is to get somewhere new by exploring a new space of interlocution: one in which, among other differences, self-relation (one's own or one's narrator's) is allowed to mingle pretty freely with intersubjectivity. Excitable, friendly daydreaming isn't a million miles from either activity, though neither are passages through hollowness or dread. The social laws that mandate a conventional Theory of Mind — at least mandate keeping up the appearance of one — are in each of these contexts significantly relaxed.

The fifth of Proust's seven volumes, *La Prisonnière* (*The Captive*), seems to represent a kind of hellish crisis in the longer novel's experiment with intersubjective relationality. This is true of the volume's content, but equally true — at least for me — of the unengaging experiences of reading, thinking about, and teaching it. As the title indicates, this is the volume in which the Proustian narrator has brought his lover Albertine, an unprovided-for orphan from a bourgeois background, to live secretly with him in his mother's apartment in Paris. Her complete economic dependence on him, along with his exacting sexual jealousy about her, seem like the defining terms of their arrangement, which he describes in exoticizing, absolute terms: the man with the Princess of China trapped in a bottle; Ahasuerus and Esther in the Bible, or Racine; or master and slave in the *Arabian Nights*, not to mention (as in fact he doesn't) Hegel.

What makes *La Prisonnière* so hard to take? For one thing, it's the only very extended section of the *Recherche* that arguably offers so banal a thing as an Unreliable Narrator. Repetitious, obsessed, haplessly explanatory and unaerated by relaxation, this narrator is as brainy and deadening as Humbert Humbert, minus his gaiety. The difference is that this late in the transferential journey with Proust (in my two-semester seminar, say, it's the baleful season of late March), there is no option of detaching your care from this narrative voice, or "placing" the narrator securely with a diagnostic epithet. Unreliable he may be, and yet it's become too late not to rely. This is like the point in therapy when you blunder hard against the area where your shrink is intractably stupid; or like a numbing childhood moment when you see that you'll never make your parents stop fighting. Possibilities of exhilaration or refreshment from such a discovery seem unimaginably distant.

And yet our narrator offers nothing if not a wealth of powerful affect theory, and plenty of just-as-decisive schematizations of Theory of Mind. Hard to tell whether it's the thought of their being quite delusional that feels so vastating; or the thought of how profoundly conventionally they're already inscribed in the whole European romance tradition, from courtly love to Freud and beyond; or of their being *true*; or simply, basally, irreconcilable. None of the individual reflections are new at this point in the novel, either, but it's here that the sense of impasse gouges the deepest. Here are just some of the elements of the impasse. To begin with, sexual possession of another person is precisely equated with a conquest of the otherness of another mind. Not just Albertine's, but any woman's (since the narrator only admits to desires for women): the otherness of that mind is exactly the thing that sexual possession overcomes. Sexual possession, though, doesn't just mean having sex with her, but conquering obstacles to obtaining her consent for sex—since it's only the obstacles that give her the otherness that makes her desirable.

> Even if the girl I found in the house of assignation were prettier than this one [I was looking at], it could not be the same thing, because we do not look at the eyes of a girl we do not know as we would look at little chunks of opal or agate. We know that the little ray which colours them or the diamond dust that makes them sparkle is all that we can see of a mind, a will, a memory in which is contained the family home that we do not know, the intimate friends whom we envy. The enterprise of gaining possession of all this, of something so difficult, so recalcitrant, is what gives its attraction to that gaze far more than its merely physical

beauty. . . . To find the midinette in the house of assignation is to find her emptied of that unknown life which permeates her and which we aspire to possess with her.[11] (5:222–23)

But then, according to the same unforgiving Theory of Mind, getting sexual possession of a woman has exactly the effect of stripping her mind of its otherness, which "slipping away from beneath . . . [women] as soon as I had approached them, made them at once collapse and fall flat on to the dead level of the most commonplace reality" (5:224).

Built into the narrator's Theory of Mind here, we can then see, is the sense of an essential flatness to reality, to whatever is actually known. The flatness of another mind is not just neutral but actually repellent, like something dead, when not animated by the projections of distance or illusion. The narrator frequently describes his possession of Albertine as suffocatingly boring to him. And then there's the issue of *her* boredom: whether it's his fear, his delusional fantasy projection, or his well-founded intuition — and we never learn the answer — Albertine's own boredom (with him, with her thralldom) is one of the main engines of *La Prisonnière*. In this hyperarticulated fantasia on the ostensible theme of Theory of Mind, to overcome the otherness of another mind, while it's the imperative to do so that constitutes almost the entirety of human motivation, is also in effect *only* a way of contaging one's own flatness or nausea across the human landscape. A very particular, monopolistic, and therefore stunningly ineffective set of monopolistic affect theories is here masquerading — as they are so wont to do — as a universalizing approach to Theory of Mind.

Actually, though, this particular dialectic, of the other mind that loses its appeal when its otherness is once conquered, has almost only a notional presence in *La Prisonnière*, albeit a heavily loquacious one. If not counteracted, it's at least fractally complicated by the narrator's fear and jealousy. Excitement — in the form of intolerable anxiety and dread — keeps swarming into every interstice of that foundational tedium. For amid it all the narrator has, of course, no stable grounds for supposing he really has gained possession of Albertine's mind. The charm of Albertine's original, internal distance from and indifference to him — inscribed as the germinal image of the visually infinite, physical distance from the horizon of a cluster of mutually preoccupied young girls at the seashore where they'd first met — lingers for him in glimpses of a possible distance in Albertine's eyes. A highly performative obsession with the possibility that Albertine is "really," "basically" a lesbian, and a sexually ravenous one, spins out this motivating image into the endlessly productive, narratogenic form of jealousy—jealousy toward Albertine's future and toward every instant of her past.

Further and even more recursively, Albertine's boredom, despondency—and eventual fury—are conceived to be generated by the very completeness of the narrator's knowledge of her mental apparatus, breeding privacy, resistance, and explosive power in the very dependence and silence that he enforces. Furthermore, the situation—as he sees it—imperiously demands that he weave an endless system of lies. ("To make her chain appear lighter, the best thing was no doubt to make her believe that I was myself about to break it.")[12] Which necessitates that, correspondingly, he interpret every word she utters to him as part of a correspondingly methodical and extensive system of deception.

So far, so conventionally Petrarchan, or Hegelian, or Sartrian, or Lacanian, or whom you please. And clearly, it's beyond my remit here—as well as probably still beyond my power—to offer anything like a full reading of La Prisonnière.[13] But I think I've said enough to forcefully suggest several things about its relation to Theory of Mind. I've tried to show how the volume is pointedly, even obsessionally, about Theory-of-Mind issues. Then, according to Proust's showing, Theory of Mind is in no degree a purely cognitive issue, even though Proust's narrator (like many of Poe's) often seems to insist that his every mental event, his every premise and conclusion, emerge from sheer ratiocination. Instead, his Theory of Mind is so deeply imbricated with affect that there is no motive in the book—however fleeting or however deep-dyed—that can be separated from the question of others' and one's own mental opacity. (I'm following Tomkins here in equating the affect system with motivation tout court.) Additionally, I hope I've succeeded in making you feel that if you had to be a character in La Prisonnière, you might not be all that eager to occupy Albertine's position in this particular household.

But here's what I'm afraid is the furthest thing from clear about our narrator's Theory of Mind: does he, in the neuroscientists' and the philosophers' sense, have one? For all his obsession with Theory of Mind—or maybe because of his obsession—the very least obvious question about this narrator is whether he actually possesses the knowledge that other people have mental states that can differ from his. I can see at least two reasons why we might be left uncertain as to this. The first is that, as the narrator tells us, the news that he has not in fact taken possession of Albertine's mind seems to have to be learned over and over again—and each time as if for the first time, with the same existentially threatening shock of betrayal and dismay.

It also seems tempting to suggest that the sheer monstrousness with which the narrator treats Albertine raises the question of whether he can possibly have a Theory of Mind. In a way this ethical question is a non sequitur—simply knowing that she has mental states wouldn't guarantee that he'd want to respect them, or would wish her well in any way. From one point of view it seems as if his rage to know what's in Albertine's mind must be the surest proof that he knows it to be separate from his. But then—and even beyond the question of what makes the epistemological issue a matter of *rage*—we can wonder at how hard or impossible it apparently is to find the difference between, on the one hand, his rage to know her mind; and, on the other hand, the paranoid calculations, attributions, and projections that he silently and fatally hurls into her. His analyses seem so vastly less effective at sounding the depths of her mind than at jamming and preempting her every signal. As who should stuff his fingers in his ears and sing out, "La la *la*! I can't *hear* you!"

My students sometimes attach their sense of outrage on Albertine's behalf to Proust's choice of a rigorously first-person narrative point of view. It's certainly true that no voice in the novel offers Albertine's point of view to the reader, or even makes a pretense of doing so. That's why a text like Jacqueline Rose's novel *Albertine*, written in Albertine's own dense and involving first person, can seem so new as an avenue into the *Recherche*.[14] The radicalness of Proust's choices comes into particular relief when one remembers, for instance, his profound indebtedness, as both psychologist and stylist, to George Eliot. Notoriously, if there's one novelist whose practice could be said to represent the fullest, most mature imaginable version of Theory of Mind, that one would be Eliot. Her essentially omniscient narrative voice seems to distill an essence of humanity, at its most intelligent, as a whole; her use of free indirect discourse offers an almost magically intimate illumination of the motives, feelings, and ideas—however inchoate—of a range of characters whose variety beggars Dostoevsky's; and her explicit reflections on the irreducible otherness of other people's minds have enabled refinements of ethical thought across the ambit of her literary influence. If her great admirer Proust turns so decisively away from her mode of narration, it's not because his psychological preoccupations are so very different from hers; nor yet the bent of his aptitudes as a writer.

But I wonder whether he may not have been, or become, specially alert to the ways in which — even in Eliot's writing, even with the most scrupulous imaginable, all-but-religious respect for the privacy of the individual mind — caring so very much for Theory of Mind may not always be quite distinguishable from preempting, presuming, or even quite undoing it. Eliot's endlessly engaged narrator could never display the same frontally invasive epistemological violence as Proust's. But I think Proust might have agreed with Neil Hertz, another of Eliot's best readers, who writes that sometimes "the best advice to give someone on the receiving end of George Eliot's narrator's sympathy would be: 'Duck!'"[15]

So maybe it's true that Theory of Mind and Lack of Theory of Mind — or, to borrow the psychiatric jargon, ToM and LoToM — can work so much alike as to be indistinguishable. At least, that is an argument that's made in a very powerful, multivocal paper published in 2000, "A Discussion about Theory of Mind: From an Autistic Perspective." It's a group-authored paper that emerged from the members of an online listserv that is mainly for autistic people and those with autistic-related conditions. (The eight members whose work comprises the paper have all received such a diagnosis.) The paper is available on the Web through the site autism.org, "the real voice of autism," one of several sites that reflect a loosely organized international movement often called the neurodiversity movement. Neurodiversity began as, and remains, a rights movement for people disenfranchised by a certain range of particular mental diagnoses. At the same time, like so many seemingly minoritarian rights movements, it has become the source of a kind of analysis whose limits of applicability would be very hard to circumscribe.

The paper begins with a discussion of how Theory of Mind has been defined, and several people consider what they would have made, in childhood, of the Sally-Anne test I mentioned, the one with two dolls retrieving a marble from a basket. Although the test is often treated as defining for both autism and, inversely, Theory of Mind, these list-members' responses are so divergent that it becomes impossible to see "Sally-Anne" as a test of any single faculty. One of the writers, for instance (Niki L), wrote:

I believe that I had some sort of theory of mind problem . . . when I was younger, but the problems I had were something that Sally Anne test cannot show. What you can detect by [the] Sally Anne test is lack of "theory of others' knowledge," not lack of "theory of mind" in general. I had theory of others' knowledge when I was very young, possibly I might even have attained it earlier than many NT [neurotypical] kids. However, . . . I completely lacked "theory of people's (including my own) will and decision making." . . . It was not because of ignorance, but because of . . . something similar to determinism, which I had formed when I had been very young, reasoning by analogy of TV program time-tables I saw on [*sic*] newspapers, train timetables, weekly lunch menu at nursery school, and so on. I assumed that everything is predetermined and that adults were taking care of us according to some sort of pro-gram, without their own decision making. That is why I stopped making requests to [my] parents. . . . I would have passed [the] Sally and Anne test even when I was two years old, if only [the] two puppets were made to be [the] same in size. But if Sally were taller than Anne and looked like an adult, I would not have been able to answer correctly until third [grade]. . . . That is why I did not tell lies to my parents, not because I could not deceive [them], but because I thought it [would be] useless anyway. I thought adults know everything like god, though they can-not change anything [through] what they know. . . . I derived the wrong theory from the fact [that] adults say something like "you will like it," "you are going to have fun," "it won't hurt," and so on. Here, the pri-mary problems were [a] semantic-pragmatic problem and lack of intu-ition (or too narrow focus of attention).[16]

It is Jared Blackburn who reflects explicitly on "why Autistic people often seem to lack 'Theory of Mind' to normal people." The problem, he writes, is

basically a social form of the "availability heuristic," an assumption that what is readily available to the mind is typical—in practice this means that whatever is typical of one's own experience is considered typical in general, and can be assumed true as default (unless known otherwise). Since people have more experience with their own behavior, much more knowledge of their own thoughts and feelings, and direct knowledge *only* of their own thoughts and feelings, this is what is available to them. Thus, they use this assumption to guess motives and predict action of others. The results may not always be right, but it works enough (with perhaps some moderation some of the time) to be useful.

I believe that for people who are relatively typical—particularly nor-mal people in their own culture—it works enough of the time to be very efficient, and this makes it rewarding, thus reinforcing the use of this heuristic—thus, this kind of thinking becomes pervasive and automatic. It may not work (or may even backfire) occasionally, but is mostly adaptive.

Since Autistic people are less likely to see things as connected, we may be less likely to make this assumption. Further, since our sensory experience and thinking may be different, and we may lack many socially learned assumptions, we may not be a good "model" for the behavior of most people around us. As a result, this heuristic may not give accurate or useful results for us—thus, this type of thinking is neither adaptive nor reinforced for most Autistic people—so even if an Autistic person does try this approach, it is not likely to be repeated much. . . .

I think my view of other people was/is unusually flexible because I lack a specific "people" way of thinking (separate from objects), so I do not "see" myself in others. Instead, it is all processing abstract concepts and systems—much like computer programs or physical forces. However, I have been quite aware for a long time that others had (different) knowledge and motives.[17]

Jane Meyerding describes a specific, phenomenological difference in her experience of perceiving others' minds.

Speed is a good analogy here, I think. People often impress me as a speed, a frequency. As Hal says, it takes time. NT people (some of them, anyway) are busy absorbing all the ripples on the surface of a person and making a judgment on that basis. Meanwhile, I see the ripples as blinding or irritating flashes in my eyes (so I close my eyes, if I can get away with it), but/and some other part of me, some sense, is becoming aware of the frequency at which the core of the person is vibrating. Some people resonate well with me. They tend to be the slower (in frequency) bear-like people. Others have a frequency that, as my sister would say, makes my teeth itch. They tend to be the flashier, more impressive (to NTs) people.

My slow way of apprehending people can be (or seem) quite "penetrating" when NTs become aware of it. (I don't like that way of describing it. Seems to me more a case of resonance tha[n] of penetration.) They don't realize anything is happening in/with me because I am not reacting (positively) to all those ripples and they assume I am not sensitive to other people. Well, I am. But I am *slowly* sensitive.[18]

Elsa George generalizes:

The way I understand Theory of Mind now, Lack of ToM = a belief that everybody shares your knowledge of things / everybody thinks the same way you do / [everyone] experiences everything the same way you do. If this is so what makes anyone think that it's ACs [autistics] who lack theory of mind? Uta [Frith] also says that ACs don't understand social rules and appear not to have any knowledge of them. In this case problems are caused by the fact that NT's assume such knowledge is universal (= LoToM). Personally I have little doubt that I think differently to most others. This has caused problems at school sometimes when teachers have automatically assumed I'm wrong without bothering to understand what I did (= LoToM). . . . Finally, I wonder how many of us have been "accused" of being oversensitive. How true! But this does not mean our experience was deluded or wasn't really experienced this way. People can be very nasty in their belief that it does (= LoToM).[19]

Or as Blackburn summarizes, "Because Autistic people see most normal people as seeming to assume everyone is like themselves, and would react as they would in the same situation, normal people may often seem to lack 'Theory of Mind' . . . to many high functioning Autistic people. On the other hand, normal researchers are tempted to assume lack of or deficiency in 'Theory of Mind' when Autistic people don't automatically jump to [the same] conclusions."

The neuro-atypical authors of this essay express a clear, careful, and bounded understanding of intersubjective relationality. Without any of the violence that propels Proust's narrator in *La Prisonnière*, they bring home that Theory of Mind is not the most, but actually one of the least, stable and stabilizing of concepts. And yet, how much there is still the need for some usably formulated, theory of mind–relevant tools of analysis. I feel the need at present, for only one example, in the face of current new imaging, and new popularization, of the so-called mirror-neuron system in the brain, which is today's prestigious place holder in the game of biogenetically regularizing a single, normative understanding of how the structure of one mind interdigitates with the structure of another.

Finally, while the centrality of affect for theory of mind–type projects seems obvious enough (famous last words), I can't say whether it would seem to make more sense to conceptualize one nested within or embracing the other, or to conceptualize them as being, in some senses, parallel systems—albeit with a full suffusion of cross talk and mutual feedback. It does seem to me, though, in any event, that current understandings of affect—and especially those based on Tomkins's work— have many lessons for ways of thinking about Theory of Mind. I'd summarize these under the following rubrics:

1. Don't work toward, or depend on the model of, development of a

single, normative outcome — with differences from that outcome analyzed in terms of deficiency or at best detour.

2. Instead, find ways of discerning and describing a variety of outcomes, qualitatively and phenomenologically distinct; not understood in terms of a preimagined evolutionary teleology, but instead in terms of a diversity of potentials. Only the latter mode can be relevant to a range of possible futures and to the rules of contingency and plurality that remain at the center of evolutionary process.

3. To maximize a sense of diverse outcomes, try to conceptualize a system in terms of a distinct plurality of working parts, both semantically and syntagmatically. At the syntactic level, the ideal is to be working with more than one, indeed more than two or three, constitutive elements, but finite in number, and once again, qualitatively differentiated.

4. Such qualitative differences may or may not be rooted in detectable, hard-wired, and/or immutable biological difference. Conceptually it doesn't matter much — especially as thresholds of detectability are constantly changing. So too, importantly, are understandings of neural plasticity — with regard to genetics, prenatal environments, and the overall lifespan, and equally with regard to the temporary, nonce, and provisional.

5. Take advantage of an understanding of theories *as* theories. In Tomkins, while everyone has affect theories, they remain plural; they are continually tested and, in a number of possible ways, modified; they may also be discarded in favor of alternative affect theories. None of these things is true of Theory of Mind, which its researchers also refer to as a kind of "folk knowledge" that relies on "everyday mindreading"[20] — as though anything so widespread could only be something rather simple, and solidly knowable.

And hence also: feedback, feedback, feedback — at every level of individual and social processing. Equally there needs to be lots of room for the productivity of error, of feedback distorted whether contingently or consistently, and for the articulation of contingencies with consistencies. Maybe it's easy to take them for granted, these conceptual legacies of the cybernetic moment, but it's never safe to do so, whether the framework of research be empiricist or even postmodernist.

6. Epistemological modesty. If that can't be found with regard to Theory of Mind, then where to look for it?

NOTES

"Affect Theory and Theory of Mind" was delivered on April 14, 2008, at a conference at the University of Leiden titled "Affective Operations in Art, Literature, and Politics," organized by Ernst van Alphen, whom EKS thanks in a penciled notation for a "productive invitation for thought (even tho[ugh] no sense of 'present moment')" and "for very interesting and *careful* historical discussion of recent discourse on affect." She prepared an abstract of her paper, which reads as follows:

> This talk will discuss two usages of the term "theory" that have some attractive commonalities. When Silvan Tomkins writes about "affect theory" in the first two volumes of *Affect Imagery Consciousness*, his main reference is not to the activity of psychologists like himself who discuss affect at an abstruse level. Instead, "affect theory" is lay theory in the first place. Given that—as Tomkins posits—the affect system is imbricated in complex and sensitive feedback processes, people's affective experience will be structured according to their theories and expectations about affect, and those theories in turn will respond to the quality of their encounters. For Tomkins, the ability of individuals to be wrong about their feelings and motivations is crucial to the human capacity for affective and cognitive freedom, development, and depth. Furthermore, scientific or philosophical theorizing about affect doesn't take place at a different, metalevel from lay theorizing, but represents a further instance of it.
>
> This democratic understanding of "theory" also characterizes Theory of Mind. Introduced in an article on animal behavior in 1978 [David Premack and Guy Woodruff, "Does the Chimpanzee Have a Theory of Mind?" (*Behavioral and Brain Sciences* 1, no. 4 [December 1978]: 515–26)], the term "Theory of Mind" doesn't designate a philosophical field, like Philosophy of Mind, but rather a particular cognitive ability that develops in most people and a few animals: the understanding that another may know or intend different things from what I know and intend. And Theory of Mind, like affect theory, also emerges from the possibility of wrongness; Daniel Dennett early posited that Theory of Mind is present when a child understands that someone else can believe something that the child knows to be untrue.
>
> Finally, my text for exploring how these two kinds of theory can interact: probably the strangest volume of Proust's *A la recherche du temps perdu*, the one called *La Prisonnière*, which recounts the narrator's virtual imprisonment of his mistress Albertine. Structured around the narrator's increasing paranoia and the resulting, multiple stereotyped layers of mind-reading fake outs, the volume also, unexpectedly, offers a gradual but marked enrichment of his vocation and sensibility, and an access to ranges of emotion that are anything but predictable.

1. Eve Kosofsky Sedgwick, *Epistemology of the Closet* (Berkeley: University of California Press, 1990), 22.

2. Jared Blackburn, quoted from Jared Blackburn et al., "A Discussion about Theory of Mind: From an Autistic Perspective," in *Proceedings of Autism Europe's 6th International Congress*, Glasgow, May 19–21, 2000 (www.autistics .org/library/AE2000-ToM.html).

3. Simon Baron-Cohen, *Mindblindness: An Essay on Autism and Theory of Mind* (Cambridge: MIT Press, 1995), 51.

4. See Simon Baron-Cohen, "The Autistic Child's Theory of Mind: A Case of Specific Developmental Delay," *Journal of Child Psychology and Psychiatry* 30, no. 2 (March 1989): 285–98.

5. See Peter Carruthers and Peter K. Smith, eds., *Theories of Theories of Mind* (Cambridge: Cambridge University Press, 1996).

6. In the thirty years between the appearance of volumes 2 and 3 of Silvan Tomkins's definitive, four-volume *Affect Imagery Consciousness* (New York: Springer, 1962–92), his vocabulary developed so that the term "script" supplanted the term "affect theory"; the latter is now better known. But the "scripts" of volume 3 retain features of the "affect theories" from which they emerged—signally, their complex circulation of feedback processes. The citation below is from this edition.

7. See Eve Kosofsky Sedgwick and Adam Frank, eds., *Shame and Its Sisters: A Silvan Tomkins Reader* (Durham: Duke University Press, 1995), 75–80. Further citations from this are cited in my text as *Tomkins Reader*.

8. Although Tomkins's use of "stimulus" here makes him sound, superficially, like a behaviorist, he makes clear elsewhere that stimulus is already a complex concept and can include not only external but also internal events, such as other affects, ideas, feedback, and long-term states; nor can there be a stable distinction between stimuli and responses (see *Tomkins Reader*, 11).

9. Blackburn et al., "A Discussion about Theory of Mind."

10. Lisa Zunshine, *Why We Read Fiction: Theory of Mind and the Novel* (Columbus: Ohio State University Press, 2006), 34.

11. Unless otherwise noted, all citations from Marcel Proust are to book and page number in the six-volume *In Search of Lost Time*, trans. C. K. Scott Moncrieff and Terence Kilmartin, rev. D. J. Enright (New York: Modern Library, 2003).

12. Marcel Proust, *The Prisoner and The Fugitive*, trans. Peter Collier (London: Penguin, 2002), 136. The sentence in the Moncrieff and Kilmartin translation reads: "To make her chains lighter, the clever thing seemed to me to be to make her believe that I myself was about to break them" (5:236).

13. There are several elements I haven't mentioned, for instance, that variously seem to run athwart the project of reading *La Prisonnière* entirely through Theory of Mind problematics. One is the very explicit and contagious sadness in which the volume is steeped. Probably related is the narrator's intermittent attention to the sensations of Albertine's actual companionship, her "sisterliness." And there's the persistent impression that, if the *Recherche* displays an overarching teleology toward writerly vocation, this is the volume in which

that vocation most thickens and deepens. But where does that happen and how?

14. See Jacqueline Rose, *Albertine* (New York: Vintage, 2002).

15. Neil Hertz, *George Eliot's Pulse* (Stanford: Stanford University Press, 2003), 96.

16. Blackburn et al., "A Discussion about Theory of Mind."

17. Ibid.

18. Ibid.

19. Ibid.

20. Daniel Dennett, *The Intentional Stance* (Cambridge: MIT Press, 1987), 48.

Anality

News from the Front

In "The Danger of Desire: Anal Sex and the Homo/Masculine Subject," Jeffrey Guss is working at some of the most important and under-examined seams of sexuality theory (which I seem to picture as something like a skull, oddly asymmetrical, rich with the traces of both ontogenetic and phylogenetic process, full of sutures and cavities and outcrops, soft spots where the bones haven't fused yet and thick spots where an early fracture has over-healed). Although the anus—the male one—announces itself as the central site of fissure in his essay, Guss's other defining term, danger, seems to explain even more of its tectonic seams.

Like Stephen Botticelli, Guss makes the challenging choice of grounding his historical discussion of anality in the work of the French writer Guy Hocquenghem—specifically, in the 1972 volume that was translated into English in 1978 as *Homosexual Desire*.[1] From the point of view of Hocquenghem's book, like others emerging from that pregnant post-1968 moment in France and internationally (cf. Paul Hoch in Britain, Mario Mieli in Italy), "danger" was a word as fraught with promise and excitement as it was with threat.

It's worth underlining some distinctive features of the historical moment out of which such thinking emerged in Europe. For the post-68 cultural theorists, unlike present workers in these fields, psychoanalysis was an overarching matrix of culturally available concepts, much more than it was a profession, a specialization, or a set of techniques to facilitate individual change and development. In France, all kinds of leftist thought—such as that of Sartre or of Frantz Fanon, himself a psychiatrist—had long found expression through critiques and reformulations of Freudian ideas. And in public discourse the concept of repression, along with a few other psychoanalytic concepts, was so magically valued and endowed with such unquestioned efficacy that to break through societal repression, e.g. to bring to collective consciousness a repressed bodily zone (the anus) and its pleasures, might be thought to catalyze complete social breakdown and reorganization.

But psychoanalytic ideas were not the only ones to carry such widespread intellectual authority. Hocquenghem's book and those that formed its immediate context were equally responsive to a Marxist imperative that would interrogate and, if possible, dismantle or explode the abusive inequalities of class and capitalism. The grounds and, indeed, the possibility of a Freud/Marx synthesis, within or against the Marcusian tradition, greatly preoccupied these writers and, for several, remained a prime motivating force. Hocquenghem's own career began with his Communist Party–affiliated participation in the events of May 1968, encompassed his expulsion from the Party for homosexuality, but was propelled by the urgency of his continued commitment to Marxist questions if not answers. In its contradictions his career exemplifies the endlessly difficult but deep-rooted leftism underlying that theoretical moment. Consider Mario Mieli, who resisted the integration of Italian gay liberation into the left-right party system, but who is best known among English speakers for his pamphlet "Towards a Gay Communism" (1980).[2] Or think of the extremely generative work of the Gay Left Collective (1974–80) in Britain, whose tireless theoretical as well as activist work mediated the gaps between "Gays and the Trade Union Movement" on the one hand (Bob Cant, *Gay Left #1*, Autumn 1975), and on the other, a manifesto "In Defense of Disco" (Richard Dyer, *Gay Left #8*, Summer 1979).

A further important component of that theoretical context was its antiracism and the attendant colonial consciousness. Like Jean Genet, Hocquenghem was involved with the defense of the Black Panthers in the United States, and wrote about the situation of Arab immigrants in France as seen through the lens of his sexual politics.[3] Paul Hoch, in *White Hero, Black Beast* (1979), is the most explicit of these writers both in his antiracist program, and in placing anality at the center of his theoretical work. His subtitle for that book is *Racism, Sexism, and the Mask of Masculinity*—and what's masked (Latin *masca*) by racist heteromasculinity, as he etymologizes, is specifically the *culus* (Latin for arse; in French, *le cul*).[4]

Nor is Hoch unusual in placing sexism among the social constructs that can be understood and, ideally, undone through the "dangerous" work of a sexual liberation movement. It is very explicit in each of these authors' projects that the women's liberation movement is more than a provocation or inspiration for nascent work in gay liberation. Instead, the inequity of the gender system itself remains quite central to each of these analyses of the sources and dynamics of sexual oppression. One can, like Leo Bersani in *Homos*, be fascinated by the explosive potential of anal sensation without being a feminist.[5] For such theorists, however, the undoing of patriarchy, of homophobia (though the term wasn't widely used at that time), of capitalism, and of racist colonialism were seen as not only contiguous or congruent undertakings, but completely inextricable ones. Some figures — notably the men attached to the Gay Left Collective in London, working closely with the pioneer theorists of British socialist feminism — had a much more sophisticated view than others of the tensions built into so comprehensive a vision. But the systemic relatedness of these different forms of oppression — the ways in which they necessitated, generated, and potentially supported one another — were both axiomatic for our theorists and also powerfully illuminated by their work.

To be systemic, in fact, to get to the heart of systems as such, was a great hallmark of all this writing and its ambitions. This was a theoretical and political time that showcased a distinctive aesthetic of knowing — you might call it radicalism, in the root sense as well as the leftist sense. At that international moment of (what seemed) revolutionary possibility there was a great premium placed on economy of theoretical means, the elegance of understanding how exactly the most defended aspects of a culture were also those that could most readily be turned against it. As Guss puts it, for example, even in arguing against such radical formulations: "If anal sex is rebellious and subversive, it is also a double agent: it reflects a refusal of compulsory heterosexuality while its rejection through disavowal sits as a cornerstone of that exact mechanism of masculine gender production. . . . It serves as a location through which binaries of gender are sustained, enacted, and overthrown — it is precisely these protean effects that constitute its dangerousness." The radical promise of both women's and gay liberation at that time was that a very small body of concepts and questions could give unique access to a wildly disproportionate force field of social relations. And such access would be not only analytic but through-and-through performative. Invoking "danger" in this context was far from being a go-slow signal but instead an incitement and rallying cry.

The reason I'm pausing on this historical evocation is to highlight what I take to be an important, though somewhat submerged organizing principle in Jeffrey Guss's essay. In it, danger seems to have undergone a metamorphosis—relatively unmarked—from a revolutionary flash point to be sought out and exploited, as it is for Hocquenghem's cohort, into a subjective threat that needs to be avoided at almost any cost. In the face of such risk aversion, one rhetorical strategy might be a leftier-than-thou wallow of accusatory nostalgia for a systemic gender-sexuality-class-race revolution that never happened. Not wanting to take up such projectile armaments (at Guss's expense), I do still want to look at some aspects of his argument that may prove to be either strengthened or circumscribed by this danger-avoidant mode of thought.

For one example, in his otherwise eloquent discussion of the Hocquenghem moment, and his critique of the absence from it of a gay male subjectivity per se, I think Guss forgets (or may be too young to have experienced) how fully a utopian motive, or a catastrophe-seeking or otherwise revolutionary one, actually could have come to imbue many people's sexual pleasures as well as their theorizing and, perhaps, activism. (A note from January 2009: maybe the global outpouring of positive affect that is currently clustered around the person of Barack Obama can give an idea of the sexy potential of so apparently abstract an emotion as hope.) Given Hocquenghem's analysis of all the ghastly uses that privatizing, patriarchal capitalism has for anality—as the chosen object of masculine projection, abjection, and violence, in the service of stabilizing a defined masculinist heterosexual identity—Guss asks: "What could instigate this costly plunge into identity destruction and cultural destabilization? With so much to lose, what constitutes the robust drive toward this particular kind of sex?" And later, "What would motivate a desire that evokes the assignment of a profoundly abjected, debased identity?" These aren't posed as entirely rhetorical questions; they imply that some needed explanation, via individual subjectivity or agency, is lacking from analyses like Hocquenghem's. Yet given the apparent transhistorical robustness of many people's desire for anal sex regardless of the extreme proscriptions so often attached to it, I'm not sure these are unanswerable questions.

Or put another way: in a psychoanalytic context, why does a desire — never mind a drive — need to be motivated or constituted, rather than itself serving to motivate or constitute the actions of a person? (And a person, one might have thought, who is thereby understood as having at least a modicum of subjectivity and agency.) It seems as though at least in Freud, the libidinal drive/desire is understood as already having such originary and explanatory force. Guss looks to the neuroscience of Solms and Turnbull, recruiting consciousness and, apparently, cognition and narrative as well, in an attempt to fill in more of the links that lead (in their view) from physical sensation to mental signification to intention and action. I think a more direct use of neuroscience here would be one that focused on affect, in the tradition that extends from Darwin up to Silvan Tomkins and has been furthered in some respects by Ekman, Izard, and others.[6] In the latter tradition, affect is somatically grounded (though for Tomkins, in a way that also incorporates cognition, association, and so forth) and constitutes motivation *tout court*; and even the most basic drives require affective amplification in order to be instantiated.

While Tomkins never posits a one-to-one relation between any affect and any act, he considers both enjoyment-joy and interest-excitement good candidates (among the primary affects) for motivating sexual behavior in most people.[7] While hope would count for Tomkins as a (secondary) emotion in the vicinity of these (primary) affects, hope, which is intoxicating in itself and protean enough to lend an aphrodisiac glow to many different scenarios, is only one of the ways in which strong subjectivity and agency found their way into a context where Guss is more inclined to see pure reactivity, self-betrayal, and existential danger. Through an affective lens it's not hard to see how, given the post-68 political zeitgeist, a hopeful as well as explosive revolutionary consciousness could increase the interest-excitement attaching to particular modes of sexual expression. And once interest-excitement is admitted as a likely constituent of sexual desire, the door is also open to such untraditional extra constituents as disgust (e.g. at the suffering caused to a great many other people by the status quo); shame-humiliation (based on the society's contempt for sexual expression); anger; and even fear-terror. A number of the sexual manifestoes of this period (and even earlier, e.g. those of Jean Genet) explicitly touch on the sexual relevance of each of these affects. I don't think one has to go far from these men's radicalism in seeking "a basis for anal erotic desire" whose motives go distinctly beyond "the system that disavows it."[8]

"Indeed," Guss admits, "some gay men embrace just such an out-sider status, seeing themselves as sexual outlaws, hooked on the trans-gressive thrill of gender misbehavior." He suggests that such men are in the minority among gay men—as perhaps they are today, and in-deed they may have been even in 1980. But being in a minority is one thing, not incompatible with a certain level of dignity. I'm struck on the contrary by the diminishing language that Guss summons for his dismissal of such queer types, who by implication are uncritically mas-ochistic (*embracing* outsider status), self-deluded (*seeing themselves*), histrionic (*outlaws*), addicted (*hooked*) to a form of pseudo-satisfaction that is neither authentic (being purely reactive, *transgressive*) nor ac-cordingly, as a mere "*thrill*," sustainable or productive over time (em-phases added).

I feel stupid admitting this, but it was only the climactic placing of "gender misbehavior" in this negatively toned sentence that made me notice how thoroughgoing the reactionary gender polemic of Guss's essay seems to be. Up until there—and indeed later, in the sympathetic and fairly wide-ranging discussion of barebacking, which does not di-rectly engage gender—the direction of his writing had seemed much more exploratory and less tendentious. But beyond this point, I found myself increasingly alert, and increasingly resistant, to several aspects of Guss's argument that seem to converge on a desire that women (or that challenges to the gender system itself) be eclipsed from gay male experience and discourse at every level. I can only deal briefly with the substance of these several converging elements, but am most im-pressed by the way they seem collectively to give a shape to the second half of Guss's essay.

Most striking, still, is the changed status of "danger." It is only in the course of finishing Guss's essay that one comes to see clearly that in his view, danger now is altogether a thing to be decried and avoided. To begin with, as his focus narrows to the twenty-first century, Guss jettisons the concerns that, in their ostensibly systemic relatedness, ani-mated Hocquenghem's generation of European thinkers. Guss leaves no trace of their engagement with racism, colonialism, and economic exploitation—neither the theorists' motivating disgust at those prac-tices nor their continuing struggle with the way gay people can also be endangered by Stalinist strains of radicalism. Between then and now any possible systemic dangers to racism, colonialism, and eco-nomic exploitation seem to have entirely lost their power to invigorate or quicken a sexual movement. In fact, the intuition of their having any relation at all to sexuality seems to have quietly disappeared from mainstream gay discourse. The likelihood or valuation of "systemic" insight is itself tremendously diminished.

For Guss at least, however, it may remain true that issues of sexuality and those of gender identity are related or relatable to one another. And yet the grounds for even this connection are unclear. He writes, for example, "It seems obvious to us now that male anal erotic desire, felt or acted upon, does not destroy the subject, but it does destroy the conflation of phallic hegemony and masculinity." I, for one, found this formulation puzzling rather than obvious, so long as I understood "phallic hegemony" to mean, Kate Millett–style, something like "male privilege": male privilege over women. Silly girl. After a while I hypothesized that "phallic hegemony" might instead mean the penis/phallus's position—as opposed to that of the male anus—as the guarantor of masculinity. Still, what about male desire for a woman's anus—is that anal desire? Finally I saw that the only condition that would make Guss's contention true, never mind "obvious" (to "us"), would be the prior and entire exclusion of women from the general population of desirers, desirees, anus-possessors, and even readers. Explicitly for Guss, the significant meanings of anality emerge only "when anal sex occurs *between men*, [and] when anal arousal occurs *in a homoerotic context*" (emphases added).

I know some people have trouble with scenes that don't include them, or that don't include women. I don't mind them—in fact, some are among my favorite scenes. A lot can depend on one's sense of why the women aren't there, and in particular, whether theirs is an invidious absence. Many writers on intimate subjects such as the anus manage to offer readers some appealing, well-lighted glimpses of their personal utopias, and I found an unexpected and initially welcome one in Guss's compassionate discussion of Holmes and Warner's 2005 work on communities of men who have anal sex without practicing HIV prevention.[9]

In exploring the meaning of anal erotic activity and semen transmission, the subjects' responses organize into a familiar theme: the oedipal longings of a protogay boy for his father *and as well* the father's reciprocal desire for his son, both actively taking pleasure as well as giving it. In so doing, they create a relational context that contains an intensely intimate relatedness, whether the actors are long-term partners or strangers to one another. These subjects, allowed to narrate their own subjective stories, describe a self-contained system of giving and receiving, outlining an Oedipal narrative that is fecund rather than destructive. There is a notable absence of destructive, threatening wishes toward phallic hegemony. No one's masculinity is destabilized or destroyed, quite the contrary. Allowed to speak, these anal erotic, semen-transmitting men describe feelings of closeness, trust, kinship, acceptance and masculine communion as vital aspects of anal sexuality and semen transmission. They do not locate the origins of homoerotic anal desire in subversion.

Holmes and Warner make clear from the start that their subjects are specifically men and specifically gay men — in this Spenserian glade even one's father is reborn as a gay man — so the identitarian coordinates of each person are relaxingly clear. (None of Hocquenghem's fierce anti-identitarianism here, nor even the mildest deconstructive ambiguity.) Also clear, also relaxing is the fact that sexuality in this Garden of Venus and Adonis is affectively motivated much more by enjoyment-joy than by interest-excitement. (Not That There's Anything Wrong With That. I swing pretty vanilla myself.) Magically endowed terms here seem to be reciprocity and relationality ("a relational context that contains an intensely intimate relatedness"), self-contained systems, "masculine communion," and pretty much anything that conveys "closeness, trust, kinship, acceptance," and whatever the exact opposite of challenge is.

If any contemporary readers are startled to know that Oedipal narratives and Oedipal longings are possible in the complete absence of women and mothers, they need to know that since at least the 1989 publication of Richard A. Isay's *Being Homosexual: Gay Men and Their Development*, and the 1990 publication of Richard Friedman's *Male Homosexuality: A Contemporary Psychoanalytic Perspective*, it's been increasingly true that psychoanalytic approaches toward gay men have dissolved their former focus on maternal relation and replaced it with a focus on the father — even where the real father has been mostly absent or alienated by the child's apparent gayness.[10] It's easy to see what could motivate a conscientious wish to banish the mother from these psychoanalytic narratives. Both psychoanalysis and popular culture in the postwar United States had been marked by such a hideously abusive consensus, crystallized in the work of Lionel Ovesey, Irving Bieber, and Charles Socarides, about the role of the mother (smothering, seductive, histrionic, too much and yet not enough, equally incapable of really loving her son and of letting him go) in generating gay men, that it must have been impossible to run away from it fast enough.[11] The homophobic force of this set of psychoanalytically sanctioned stereotypes must have been even more salient than its misogynistic force; at least, that's how I (perhaps wishfully) interpret the present situation if, as appears from this article, the entire exclusion of women from narratives of gay male development remains in effect after so long, as apparently the only way of avoiding the outrages of the postwar analysts. (It's not that there is *no* mother in Guss's world. There is a pre-Oedipal mother, in relation to whom the boy-child is demeaningly passive; but Guss argues, contra Diane Elise and Judith Butler, that separation from this mother can occur smoothly and efficiently enough that there remains not even a mother-shaped scar in the well-adjusted, post-Oedipal gay man's psychic life.)

What remains, then, of the supposed Oedipal moment, or of Oedipal challenge, in this womanless idyll? As we've seen in Guss's approving paraphrase of Holmes and Warner, it involves

> the oedipal longings of a protogay boy for his father *and as well* the father's reciprocal desire for his son, both actively taking pleasure as well as giving it. . . . outlining an Oedipal narrative that is fecund rather than destructive. There is a notable absence of destructive, threatening wishes toward phallic hegemony. No one's masculinity is destabilized or destroyed, quite the contrary. Allowed to speak, these anal erotic, semen-transmitting men describe feelings of closeness, trust, kinship, acceptance and masculine communion as vital aspects of anal sexuality and semen transmission. They do not locate the origins of homoerotic anal desire in subversion.

Clearly, this Oedipal transaction is a lot sunnier than the hetero version. May I admit to not putting a great deal of stock in the hetero version either? But at least it does get the young Freudian subject introduced to some facts of life. That the law of plenitude is not the only economy in which human relations occur, for example. Or that a seemingly straightforward love for two people can necessitate something like betrayal of one or both. That people sometimes learn to substitute one love object for another. Or that relations that don't seem to involve competition can turn out to do so. Even "he may not be all that into you," and there may be other fish in the sea. For better or worse, on the other hand, graduates of Guss's gay and happy (though hardly campy) Oedipal day camp have yet to encounter such initiations. As far as I can see, the only Oedipal thing about it is that the lines of desire traverse generational boundaries—but here they do so freely.

Just as arresting as the affirmative features of this utopian scene, though, are its negative ones. Somewhere, Guss implies, though not here, there is a different Oedipal narrative that is far from benign; unlike the fecund gay version, it is marked by destructive, threatening wishes toward (against) phallic hegemony. (Phallic hegemony may have its full double meaning in this passage: somewhere there seem to be threats against the patriarchal power of men; but among the male sexual organs, penile primacy is especially threatened. Hence, doubtless no fecundity.) In that dystopian other place, too, masculinity is destabilized and destroyed, and the very origins of homoerotic anal desire are attributed to subversion.

It's important not to get one's allegorical meanings too mixed up when reading Guss. But I'm already wishing I could tell who deserves the blame for that grim, disastrous straight Oedipal drama (all those castration threats!) that we might have had to undergo in place of the actual, jolly all-male version. At one level, it's obviously women as a group who must be to blame. Oedipal narratives without women are so much more benign and less threatening — who wouldn't hanker for them? But at the same time, in the context of Guss's essay, a second layer of meaning keeps poking through. For wasn't it Guy Hocquenghem, that queer theorist *avant la lettre*, who first insisted that gay men's anal sex might somehow involve a subversion of "phallic hegemony" — again in, seemingly, both meanings of the phrase? Or even some subversion of racism, colonialism, private property, and the state? Who but Hocquenghem and his emasculated spawn could want to see masculinity destabilized or destroyed? Wouldn't it be better to have masculinity tolerantly broadened and broadened, exalted and exalted until, ultimately, it encompasses all? Nothing human is alien to masculinity. Or as Whitman writes:

Do I contradict myself?
Very well then I contradict myself,
(I am large, I contain multitudes.)[12]

And so does masculinity itself contain multitudes.

The only question that doesn't want to be asked in this expansive context would seem to be, of course, about women and femininity. Can masculinity expand to contain women and femininity as well? And if so, how does it and why should it? Does one want to say about Thomas Beatie, the F-to-M who became briefly famous as the tabloids' "pregnant man," "He must be so secure in his masculinity!"? Maybe it's something else besides masculinity in which, giving birth, he seems secure; but since he is a man, it seems disrespectful to call him secure in his femininity. Can his visible self-possession reside in some broader ontological status — in his human self-knowledge, maybe? In a mature resilience, with regard to childbearing among other incidents that contemporary mammalian subjectivity may encounter? Masculinity alone hardly seems elastic enough to suit the case.

From a clinical point of view, I find it easy to picture Dr. Guss as an ideal analyst for certain kinds of young men, and a much less apt choice for some others. Those who were born to be his clients (Youth A) are the ones you might call gay but not queer. With a strong core gender identity they've never found it strange to see themselves as male, nor to identify with the abilities and privileges enjoyed by other men. Redefining identities and fooling around with categories, in general, are not among their pleasures and needs, however much anal sex may be. Yet they approach Dr. Guss with real vulnerabilities. His talent for helping them understand a very wide range of feelings and aptitudes *as* forms of masculinity, and as ego-syntonic with themselves in their individual understandings of their masculinity, opens many doors for them, internally and also in the larger world. Guss is good at recognizing such youth and allowing himself to be recognized by them. His nurturance of them is distinctly maternal—a good thing, as Youth A are no longer close with their mothers, nor accompany close women friends into adulthood. Once they develop a firm, conventional sense of how gay men can interact with fag hags, however, Youth A can become—to a limited extent—participants in that or some similarly stylized form of cross-gender interaction, if they want to do so.

Youth B, young men who are less successful at working with this imaginary Dr. Guss, would be unmistakably queer, though they might not be as sure of being gay. (Indeed some, as adults, are not gay.) They have been stigmatized by boys and men for as long as they can remember—sometimes for effeminate modes of speech or movement, other times for interests or attainments that are just eccentric (unicycles, ancient Greek). Without mostly believing or declaring themselves to be women, they are precocious in seeking out and meditating over transsexual stories, as if sure that those carry some personal message if only it can be divined. They may go through a hyperreligious phase. They are often gerontophilic: sharing a grandmother's bedroom, hanging out (if hyperreligious) with the nuns. What is certain is that they find ways of spending time with women, whether their contemporaries or older, including their mothers and aunts. Some of this is *faute de mieux* as men or boys exclude them, but their interest is increasingly in the women themselves, especially lesbians and proto-lesbians, an interest in resources that women and girls can confer—while these boys' sexual attraction may indeed prove to be toward other men, and anally couched. The adult Youth B's relation to his mother, if she survives, may grow richer over many decades—as it did for Wilde, Proust, Warhol, and even the brilliantly masculine Walt Whitman. Maybe not surprisingly, redefining identities and fooling with gender categories provide lifelong, tonic, and challenging nurturance to Youth B's imagination. Dr. Guss and Youth B don't make heads or tails of one another.

Somebody might suspect me of turning a commentary for *Studies in Gender and Sexuality* into a covert personals ad. But my description of Youth B is not of someone who is lacking from my life. Rather it celebrates friends long present there.

I could go on all night about Jeffrey Guss's paper, and up to a certain point could have found a lot to say about Stephen Botticelli's, too. Botticelli's theoretical world seems much more congenial to me than Guss's. But then I got to "Clinical Example," and that sense of pleasurable expansiveness froze in its transferential boots. The fact is that (no secret) I'm not a clinician. But it's worse than that: my sense of intense involvement with clinical scenes comes not from years of providing expertise in the course of them, but more ignominiously—as a fascinated consumer. (Years of futile toad kissing, as I always thought of it, followed much later by one intensive, terrific therapy that didn't correspond to my former theorizing in any respect whatever.)

Here's what Botticelli wrote that shut me right up. "After Ted's depression resolved he continued in therapy with me, as far as I could tell, as insurance against again becoming depressed and 'pudding headed.'" "As far as I could tell." What was there in these words to make them strike paralyzingly into the heart of someone they weren't even remotely about? As far as I could tell.

"AFAIK," as younger people nowadays text it, the problem seemed to be in how Botticelli's words responded with what sounded like withering near-indifference to the questions I used to ask my shrink with humiliating urgency—or wouldn't even be able to make myself ask — at the very darkest, most lost times in that therapy. Those were times when the question of trusting him became conflated with the question of trusting anything on earth, including myself, and yet I felt I all but patently didn't and *shouldn't* trust him. They were questions, the ones I asked, phrased with this awful Dickinsonian smallness, chastened to almost nothing by hundreds of corrosive rehearsals to myself. "You don't have to tell me what you're actually thinking BUT"—But do you know where we are in this therapy? Do you feel as if you have anything remotely like a map of the territory? Do you (I really felt myself to be asking) know what you're doing? Is there a distinct *thing* going on in this therapy, something you recognize? Are you as far out of your depths here as I am?

I certainly dreaded the answer that he didn't know much more than I did. Yet I quite nauseously dreaded any reassurance that would sound the slightest bit defensive or slick. The right answer — the one he gave, actually, but also the only one I can picture relieving or interesting me — was very calm. Yes (he could answer and did), it does feel shitty, but I do know where we are. I've been here a few times, he said, and I'm pretty sure I see how we can figure a way out. Characteristically he added, "I shouldn't say this, but it's actually the kind of juncture I can get a kick out of."

The worst answer would have been surprise to learn that I felt there was anything going on at all.

I needed to know he had the capacity to, and would, take responsibility for our times in this room, and also for relevant parts of the time in between. I needed to know for sure that he could and did mentalize, if you want to put it that way, me, and also the course of the therapy itself. I uglily found myself fearing that the only "object permanence" involved was that of my insurance payments accumulating in his bank account.

So without identifying personally with Ted, when I read Botticelli's account of his own proceeding, I identified so strongly against *him* that it was hard for me to do much with his essay beyond enumerating a bill of particulars against him. The voiced version of my complaint went something like: So it's all true. They can let the paid hours accumulate forever without having any plan or vision of getting somewhere else, or taking any responsibility for the patient's being in therapy — or even remembering the patient's existence from one week to the next. "Apparently," Botticelli wrote — with what I judged was excessive understatement — "I had played my part as well, having recreated Ted's experience of parental neglect."

By that point in the narrative it was already clear that Botticelli didn't like Ted, didn't feel warm or forgiving toward him. The story he couldn't refrain from telling first against Ted is that Ted likes to boast of "ruining" other men — in the sense of giving them such satisfying sex that they may never get its like again. Botticelli adds, "While this conceit conceivably could be charming in some, with my knowledge of Ted's psychology I had to hear it with the full force of its aggressive and destructive implications." Now while I don't picture how the re-peated boast of "ruining" sexual partners could quite be charming, it struck me there was also a kind of "ruining" of Ted himself going on here, as if every time he made his unpleasant joke he had in fact, instead of giving memorably good anal sex, actually performed anal rape on a resisting man. (And I resented Botticelli's circular recourse to profes-sional authority in denigrating his patient this way. "With my knowl-edge of Ted's psychology . . .")

Later things got more interesting between me and this imagined therapist. More interesting—hence meatier—but at the same time, much more fragmentary. I'm not sure whether that quality reflects some strong transferential dissociations that remain from my own therapy (or may have accumulated retrospectively around it). It may also, though, reflect what I perceive as a certain nonlinear, or under-determined, relation between the apparent argument of Botticelli's essay on the one hand, and on the other, the unresolved, transferential and countertransferential blockages that I seemed to keep finding in his clinical narrative. Another conceivable factor: what if the famous "shattering effect" of receptive anal sex also adheres to the mere acts of reflecting and writing about it?

At any rate, I noted Botticelli's mention of Buddhist ideas about loss of self. The Buddhist idiom is congenial to me, and I rather abruptly thought: "He's never had a vision of Ted's Buddha nature that he could fall in love with." Partly this thought echoed the other reproaches with which I'd been heaping Botticelli, since in my mental shorthand, getting a sense of a student's or patient's Buddha nature (that is, of some un-spoiled hum or pulse of perfection in the person, to which further inter-actions—even some necessary idealizations—can be tuned) does seem like a fundamental task for that person's would-be teacher or therapist.

But then I found I felt sorry for this doctor who'd missed the plea-sure of seeing his patient, even briefly, transfigured. It seemed his work must feel excessively bleak without that glimpse of an embodied pur-pose. Other instances of Botticelli's bleakness came up too—as if he'd misunderstood the genre of a TV series that really wanted to be a com-edy. For instance, he said Ted had "told me of a recent dream in which he and another man walk along a boardwalk. The other man slips a finger into his ass, and Ted feels both a rush of pleasure and a sense of danger, aware of the risk that he and the man are taking in this pub-lic space." Quite a nice-sounding dream, and one in which, Botticelli notes, Ted considerably aerates his rigid insistence on being an exclu-sive top.

When Ted (maybe) steals a *New York* magazine from Botticelli's waiting room, it seems to Botticelli like a reenactment of this dream that Ted has just narrated. But note how the dream's "rush of pleasure" and its sense of experimental fun have utterly drained out:

> Some time after the session ended I went out to the waiting room to look for the current issue of *New York* magazine that had caught my eye, one featuring some typically lurid cover story about the sexual and romantic lives of teenagers at an exclusive Manhattan high school. Not finding it on top of the magazine pile, I rifled through the pile several times with growing agitation—had Ted taken it? By the time I determined the magazine was missing, I felt violated and enraged, as well as angry at myself for my easy, nearly unthinking assent to Ted's request [to borrow some old issues of magazines]. In so doing I had put out of my mind what I knew, or thought I knew, about Ted's capacity to do harm.
>
> . . . Ted had "flipped" me, putting himself back in the role of the ruthless top. I thought also of what I had started to think of as his dissociated rage . . . emergent in his sexual episodes of "ruining" other men.

Me here reflecting: how can there not be even the least bit of Puck in him, bubbling over at the image of this learned Doctor B., all raw and violated, enraged but endlessly *intelligent*, bent totally out of shape over missing a lurid cover story about the sexual and romantic lives of teenagers at an exclusive Manhattan high school?

If Ted had really stolen, then returned, the magazine, wasn't it his way of trying (successfully) to get Botticelli to mentalize him, a thing that hadn't previously happened? All those previous absences couldn't convey any message to Botticelli so long as Ted's presence had never properly registered with him. But then beyond that, hadn't Ted also been making another attempt, one that didn't come anywhere near succeeding? I picture it as his creative and seemingly generous effort to make contact through, not reproach or anger, but *a joke*. He wants to evoke if only for an instant—in the quick recognition of a tease or a wink—their possibly shaming, tacky, secret shared identities as—what to call them?—say, as Gossip Girls.

The joke goes ungotten, and needless to say, Ted's (imagined) fantasy masque of mutual recognition goes unperformed.

Botticelli worries in this essay about a something in his writing that some other people have perceived as mean, harsh, or sarcastic. His is an anxiety that seeks out parallelisms: "What Ted did to other men in a cubicle at the baths, did I do to people on the page?" (Gosh, many readers may hope so!) Still, I couldn't tell whether he was trying to avoid that abrasive tone in this particular piece; or even whether he really feels his writing ought to rise above such dangerously evocative textures or motives. The nicely lubricated and the un-: aren't they, among other things, textures and motives that are built into the forms (as well as fantasies) of anal pleasure and excitement?

Botticelli seems to perceive many things as essentially forms of violence, and violence itself as all but equivalent to homophobia. I wondered how much the sourness, the inffectuality of the clinical interaction Botticelli records and reflects on here may be tied to the circularity, the disproportion, the purism of his need to set violence altogether out of even the bounds of imagination. His writing made me miss a worldlier or more tricksterish analytic voice — a more Nietzschean or even Freudian one, that could allow for broader consolations to be applied in such cases.

Maybe few people find Melanie Klein consoling, but at such a juncture she can satisfy. One thing Klein offers is an understanding that the need to destroy and ruin is as endogenous as the need to relate and repair. Not for her a blank-slate subjectivity in whose mouth butter wouldn't melt. For Klein, as opposed to (say) Winnicott, there's no assumption that the nature of any infant is to be innocent, resilient, or even viable; it is not only the mother's depression or abstraction, the father's intolerance, that introduce psychic danger and violent cross-purposes into this small world. At one point Botticelli speculates almost with wonder, "Might I too harbor some dissociated anger, some unacknowledged wish to harm?" A Kleinian, or for that matter a Buddhist, would find his speculation grimly funny: Ya think? Aren't such angers and wishes unnumbered as the sands of the ocean? And isn't there any place to go from there? Yet it's hard to figure a politics or therapy that could refrain from trading the rich, stinky humus of the elastic everyday for imagined fidelity to a fantasy of vindicated innocence.

NOTES

A version of this essay appears in *Studies in Gender and Sexuality* 11, no. 3 (July–September 2010): 151–62, in which also can be found Jeffrey R. Guss, "The Danger of Desire: Anal Sex and the Homo/Masculine Subject," 124–40, and Stephen Botticelli, "Thinking the Unthinkable: Anal Sex in Theory and Practice," 112–23, as well as responses to commentaries by Guss and Botticelli, 163–72.

1. Guy Hocquenghem, *Homosexual Desire*, trans. Daniella Dangoor (London: Allison and Busby, 1978).

2. Mieli's pirated pamphlet appeared in London.

3. Guy Hocquenghem, *La beauté du métis, réflexions d'un francophobe* (Paris: Ramsay, 1979).

4. Paul Hoch, *White Hero, Black Beast: Racism, Sexism, and the Mask of Masculinity* (London: Pluto, 1979), 96.

5. Leo Bersani, *Homos* (Cambridge: Harvard University Press, 1995).

6. See Charles Darwin, *Expression of the Emotions in Man and Animals*, ed. Paul Ekman (New York: Harper Collins, 1998); Carroll E. Izard, *The Psychology of Emotions* (New York: Plenum, 1991).

7. Tomkins gives double names to most of the nine basic affects, names that designate the qualitative spectrum of that affect from least to most intense. See Eve Kosofsky Sedgwick and Adam Frank, eds., *Shame and Its Sisters: A Silvan Tomkins Reader* (Durham: Duke University Press, 1995).

8. There are a number of reasons for doubting how substantial the putative alignment of Foucault's work was with that of these sexual dissidents. In fact, activists of many kinds have long recognized that (as Guss shows) Foucault's work creates constant problems for anyone interested in agency or subjectivity. I've written about what seems to me the inapt choice of Foucault as a French exemplar for American queer theory as well, on closely related grounds in *Touching Feeling: Affect Pedagogy, Performativity* (Durham: Duke University Press, 2003), 9–13; "Melanie Klein and the Difference Affect Makes" [earlier in this volume]; as well as in "Gender Criticism," in *Redrawing the Boundaries: The Transformation of English and American Literary Studies*, ed. Stephen Greenblatt and Giles Gunn (New York: Modern Language Association of America, 1992), 271–302, especially 278–94. The invigorating perspectives that come into focus through an emphasis on affect, à la Tomkins, make Foucault look particularly marmoreal.

9. Dave Holmes and Dan Warner, "The Anatomy of a Forbidden Desire: Men, Penetration, and Semen Exchange," *Nursing Inquiry* 12, no. 1 (March 2005): 10–20.

10. See Richard Friedman, *Male Homosexuality: A Contemporary Psychoanalytic Perspective* (New Haven: Yale University Press, 1990) and Richard A. Isay, *Being Homosexual: Gay Men and Their Development* (New York: Farrar Straus and Giroux, 1989).

11. See Lionel Ovesey, *Homosexuality and Pseudohomosexuality* (New York: Science House, 1969); Irving Bieber, *Homosexuality: A Psychoanalytic Study of Male Homosexuals* (New York: Basic, 1962); Charles W. Socarides, *The Overt Homosexual* (Lanham, Md.: Jason Aronson, 1968).

12. Walt Whitman, "Song of Myself," ll.1324–26, in *Leaves of Grass and Other Writings*, ed. Michael Moon (New York: W. W. Norton, 2002), 77.

Making Gay Meanings

Some intellectuals do a lot of foreign travel, some don't; I'm one of the latter, so my ideas tend to get very defamiliarized every time I cross a national border and speak with an audience outside the United States. Given France's fame or notoriety as "the country that doesn't have identity politics," the present occasion seems like an especially good chance to revisit and think further about some implications of gay men and lesbians viewing ourselves, and being viewed by others, as a distinct minority population.

The question of minority status, or minority identity, has a kind of fatal pseudo-intelligibility in the United States. The lens of political history through which the gay/lesbian movement views itself there is an extremely selective one, and the history that it narrates is very short. It begins with the successes of the black civil rights movement in the American south in the 1950s and 1960s, successes that led to new legislation, new constitutional interpretation, and, to some degree, new prestige and mobility for many African Americans. The feminist movement is seen as taking its form from the civil rights movement, in making audible the claims and historical grievances of an additional distinct, circumscribed, physically recognizable, and ontologically immutable group of citizens. And other racially or ethnically based advocacy movements in the United States, as well as other movements such as disability rights, are seen as having followed the same model. Paradoxically, these movements claim the right of seamless social assimilation for a group of people *on the basis of* a separatist understanding of them as embodying a stable ontological difference. An infinitely additive version of such separatist assimilationism is widely understood to form the basis of American "identity politics," "multiculturalism," and "diversity," including most components of the contemporary gay movement.

From a European vantage point, it is probably easy to spot one weakness of the American conception of identity politics: its dependence on the historical occlusion of any analysis of class. It is true that American identity politics has been shaped by the gaping absence of a significant postwar Left. There are other problems too, however, in understanding identity politics in this way. The most important is that it simply fails to describe important political currents that are not in the first place structured in terms of stable identities. It is true that the identitarian momentum of American political geography has resulted in the invention of newly spatialized, postmodern pseudo-identities, so that someone who is stingy will now make their claims "as a taxpayer," or who is repressive will speak "as a Christian," with all the self-righteous certitude of representing a distinct, embattled, and long-oppressed minority (this in an overwhelmingly Christian country where everyone pays taxes except the very rich). The language of minority identity, however, although it is rhetorically very potent and may even have a certain credibility for those who use it in these postmodern ways, is entirely useless for historicizing or conceptualizing, and therefore for opposing, the real politics of such movements.

It is not only postmodern politics, however, that damagingly escapes the analytic grid of fixed minority identities. Today's identitarian gay movement likes to date its inception from the late 1960s, specifically of course from the Stonewall riots of 1969. What has disappeared from this history is the completely nonidentitarian nature of so much of the politics that surrounded, supported, and indeed constituted the nascent gay liberation movement of that period. While it is true that the black civil rights movement offered one important model and motive, the rest of the late-1960s social context in the United States was more similar, perhaps, to that in France. Its main constituents included the anti-war movement, the student and youth movements, the new drug culture, and the sexual liberation movement—none of them, certainly, defined by any immutable or separatist criterion of identity. Perhaps by the same token, none of them was assimilationist in aim. For Americans in the 1990s, to remember the real political ecology of the late 1960s would be far more difficult than to conjure up, with Steven Spielberg, the lost world of the dinosaurs: there remains nothing now to remind us, and nothing either that resembles or in any way takes the place of such vanished, indispensable energies as the children's liberation movement, the mental patients' liberation movement, or even (though America now incarcerates more of its population than ever before and more than any other nation) the 1960s movement for prisoners' rights. Age-based movements, such as the children's rights and student movements, are perhaps by definition the most clearly resistant to a separatist, identitarian, minority conceptualization; surely it's significant that the only explicitly age-based American political movement that is active today also represents the only stage of life whose constituents will never outgrow it: the immensely powerful and organized lobby of the (immutably) aged and retired.

In fact, however, the tug of war about whether homosexuality, at any rate, constitutes a minority identity goes much farther back than the 1960s; it is at least as old as the twentieth century. Foucault famously offered 1870 as the date of birth of modern homosexual identity; even if that is true, it does not erase the impacted mass of nonminoritizing understandings of same-sex desire, such as classical pederastic relations, early-modern sodomitical ones, or the psychoanalytic concept of universal bisexuality, that continue to coexist with the minoritizing concept of homosexuality. As I argued in my 1990 *Epistemology of the Closet*, there is now a widespread, yet deeply incoherent Western consensus shared by both antihomophobic and homophobic common sense. It holds the minoritizing view that there is a distinct population of persons who "really are" gay; at the same time, it holds the universalizing views that sexual desire is an unpredictably powerful solvent of stable identities; that apparently heterosexual persons and object choices are strongly marked by same-sex influences and desires, and vice versa for apparently homosexual ones; and that at least male heterosexual identity and modern masculist culture may require for their maintenance the scapegoating crystallization of a same-sex male desire that is widespread and in the first place internal.

There are already good reasons to believe that the contemporary American understanding of minority identity, at once separatist and assimilationist, is damagingly inadequate to the historically varied and definitionally permeable experiences of any group, whether that group defines itself by race, gender, ethnicity, nationality, or another criterion. As I've been suggesting, in the particular area of sexuality this inadequacy is, if anything, even more dramatically obvious. "Sexual orientation" in the sense of gay versus straight is, to put it mildly, not a sharply descriptive analytic tool. I assume that most of us already know the following simple facts that can crucially differentiate even people of identical gender, race, nationality, class, and "sexual orientation" — each one of which, however, if taken seriously as a difference, retains the unaccounted-for potential to disrupt many forms of the available thinking about sexuality:

—Even identical genital acts mean very different things to different people.

—To some people, the nimbus of "the sexual" seems scarcely to extend beyond the boundaries of discrete genital acts; to others, it enfolds them loosely or floats virtually free of them.

—Sexuality makes up a large share of the self-perceived identity of some people, a small share of others.'

—Some people spend a lot of time thinking about sex, others little.

—Some people like to have a lot of sex, others little or none.

—Many people have their richest mental/emotional involvement with sexual acts that they don't do, or even don't *want* to do.

—For some people, it is important that sex be embedded in contexts resonant with meaning, narrative, and connectedness with other aspects of their life; for other people, it is important that it not be; to others, it doesn't occur that it might be.

—For some people, the preference for a certain sexual object, act, role, zone, or scenario is so immemorial and durable that it can only be experienced as innate; for others, it appears to come late or to feel aleatory or discretionary.

—For some people, the possibility of bad sex is aversive enough that their lives are strongly marked by its avoidance; for others, it isn't.

—For some people, sexuality provides a needed space of heightened discovery and cognitive hyperstimulation. For others, sexuality provides a needed space of routinized habituation and cognitive hiatus.

—Some people like spontaneous sexual scenes, others like highly scripted ones, others like spontaneous-sounding ones that are nonetheless totally predictable.

—Some people's sexual orientation is intensely marked by autoerotic pleasures and histories—sometimes more so than by any aspect of alloerotic object choice. For others the autoerotic possibility seems secondary or fragile, if it exists at all.

—Some people, homo-, hetero-, and bisexual, experience their sexuality as deeply embedded in a matrix of gender meanings and gender differentials. Others of each sexuality do not.[1]

With these differences in mind, think, then, of all the elements that are condensed in the contemporary notion of sexual identity, something that the common sense of our time presents as a unitary category. Yet, exerting any pressure at all on "sexual identity," you see that its elements include

> your biological (e.g., chromosomal) sex, male or female;
>
> your self-perceived gender assignment, male or female (supposed to be the same as your biological sex);
>
> the preponderance of your traits of personality and appearance, masculine or feminine (supposed to correspond to your sex and gender);
>
> the biological sex of your preferred partner;
>
> the gender assignment of your preferred partner (supposed to be the same as her/his biological sex);
>
> the masculinity or femininity of your preferred partner (supposed to be the opposite of your own);
>
> your self-perception as gay or straight (supposed to correspond to whether your preferred partner is your sex or the opposite);
>
> your preferred partner's self-perception as gay or straight (supposed to be the same as yours);
>
> your procreative choice (supposed to be yes if straight, no if gay);
>
> your preferred sexual act(s) (supposed to be insertive if you are male or masculine, receptive if you are female or feminine);
>
> your most eroticized sexual organs (supposed to correspond to the procreative capabilities of your sex, and to your insertive/receptive assignment);
>
> your sexual fantasies (supposed to be highly congruent with your sexual practice, but stronger in intensity);
>
> your main locus of emotional bonds (supposed to reside in your preferred sexual partner);
>
> your enjoyment of power in sexual relations (supposed to be low if you are female or feminine, high if male or masculine);
>
> the people from whom you learn about your own gender and sex (supposed to correspond to yourself in both respects);
>
> your community of cultural and political identification (supposed to correspond to your own identity);
>
> and—again—many more.[2]

Even this list is remarkable for the silent presumptions it has to make about a given person's sexuality, presumptions that are true only to varying degrees, and for many people not true at all: that everyone has a sexuality, for instance, and that it is implicated with each person's sense of overall identity in similar ways; that each person's most characteristic erotic expression will be oriented toward another person and not autoerotic; that if it is alloerotic, it will be oriented toward a single partner or kind of partner at a time; that its orientation will not change over time. Normatively, as the parenthetical prescriptions in the list above suggest, it should be possible to deduce anybody's entire set of specifications from the initial datum of biological sex alone—if one adds only the normative assumption that "biological sex of preferred partner" will be the opposite of one's own. With or without that heterosexist assumption, though, what's striking is the number and *difference* of the dimensions that "sexual identity" is supposed to organize into a seamless and univocal whole.

And if it doesn't?

It is only here, I think, that a politics can begin that is both nonseparatist and nonassimilationist. That's one of the things that the American usage "queer" can refer to: the open mesh of possibilities, gaps, overlaps, dissonances and resonances, lapses, and excesses of meaning when the constituent elements of anyone's gender, of anyone's sexuality aren't made (or can't be made) to signify monolithically. The experimental linguistic, epistemological, representational, political adventures attaching to the very many of us who may at times be moved to describe ourselves as (among many other possibilities) pushy femmes, radical faeries, fantasists, drags, clones, leatherfolk, ladies in tuxedos, feminist women or feminist men, masturbators, bulldaggers, divas, Snap! queens, butch bottoms, storytellers, transsexuals, aunties, wannabes, lesbian-identified men or lesbians who sleep with men, or . . . people able to relish, learn from, or identify with such.[3]

In the quick-change American marketplace of images, maybe the queer moment, if it's here today, will for that very reason be gone tomorrow. But many of us feel the need to make, cumulatively, stubbornly, a counterclaim against that obsolescence: a claim that something about queer is inextinguishable. Queer is a continuing moment, movement, motive—recurrent, eddying, *troublant*. The word "queer" itself means across—it comes from the Indo-European root -*twerkw*, which also yields the German *quer* (transverse), Latin *torquere* (to twist), and English athwart.[4] A lot of queer writing tends toward "across" formulations: across genders, across sexualities, across genres, across "perversions." The concept of queer in this sense is transitive—multiply transitive. The immemorial current that "queer" represents is antiseparatist as it is anti-assimilationist. Keenly, it is relational, and it is strange.

NOTES

EKS delivered this paper at an international colloquy on Gay and Lesbian Studies at the Centre Georges Pompidou on June 23 and 27, 1997. The proceedings of that event can be found in *Les Etudes gay et lesbiennes*, ed. Didier Eribon (Paris: Centre Georges Pompidou, 1998), including this talk in Eribon's translation, "Construire les significations *queer*," 109–16.

1. Eve Kosofsky Sedgwick, *Epistemology of the Closet* (Berkeley: University of California Press, 1990), 25–26.

2. Eve Kosofsky Sedgwick, "Queer and Now," in *Tendencies* (Durham: Duke University Press, 1993), 7–8.

3. The preceding sentences draw on Sedgwick, "Queer and Now," 8.

4. The preceding sentences draw on the foreword in Sedgwick, *Tendencies*, xii, which is the source as well for some of the phrasing in the lines below.

Thinking through Queer Theory

To begin with, I would like to thank all my hosts at Ochanomizu University for their very kind invitation to speak to you today. I am most grateful for the opportunity to do so, as well as for all the generous hospitality I have encountered here.

But besides being exciting, it is also sobering to speak about important cultural issues while visiting a country with whose history and institutions I am so sadly unfamiliar. Please believe that the insistently American emphasis of these comments does not represent any lack of interest in the very different Japanese experience. Instead, I hope you will hear my lecture as a very heartfelt invitation to join in a comparative conversation that will enable us to share more fully.

It seems like a great privilege now to be able to look back at twenty years of close involvement with feminist and queer thought, writing, teaching, and activism in the United States. In retrospect, I can see that there are two basic principles that have animated all my work in these areas. These are not so much ethical principles as, I suppose, something like character traits, a mental idiom, or a consistent intellectual aesthetic.

The first of these is a very thoroughgoing conceptual habit of nondualism. As soon as anybody posits "concept X as opposed to concept Y," I'm always the person who reflexively responds, "But maybe X and Y aren't so distinct from each other after all." Because of this nondualism, the methodological tools of deconstruction have always been congenial to me. I'm also extremely interested in Buddhist thought for the same reason.

The second mental habit is closely related to nondualism, but transferred into a more political sphere: that is, I have very little patience with separatism of any kind. This is true both for groups within which I could be included, such as separatist feminism or Jewish nationalism, and also those from which I would be excluded by definition, such as black nationalism. The impulse toward forming homogeneous groups of any kind feels politically retrograde to me and, even more, intellectually stultifying.

Of course, the only predictable thing about the landscapes of critical thought is how they change—constantly and almost kaleidoscopically. With each new twist of the kaleidoscope, a particular theoretical orientation will reveal both useful new relevances and, unfortunately, often new ways of being beside the point. It is because of these frequent changes of gestalt that the ongoing outlines of a given person's theoretical work often become visible only in retrospect.

My interest in feminist theory began in 1970, as an undergraduate student in the very first women's studies course offered at Cornell University. Interestingly, this very challenging course was offered by the College of Home Economics, rather than the College of Liberal Arts! At Yale University, where I did my doctoral work in the English department, there was no encouragement to pursue feminist work, to put it mildly. But in 1978, my first full-time teaching position plunged me and my new colleagues into an unusually turbulent and productive political situation. I went to teach at Hamilton College, a small, isolated, men's liberal-arts college that had just taken over a nearby all-female college. Thus, a very conservative male establishment was suddenly confronted with the entire range of gender issues that had been suppressed for the preceding century or more. All at once there were not only women students to be taught, but a critical mass of women faculty to be acculturated, and enormous changes to be made both in student life and in the college's curriculum. Furthermore, the male faculty and administrators had had no suspicion whatsoever that any of these adjustments would be necessary.

The result was that the small group of women faculty embarked together on an exhausting, but also immensely exhilarating, project of intensive education in feminist thought. We had to educate ourselves, our students, our colleagues, and our institution, all at the same time. One factor that made things easier was that many of us had been hired on a long-term (four years) but terminal basis—so there was nothing to deter us from taking professional risks in our adversarial relation to this college.

In the period around 1980 in the United States, feminist theory was at a particularly exciting, almost reckless, juncture. After a certain amount of additive scholarship in various disciplines, in which the writings or other achievements of a few women were simply added to the existing male canons, this was a time, instead, of very basic feminist challenges to the conceptual roots of the disciplines themselves. It was at this time that the claims of gender-free objectivity in the sciences, of phallic privilege in psychology, of the exclusive importance of statesmen and warriors in history, of purely stylistic value judgments in literature were all subjected to feminist attack at a radical level. A few big concepts, such as patriarchy, seemed to offer a lot of new critical leverage across disciplinary boundaries. As was the case with my colleagues at Hamilton College, the scholars pursuing this new knowledge were virtually all women, and our scholarship dealt almost exclusively with women's experience and women's oppression at the hands of men. In this heady context, I found myself developing the discussion of homosocial desire that underlies my 1985 book, *Between Men*.

The germ from which this work developed was a rather everyday psychological observation: I had noticed from personal experience and from my reading of British and American literature that whenever two men were in love with the same woman, the two men seemed to care much more about each other, as rivals, than they actually cared about the woman upon whom their desire was supposedly fixed. The more I thought about this observation in the context of emerging feminist theory, the more potentially significant it seemed — and the more disruptive, as well.

In the first place, it was disruptive to the implicit gender separatism that had been underlying most feminist theory to this point. Although it emerged from a context in which a group of women scholars were struggling to survive in a male-dominated academic situation, the book's paradigm of male homosocial desire suggested that in order to understand the fates of women, it was equally necessary to understand not only the relations between men and women but also, in fact, the structuration of men's relationships with other men. In this respect, my work, along with other work such as Gayle Rubin's analysis of the "traffic in women" paradigm in anthropology and psychoanalysis, prefigured the larger-scale transition in American scholarship from women's studies to gender studies. Its implication was that gender needed to be studied as a complex representational system, a dynamic one with many levels of feedback and interaction, rather than just as the sum of its additive, apparently incompatible components (male and female).

"Male homosocial desire": the phrase in the subtitle of *Between Men* was intended to mark both discriminations and paradoxes.[1] "Homosocial desire," to begin with, is a kind of oxymoron or contradiction in terms. "Homosocial" was at that time a word that had been occasionally used in history and the social sciences, where it described social bonds between persons of the same sex; it was a recently made up word, obviously formed by analogy with "homosexual," and just as obviously meant to be distinguished from "homosexual." In fact, it was applied to such activities as male bonding, which may, as it often is in American society, be characterized by intense homophobia, which is the fear and hatred of homosexuality. To draw the homosocial back into the orbit of desire, of the potentially erotic, then, was to articulate a new hypothesis. I was suggesting the potential unbrokenness of a continuum between homosocial and homosexual — a continuum whose visibility for men, in American society, is radically disrupted. "Male homosocial desire" was the name I gave to the entire continuum.

I chose the word "desire" rather than "love" to mark the erotic emphasis because, in literary-critical and related discourse, "love" is more easily used to name a particular emotion, and "desire" to name a systemic structure; in this study, a series of arguments about the structural permutations of social impulses fueled the critical dialectic. For the most part, I was using "desire" in a way analogous to the psychoanalytic use of "libido" — not for a particular affective state or emotion, but for the affective or social force, the glue, even when its manifestation is hostility or hatred or something less emotively charged, that shapes an important relationship. How far this force is properly sexual (what, historically, it means for something to be sexual) was an active question.

My formulation was specifically about *male* homosocial desire for a particular reason. It was one of the main projects of this study to explore the ways in which the shapes of sexuality, and even what *counts* as sexuality, both depend on and affect historical power relationships. A corollary is that in a society where men and women differ in their access to power, there will be important gender differences, as well, in the structure and constitution of sexuality.

For instance, the significant opposition between the homosocial and the homosexual seems to be much less thorough and dichotomous for women, at any rate in American society, than for men. At this particular historical moment, an intelligible continuum of aims, emotions, and valuations linked lesbianism with the other forms of women's attention to women: the bond of mother and daughter, for instance, the bond of sister and sister, women's friendship, networking, and the active struggles of feminism. The continuum is crisscrossed with deep discontinuities — with much homophobia, with conflicts of race and class — but at the same time, for many women it seems a matter of simple common sense. However bitter the politics, however conflicted the feelings, it seems to make an obvious kind of sense to say that women in American society who love women and women who teach, study, nurture, suckle, write about, march for, vote for, give jobs to, or otherwise promote the interests of other women are pursuing congruent and closely related activities. Thus the adjective "homosocial" as applied to women's bonds need not be pointedly dichotomized as against homosexual; it can intelligibly denominate the entire continuum.

The apparent simplicity — the unity — of the continuum between "women loving women" and "women promoting the interests of women," extending over the erotic, social, familial, economic, and political realms, would not be so striking if it were not in strong contrast to the arrangement among males. When conservative male politicians get down to serious negotiations on "family values," they are men promoting men's interests. (In fact, they embody Heidi Hartmann's definition of patriarchy: "relations between men, which have a material base, and which, though hierarchical, establish or create interdependence and solidarity among men that enable them to dominate women."[2]) Is their bond in any way congruent with the bond of a loving gay male couple? The conservative politicians would say no — disgustedly. Most gay couples would say no — disgustedly. But why not? Doesn't the continuum between "men loving men" and "men promoting the interests of men" have the same intuitive force that it has for women?

Quite the contrary: much of the most useful 1970s writing about patriarchal structures suggests that "compulsory heterosexuality" is built into male-dominated kinship systems, or that homophobia is a necessary consequence of such patriarchal institutions as heterosexual marriage.[3] Clearly, however convenient it might be to group together all the bonds that link males to males, and by which males enhance the status of males — usefully symmetrical as it would be — that grouping meets with a prohibitive structural obstacle. From the vantage point of American society, at any rate, it has apparently been impossible to imagine a form of patriarchy that was not homophobic. Gayle Rubin writes, for instance: "The suppression of the homosexual component of human sexuality, and by corollary, the oppression of homosexuals, is . . . a product of the same system whose rules and relations oppress women."[4]

The historical manifestations of this patriarchal oppression of homosexuals have been savage and nearly endless. Louis Crompton makes a detailed case for describing the history as genocidal.[5] American society is brutally homophobic; and the homophobia directed against both males and females is not arbitrary or gratuitous, but tightly knit into the texture of family, gender, age, class, and race relations. US society, I argued in 1985, could not cease to be homophobic and have its economic and political structures remain unchanged.

Nevertheless, it wasn't clear that, because most patriarchies structurally include homophobia, therefore patriarchy structurally *requires* homophobia. In fact the example of the ancient Greeks demonstrates, I think, that while heterosexuality is necessary for the maintenance of any patriarchy, homophobia, against males at any rate, is not. In fact, for the Greeks, the continuum between "men loving men" and "men promoting the interests of men" appears to have been quite seamless.

It is clear, then, that there is an asymmetry in American society between, on the one hand, the relatively continuous relation of female homosocial and homosexual bonds, and, on the other hand, the radically discontinuous relation of male homosocial and homosexual bonds. A more recent example of that in the United States is the way the Boy Scouts—the consummate male homosocial organization—have gone all the way to the Supreme Court to argue that it's essential to their mission to exclude gay male scouts and scoutmasters, while the Girl Scouts have never had a policy of excluding lesbians. But the example of the Greeks shows, in addition, that the structure of homosocial continuums is culturally contingent, not an innate feature of either maleness or femaleness. Indeed, closely tied though it obviously is to questions of male versus female power, the explanation would require a more exact mode of historical categorization than "patriarchy," as well, since patriarchal power structures (in Hartmann's sense) characterized both Athenian and American societies. In fact, *Between Men* was one of a group of theoretical projects in the 1980s that very much put in question the usefulness of the overarching concept of patriarchy. Nevertheless, it was able to offer the following as an explicit axiom: that the historically differential shapes of male and female homosociality—much as they themselves may vary over time—will always be articulations and mechanisms of the enduring inequality of power between women and men.

Besides emerging from the scholarship on feminist theory, *Between Men* was also an attempt to think through the potential relations between feminism and the relatively new gay liberation movement. As a woman and a feminist writing (in part) about male homosexuality, I felt I needed to be especially explicit about the political groundings, assumptions, and ambitions of *Between Men* in that regard. My intention throughout was to conduct an antihomophobic as well as feminist inquiry. However, most of the (little) published analysis up to that point of the relation between women and male homosexuality had been at a lower level of sophistication and care than either feminist or gay male analysis separately. In the absence of workable formulations about the male homosocial spectrum, this literature had, with only a few recent exceptions, subscribed to one of two, mutually exclusive, assumptions. The first assumption was that gay men and all women share a "natural," transhistorical alliance and an essential identity of interests — for example, in breaking down gender stereotypes. The second assumption, to the contrary, was that male homosexuality is an epitome, a personification, an effect, or perhaps a primary cause of woman hating.

I did not and do not believe either of these assumptions to be true. Especially because *Between Men* discussed a continuum, a potential structural congruence, and a (shifting) relation of meaning between male homosexual relationships and the male patriarchal relations by which women are oppressed, it seemed very important to emphasize that I was not assuming or arguing either that patriarchal power is primarily or necessarily homosexual (as distinct from homosocial), or that male homosexual desire has a primary or necessary relationship to misogyny. Either of those arguments would be homophobic and, I believe, inaccurate. I was, however, arguing that homophobia directed by men against men is misogynistic, and perhaps transhistorically so. (By "misogynistic" I mean not only that it is oppressive of the so-called feminine in men, but that it is oppressive of women.) The greatest potential for misinterpretation lay in this part of the argument. Because homosexuality and homophobia are always historical constructions, because they are likely to concern themselves intensely with each other and to assume interlocking or mirroring shapes, because the theater of their struggle is likely to occur within individual minds or institutions as well as in public, it is not always easy (sometimes barely possible) to distinguish them from each other. Thus, for instance, Freud's study of Dr. Schreber shows clearly that the repression of homosexual desire in a man who by any commonsense standard was heterosexual occasioned paranoid psychosis; the psychoanalytic use that has been made of this perception, however, has been not against homophobia and its crazy-making force, but against homosexuality itself — *against homosexuals* — on account of an association between homosexuality and mental illness. Similar confusions have marked discussions of the relation between homosexuality and fascism. As the historically constructed nature of homosexuality as an institution becomes more fully understood, it should become possible to understand these distinctions in a more exact and less prejudicious theoretical context.

Thus, I was arguing, profound and intuitable as the bonds between feminism and antihomophobia often are in our society, the two forces are not the same. As the alliance between them is not automatic or transhistorical, it would be most fruitful if it were analytic and unpresuming. To shed light on the grounds, implications, and possibilities of that alliance was one of the main aims of *Between Men*.

The result of *Between Men* that made me happiest was that it did, indeed, seem to make available some terms in which male gay and antihomophobic activists could articulate their political identifications with feminist thought. These antiseparatist, nondualist formulations were among the theoretical advances that made possible the development of a strong, exciting, theoretically sophisticated gay and lesbian studies movement in universities around the United States.

The ambition of my next project, which culminated in the book *Epistemology of the Closet*, was to focus much more closely on the specific, systemic issues of knowledge and power surrounding male homo-heterosexual definition as it emerged in Western culture around the turn of the twentieth century. In this project I was building on my earlier antiseparatist argument. Just as it did not make sense to think of women and men as self-evidently distinct groups whose histories could be extricated from one another, similarly there is not an obvious, crisp, transhistorical boundary that separates homosexuals from heterosexuals. As a result, the history of homo-heterosexual definitions and prohibitions is an important element in *any* study of history or culture. In fact, one of the key questions raised by this work is how it has come about that *the* meaning of "sexual orientation," at least in the West in the twentieth century, has come to be homosexual versus heterosexual. Consider, after all, the many, very important dimensions, other than homo-hetero, along which sexuality varies from one person to another:

— For some people, the nimbus of "the sexual" seems scarcely to extend beyond the boundaries of discrete genital acts; to others, it enfolds them loosely or floats virtually free of them.
— Sexuality makes up a large share of the self-perceived identity of some people, a small share of others'.

—Some people spend a lot of time thinking about sex, others little.

—Some people like to have a lot of sex, others little or none.

—Many people have their richest mental or emotional involvement with sexual acts that they don't do, or even don't *want* to do.

—For some people, it is important that sex be embedded in contexts that are full of meaning, narrative, and connectedness with other aspects of their life; for other people, it is important that they not be; there are others to whom it doesn't occur that they might be.

—For some people, the preference for a certain sexual object, act, role, zone, or scenario is so long-standing and durable that it can only be experienced as innate; for others, it appears to come late or to feel aleatory or discretionary.

—For some people, the possibility of bad sex is unpleasant enough that their lives are strongly marked by its avoidance; for others, it isn't.

—For some people, sexuality provides a needed space of heightened discovery and cognitive hyperstimulation. For others, sexuality provides a needed space of routine, habituation, and cognitive hiatus.

—Some people like spontaneous sexual scenes, others like highly scripted ones, others like spontaneous-sounding ones that are nonetheless totally predictable.

—Some people's sexual orientation is intensely marked by autoerotic pleasures and histories — sometimes more so than by any aspect of alloerotic object choice. For others the autoerotic possibility seems secondary or fragile, if it exists at all.

—Some people, homo-, hetero-, and bisexual, experience their sexuality as deeply embedded in a matrix of gender meanings and gender differentials. Others of each sexuality do not.[6]

All of these dimensions of difference, and many others, were suppressed when "sexuality" became synonymous with "gender of object choice."

It was in the early 1990s, around the time that *Epistemology of the Closet* was published, that some elements of the gay and lesbian movement in the United States began to use the term "queer" in place of "gay" or "lesbian." I had not actually used the term "queer" in my book. But many of the nondualist theoretical tendencies of my work were very allied to those of the queer movement, so the book became closely identified with the emergence of queer theory.

In many ways, "queer" and "gay/lesbian" are overlapping terms; but some of their implications are very different. A lot of gay and lesbian politics, for example, accepts the concept of sexual orientation without questioning it in any way. Yet, exerting any pressure at all on sexual orientation, you see that its elements are potentially quite heterogeneous. Its elements include:

—your biological (for example, chromosomal) sex, male or female;
—your self-perceived gender assignment, male or female (which is supposed to be the same as your biological sex);
—the preponderance of your traits of personality and appearance, masculine or feminine (supposed to correspond to your sex and gender);
—the biological sex of your preferred partner;
—the gender assignment of your preferred partner (supposed to be the same as her/his biological sex);
—the masculinity or femininity of your preferred partner (supposed to be the opposite of your own);
—your self-perception as gay or straight (supposed to correspond to whether your preferred partner is your sex or the opposite);
—your preferred partner's self-perception as gay or straight (supposed to be the same as yours);
—your procreative choice (supposed to be yes if straight, no if gay);
—your preferred sexual act(s) (supposed to be insertive if you are male or masculine, receptive if you are female or feminine);
—your most eroticized sexual organs (supposed to correspond to the procreative capacities of your biological sex, and also to your insertive/receptive assignment);
—your sexual fantasies (supposed to be highly congruent with your sexual practice, but stronger in intensity);
—your main locus of emotional bonds (supposed to reside in your preferred sexual partner);
—your enjoyment of power in sexual relationships (supposed to be low if you are female or feminine, high if you are male or masculine);
—the people from whom you learn about your own gender and sex (supposed to correspond to yourself in all respects);
—your community of cultural and political identification (supposed to correspond to your own identity);
and . . . many, many more.[7]

Ordinary gay/lesbian politics take it for granted that these dimensions will all line up neatly with each other, forming a homogeneous and univocal whole.

And if not?

That's one of the things that "queer" can refer to: the open mesh of possibilities, gaps, overlaps, dissonances and resonances, lapses, and excesses of meaning when the constituent elements of anyone's gender, or anyone's sexuality aren't made (or can't be made) to signify monolithically. The experimental linguistic, epistemological, representational, political adventures attaching to the very many of us who may at times be moved to describe ourselves as (among many other possibilities) pushy femmes, radical faeries, fantasists, fag hags or hag fags, drag queens or kings, clones, leatherpeople, ladies in tuxedos, feminist women or feminist men, masturbators, bulldykes, divas, opera queens, butch bottoms, storytellers, transsexuals, aunties, wannabes, lesbian-identified men or lesbians who sleep with men, or . . . people able to relish, learn from, or identify with such folks.[8]

Again, "queer" can mean something different: a lot of the way people use it is to denote, *almost* simply, same-sex sexuality, lesbian or gay, whether or not it is organized around multiple crossings of definitional lines. And given the historical and contemporary force of the prohibitions against *every* same-sex sexual expression, for anyone to disavow those meanings, or to displace them from the definitional center of the term, would be to evaporate any possibility of queerness itself.

At the same time, a lot of the most important recent work around "queer" expands the term along dimensions that cannot be reduced to gender and sexuality at all: the ways that race, ethnicity, and postcolonial nationality crisscross with these and other identity-constituting, identity-fracturing discourses, for example. Intellectuals and artists of many races whose sexual self-definition includes "queer" are using the leverage of this term to do a new kind of justice to the intersecting intricacies of language, skin color, migration, state, and culture.

"Queer," to me, refers to a politics that values the ways in which meanings and institutions can be at loose ends with each other, crossing all kinds of boundaries rather than reinforcing them. What if the most productive junctures weren't the ones where *everything means the same thing*? Conventional gay/lesbian politics, for example, invests a great deal of energy in trying to create legal protections for the concept of gay families, through such issues as gay marriage, artificial insemination, and gay adoption. But a queer analysis sees the family itself as an institution that is, at best, an unstable and probably unwholesome conjunction of the following, extremely varied functions:

—a surname
—a sexual dyad
—a legal unit based on state-regulated marriage
—a circuit of blood relationships

—a system of companionship and succor
—a building [the "home"]
—a proscenium between "private" and "public"
—an economic unit of earning and taxation
—the prime site of economic consumption
—the prime site of cultural consumption
—a mechanism to produce, care for, and acculturate children
—a mechanism for accumulating material goods over several generations
—a daily routine
—a unit in a community of worship
—a site of patriotic formation[9]

–and so forth. Looking at my own life, I see that—probably like most people—I have valued and pursued these various elements of family identity to quite different degrees (e.g., no use for reproduction, much need of companionship). But what's been consistent in this particular life, and in many queer lives, is an interest in not letting very many of these dimensions line up directly with each other at one time. I see it has been a dominant intuition for me that the most productive strategy (intellectually, emotionally) might be, whenever possible, to *dis*articulate them from one another, to *dis*engage them—the bonds of blood, of law, of habitation, of privacy, of companionship and support—from the enforcement of their unanimity in the system called "family."

Looking at the current scene of sexuality politics in the United States, it appears that the insights of queer theory have become much less influential than they were in the 1990s, while the normalizing politics of the mainstream gay/lesbian movement have come to dominate the scene. The most visible political goals are demands to be allowed to conform: alongside the legitimization of same-sex marriage and families, they involve the inclusion of gay and lesbian people in the military, the Boy Scouts, electoral politics, and mainstream religions.

It seems true to say that queer politics are both antiseparatist and anti-assimilationist: antiseparatist in the sense that we don't take it for granted that the world is neatly and naturally divided between homosexuals and heterosexuals, and anti-assimilationist in the sense that we are not eager to share in the privileges and presumptions of normality. Mainstream gay/lesbian politics, on the other hand, is paradoxically both separatist and assimilationist. It is separatist in its sense of identity, but at the same time all its goals involve the uncritical assimilation of gay people into the institutions of a very conservative culture.

It has become something of a truism, at the same time, that queer theory is mainly confined to academia, as a speculative, impractical, utopian way of thinking, while the nontheoretical mainstream movement is thought to represent the only way to get real things done in terms of actual politics. This may actually make some sense, but only if politics is defined exclusively in terms of elections and legislation, or in terms of institutional assimilation. Certainly, the conservative mainstream of the gay/lesbian movement is achieving some successes, and I do not want to diminish the importance of any success in an antihomophobic undertaking. Such successes are all too rare.

Yet, when the concept of politics in the United States gets narrowed down to electoral politics, there is also a huge price to pay. The most grievous price is that after two decades of activism, mainstream gay politics has now gone into complete denial about the AIDS crisis. Believe it or not, AIDS has disappeared as a public issue, and also as a gay issue, throughout the United States. Except for a few queer activists, the entire society seems to believe that AIDS is now being cured—which it is not—and that the number of people with AIDS has gone down—which it has not. Americans, including a great many gay men, are still dying of AIDS at obscenely young ages; but now they are doing it in the midst of an uncanny public silence. The media, both gay and straight, either ignore AIDS or treat it as something that now happens only in Africa, or to a worthless, nonwhite urban underclass of drug abusers. When there is discourse about AIDS in the American gay community, it involves heaping blame on any gay youths who are still getting infected with HIV.

It seems clear to me that the failure to remain engaged with AIDS issues is closely tied to the repudiation of queer thought by the conservative gay/lesbian movement in America. After all, it is only a queer analysis, not a strictly gay one, that can give us any help with this disease that respects no simple boundaries of identity. At this point in the American epidemic, the crucial issues go far beyond homophobia; they require an understanding of how homophobia and gay identities intersect historically with issues of race and poverty, with complex and phobic ideologies concerning drugs, with epidemiological models, with profound cultural meanings associated with sexuality, risk, and death, with the burgeoning prison system, with the global economics of medical development and marketing, and with the rapidly changing force fields of America's profit-driven medical delivery system.

The reason I choose to end with this particular emphasis today is, of course, the relatively new and already gravely frightening stage of the AIDS epidemic as it now begins to impinge visibly on many Asian countries. It seems so urgent at this moment to make available any conceptual tools that can help make sense of this disease and the social and psychological matrices in which it is embedded. The continuing worldwide epidemic also, of course, mercilessly exposes every weakness in the limited and US-centered theories that we Americans can bring to bear on it. My deepest wish is that Japanese and other Asian thinkers will be able to generate fuller and more efficacious wisdom that they will be willing to share with those of us in the West.

NOTES

EKS was invited to Ochanomizu University, in Toyko, by Professor Kazuko Takemura, where she delivered this lecture on October 7, 2000. A transcription of the talk appeared in Ochanomizu University's *Journal of Gender Studies* 4 (2001): 1–11. In this version, I have restored some of the original text at several points where EKS draws on her previous publications, and have provided endnotes lacking in the previously published version.

1. See Eve Kosofsky Sedgwick, *Between Men: English Literature and Male Homosocial Desire* (New York: Columbia University Press, 1985). The paragraphs that follow draw upon the introduction, 1–5 and 19–20.

2. Heidi Hartmann, "The Unhappy Marriage of Marxism and Feminism: Towards a More Progressive Union," in *Women and Revolution: A Discussion of the Unhappy Marriage of Marxism and Feminism*, ed. Lydia Sargent (Boston: South End, 1981), 14.

3. See Adrienne Rich, "Compulsory Heterosexuality and Lesbian Existence," in *Women: Sex and Sexuality*, ed. Catharine R. Stimpson and Ethel Spector Person (Chicago: University of Chicago Press, 1980), 62–91.

4. Gayle Rubin, "The Traffic in Women: Notes Toward a Political Economy of Sex," in *Toward an Anthropology of Women*, ed. Rayna Rapp (New York: Monthly Review Press, 1975), 180.

5. See Louis Crompton, "Gay Genocide: From Leviticus to Hitler," in *The Gay Academic*, ed. Louie Crew (Palm Springs, Calif.: ETC, 1978), 67–91.

6. See Eve Kosofsky Sedgwick, *Epistemology of the Closet* (Berkeley: University of California Press, 1990). Drawing on pp. 25–26 here.

7. See Eve Kosofsky Sedgwick, "Queer and Now," in *Tendencies* (Durham: Duke University Press, 1993). Drawing on p. 7 here.

8. This paragraph draws on Sedgwick, "Queer and Now," 8. The paragraphs that follow draw on p. 9.

9. Sedgwick, "Queer and Now," 6. The paragraph that follows continues to draw on this page.

Reality and Realization

Somewhere in the background of this talk is a project I've had in mind for a year or two now — a still-unrealized project for a conference or an essay anthology whose title would be something like "Critical Theory, Buddhist Practice." I thought of the project as a way of marking and trying to understand the successive discovery that one after another of the critics I'm really interested in these days turn out also, on acquaintance, to be at some stage, whether early or advanced, in an exploration of some form of Buddhist practice or thought. I'm not just talking about Californians here, either — these recognitions have been taking place in the Bible-thumpin' south, the windy heartlands, the Manhattan cosmopole, and the Puritan fastness of New England, as well.

I've no doubt there's a *lot* to be said and thought about such encounters, both as they reflect a zeitgeist or two (or twenty) and as they intertwine with the intellectual, emotional, and spiritual destinies of a lot of really interesting individuals. Among the stories that await more telling, some of the historical ones involve American Orientalism of the nineteenth and twentieth centuries, the afterglow of a 1960s counterculture and the deep political discouragement of its cooptation, the longer reverberations of a Beat fascination with Japanese Zen, the fatuities and promiscuities of New Age marketing, the diasporic imperative impelled by the post-1959 shattering of traditional Tibetan culture, and the funny mix of humility with nativist triumphalism in the rapid emergence of something that nowadays gets called "American Buddhism," though it has barely a nominal relation to anything practiced in the Chinatowns and other Asian immigrant communities scattered broadcast over the map of the United States.[1]

Another set of stories might involve both the aptitudes and the impasses of the critical theory that has shaped these two generations of US academic critics. Aspects of Buddhist thought that initially seem counterintuitive to many people — its rigorous nondualism, for an obvious example — can seem already self-evident and invitingly *haimish* to anyone whose mother's milk has been deconstruction or, say, systems theory. Furthermore, I think many intellectuals experience a tremendous, grateful relief at encountering a deep, ramified, already long-existent history of treating these shared nondualistic understandings as more or other than a series of propositions and readings. It's probably misleading to think of Buddhism as a religion; yet, as with a religion, the distinctive bonds between Buddhism and the question of reality seem to cluster tellingly around the issue of practice rather than of epistemology.

I'll be able to point to only one of these distinctive bonds here: namely, the troubled mismatch between knowledge and realization. Let me illustrate what I'm talking about with a slight but true story. Last fall, when I was getting ready for my first trip to Asia, I was especially drawn to the sections in each guidebook that make a stab at filling visitors in on local and regional norms of behavior: don't blow your nose in public, don't wear shoes indoors, bring your own tissue paper into the toilet, don't hold hands in public *except* with someone of your own sex, walk clockwise around temples and stupas. One instruction that turns up in one guidebook after another is that gifts are supposed to be both proffered and received using both hands. This seemed important to remember, not only because it is true in all three of the countries I was visiting on that trip, but also because, as every source agreed, the giving and receiving of small gifts was going to be the warp and weft of any social interaction; so I stocked up on theory paperbacks, tins of maple syrup, and baby presents for my new nephew in Seoul, and reminded myself repeatedly that when I handed them over or received gifts in return, I should definitely remember to use both hands.

As it turned out, that trip was wonderful, and soon I was reading guidebooks for a second trip to two other Asian countries. And sure enough, it turned out that in Nepal and Thailand you're also supposed to use both hands for giving and receiving presents. Not a surprise — I already knew this rule well. What did surprise me was to look back suddenly and realize, for the first time, that in all the giving and receiving of gifts during the previous trip, I had in fact *not once* made the necessary mental connection that would have prompted me to perform those acts using both hands. Not once; and yet in some other register I certainly did and still do know the rule perfectly well, and I had firmly in mind the intent of following it.

It was just that . . .

It was just that what? I don't know how to explain it. It's just that I'm hardly ever all that self-possessed. But what does that mean? Or maybe it's that handing some particular package to Songmin or Fifi or Jo, in some particular apartment, street, or classroom, isn't easily recognized as "giving a gift" to "someone" in "Asia."

Or maybe it's a memory problem. As I get older, I do feel as if my mental filing was all done by some temp who made up a brilliant new system and then quit in a huff before explaining it to anyone else.

I want to say that I knew this rule, but still hadn't realized it—that it hadn't succeeded in becoming real to me, real in the same register as Fifi, or as my brother's living room. There's nothing necessarily transcendental about this sense of "realization"; all it would have required was someone to perform the humble, maternal office of saying, "Remember? We talked about this at home. Now, when you hand over this present, what do you do?"

Anyway, that's the sense in which I want to discuss reality today: reality not as *what's true*, but as *what's realized*, what is or has become real. Where is the gap between knowing something—even knowing it to be true—and realizing it, taking it as real?

Reality in this sense, as it happens, may be entirely orthogonal to the question of truth. The order of truth, after all, is propositional. The order of reality, on the other hand, while it might include people uttering or thinking propositions, isn't itself propositional. For example, there are many true propositions that would describe the room in which we're meeting this afternoon. Not even an infinite number of such true propositions, however, would exhaust or saturate this space in the order of reality.

Other characteristics that distinguish the order of reality from that of truth: the order of reality is spatial as much as temporal. (Maybe that's what makes real estate, *real* estate.) Reality, unlike truth, tends toward analog as much as or more than digital representation. And correspondingly, unlike truth, reality tends toward the nondual.

I wonder whether it's because of this tropism toward nonduality that the psychology of realization is so much a specialty of Buddhist thought. Whatever the reason, it does seem remarkable both how much attention Buddhism pays to the gap between knowing and realizing, and retroactively, how little attention is paid to it in Western thought.

To practice Buddhism, after all, is to spend all the time you can in the attempt to realize a set of understandings most of whose propositional contents are familiar to you from the beginning of your practice. The very existence, the multiplicity, the intensiveness of different Buddhist traditions testify to the centrality of the project of realization; to the sense of how normal it is for realization to lag behind knowledge by months or eons; and to a concern that any pedagogy of realization is likely to be a hit-or-miss matter haplessly dependent on the contingencies of the individual.

The only widespread Western practices I can think of that are even analogous to this occur in evangelical Christianity—the sometimes protracted struggle to be or to understand oneself as saved—or in psychoanalysis. These Western instances are analogous in that both of them frame realization—unlike knowledge—in terms of practices, practices that take place over time. But it's also true that to get born again is very marked, within Christianity, as depending on an act of unearned, entirely spontaneous divine grace, in the context of a radical hypostatization of agency between active and passive (the self being passive). Far indeed from the nondualistic Buddhist realization of the nature of mind: in the words of Dudjom Rinpoche,

> Samsara does not make it worse
> Nirvana does not make it better . . .
> It has never been liberated
> It has never been deluded
> It has never existed
> It has never been nonexistent.[2]

In the practice of psychoanalysis, on the other hand, while it's possible for agency, among other dualisms, to get dehypostasized in a manner that's remarkably congruent with Buddhist as with deconstructive understanding, there is still, very often, at least the pretext that progress within analysis equals the achievement of new levels of propositional knowledge, for instance about one's personal history. And meanwhile, the popularity of psychoanalysis within critical theory as a system or a language always tends toward short-circuiting its realization as practice; so its insights get added in turn to the list of *things to know* rather than becoming manifest as a *way of knowing*, never mind of doing or of being. And yet for many intellectuals, the most efficacious surprise for us in our real encounters with psychotherapy is how little our quickness of apprehension may have to do with the far statelier pace of realization and change. A humbling thing to catch on to, but only so long as one maintains the intellectual's hair-trigger, disavowing contempt for the process of realization in all its real, obscure temporality. Perhaps the most change can happen when that contempt changes to respect, a respect for the very ordinariness of the opacities between knowing and realizing.

As I noted before, anybody's engagement with Buddhism, in a culture to which it's so far from native, marks a distinct moment within many diverse histories. For me it was closely linked to that most ordinary and yet oddly privileged of encounters, the tête-à-tête with mortality: in my case, learning that a cancer I had thought was in remission had in fact become incurable. Such encounter *does* involve a privilege, though not an absolute one, with respect to reality. As advertised, it does concentrate the mind wonderfully, and makes inescapably vivid in repeated mental shuttle passes the considerable distance between *knowing* that one will die and *realizing* it. If anything, with all the very exigent lifelong uses that each of us has for the idea of dying—whether shaped by depression, hysteria, hypochondria, existential heroics—coupled with the seemingly absolute inaccessibility of our own death to our living consciousness, death offers in both Western and Buddhist thought the most heightened example of reality, where reality is taken to indicate precisely a gap between knowing something on the one hand, and on the other understanding it as real.

At any rate, this was the context in which a couple of friends passed along to me a recently published semi-bestseller by Sogyal Rinpoche, called *The Tibetan Book of Living and Dying*. Sogyal Rinpoche's book is a highly popularized, at the same time impressively inclusive, introduction to Tibetan Buddhism, and it spoke to me at that moment because it's so powerfully organized around exactly the issue of making real the encounter with death. What I found out from it is that the wisdom traditions of Tibetan culture have, if anything, a uniquely detailed focus on the experience of death as a privileged instance of reality/realization. *A* privileged instance, but not the only one: dying is one among a group of states—also including meditation, sleep, and dreams—that are called bardos, gaps or periods in which the possibility of realization is particularly available. *Bar* in Tibetan means in between, and *do* means suspended or thrown. As Robert Thurman writes, far from isolating such moments, the scheme of bardos "is used to create in the practitioner a sense that all moments of existence are 'between' moments, unstable, fluid, and transformable into liberated enlightenment experience."[3] Among these various "betweens," however, it is the one just following death, the bardo of Dharmata, that Thurman translates as the bardo of reality.

According to Sogyal Rinpoche, the bardos represent "moments when the mind is far freer than usual, moments . . . which carry a far stronger karmic charge and implication" (106). That implication, however, actually involves the possibility of stepping entirely aside from the inexorability of karmic process (which is to say, from the law of cause and effect) through a very simple achievement of recognition. "The reason why the moment of death is so potent with opportunity is because it is then that the fundamental nature of mind, the Ground Luminosity or Clear Light, will naturally manifest" (106). If at this crucial moment we can recognize the Ground Luminosity—that is, recognize it not only as itself but as ourselves and not other than ourselves—then whatever becomes of our energies after death will be entirely freed from the sordid or desperate traces of other, past *mis*recognitions.

Thus, the guidance offered to the dead in the Bardo Thodol or so-called *Tibetan Book of the Dead*, meant to be read aloud to those undergoing the bardo of reality, has very much the homely, practical structure of that maternal adjuration to "remember, this is what we talked about at home." The main thing needed by the dead, in the Bardo of Reality, is orientation amid the light shows and ostentatious projections of an anxious, dissolving identity. In Thurman's translation, for instance, on the fourth day in this bardo, the person is reminded, "On this fourth day, the red light that is the purity of the element fire dawns. . . . Do not fear it! . . . You want to flee it. . . . But . . . you must fearlessly recognize that brilliant red, piercing, dazzling clear light as [your own] wisdom. Upon it place your mind, relaxing your awareness in the experience of nothing more to do. . . . If you can recognize it as the natural energy of your own awareness without feeling faith, without making prayers, you will dissolve indivisibly with all the images and light rays and you will become a Buddha. If you do not recognize it as the natural energy of your own awareness, then pray and hold [onto] your aspirations for it, thinking, 'It is the light ray of the compassion of the Lord Amitabha! I take refuge in it!'"[4]

In the Bardo Thodol, each day's coaching ends with an encouraging note to the reader-aloud, such as, "When you thus repeatedly orient the deceased, however feeble his affinity, if he does not recognize one wisdom, he will recognize another. It is impossible not to be liberated."

As the next day dawns, though, the text resumes wearily but patiently. "However, even though you orient the deceased repeatedly in this way, still through long association with the myriad instincts, and little previous experience with the purified perception of wisdom, even though he is clearly oriented, he is pulled beyond these recognitions by [the deforming traces of cause-and-effect]."[5] So today's apparition is . . .

Now, one way in which I can imagine somebody listening to these remarks so far is with the suspicious or even alarmed consciousness, "She hasn't even *mentioned* the way all this depends on Buddhists' belief in reincarnation," or in cyclical time, or in some other doctrine that will probably sound alienating to secular critical-theoretical ears. But if I've stayed away from describing Buddhism in terms of a set of beliefs, that is not because I share Stephen Batchelor's wish for what he calls a "Buddhism without beliefs," one that could somehow be hygienically cleansed of the traces of its local and premodern histories.[6] Rather, what I'm wary of is the whole, anthropological rhetoric of ascribing "beliefs" — ascribing them always, it seems, to someone who is not oneself. Somehow beliefs are never what *I* have, only what *they* have. I suppose I've been most alerted to this by the dim, steady, destructive hail of journalistic and even scholarly pronouncements about the patent absurdities that constitute the "beliefs" of postmodernists and so-called deconstructionists. Our beliefs include things like, "Nothing actually exists," "Nothing is true outside the text," and "There is no such thing as reality." Such descriptions sound alarmingly like the mildly scandalous but comically absurd accounts of alien religious cosmologies in the *Weekly Readers* and *National Geographics* of one's childhood. Shoddy or even fraudulent as the propositional content of these anti-postmodernist ascriptions may be, it's that framing of them in terms of beliefs that does the final damage of rendering our mental process unrecognizable even to ourselves.

It's an implication of my remarks, however, that that damage is facilitated by the shrunken impoverishment of any Western psychology of knowledge and realization, whether empiricist *or* postmodern, compared with its density and richness in Buddhist thought. If anything, within the framework of the Buddhist respect for realization as both process and practice, the stuttering, exclusive perseveration of epistemological propositions in contemporary critical theory reads as a stubborn hysterical defense. Whether it comes in the form of anti-essentialist hypervigilance or, say, of the moralizing Marxist insistence that someone else is evading a true recognition of materiality, all this epistemological fixation, with all its paralyzing scruples or noisy, accusatory projections, can also seem like a hallucinatorily elaborated, long-term refusal to enter into realization as into a complex practice. Rather, it can't stop claiming mastery of reality as the flat, propositional object of a single verb, shivering in its threadbare near-transparency: the almost fatally thin "to know."

NOTES

A version of "Reality and Realization" was given at a session titled "Reality" at the MLA's annual convention on December 28, 1998; it was reworked into "Come as You Are," a talk given in conjunction with "Floating Columns/In the Bardo," a show of EKS's art at the State University of New York at Stonybrook on June 28, 1999, which also is drawn on in "Making Things, Practicing Emptiness."

1. [In "Come as You Are," EKS continues: "In fact Rick Fields, the most loving and critical historian of this movement so far, pointedly denominates it 'white Buddhism.'" See, for example, chapter 6, "The White Buddhists," in Rick Fields, *How the Swans Came to the Lake: A Narrative History of Buddhism in America* (Boston: Shambhala, 1981), 83–118, and "Divided Dharma: White Buddhists, Ethnic Buddhists, and Racism," in *The Faces of Buddhism in America*, ed. Charles S. Prebish and Kenneth K. Tanaka (Berkeley: University of California Press, 1998), 196–206.

At the end of "Come as You Are," EKS returns to Fields: "I've mentioned Rick Fields, the influential American historian and practitioner of Buddhism. Last June, Rick Fields died of cancer at the age of fifty-seven. In an obituary in *Tricycle* magazine [9, no.1 (Fall 1999): 22–23], Helen Tworkov, the magazine's editor, wrote,

I saw Rick at his house the Thursday before he died. His skin was sallow and buttery soft, his eyes luminescent. With scratchy, slurred words, he explained that he was feeling woozy. . . . Then came a moment when we were alone. In a clear voice suddenly delivered of static, he spoke of the interview that we had done for *Tricycle* [two years before]. 'Do you remember what you said to me,' recalled Rick, 'you're dying and I'm dying. And you have cancer and I don't. Is there a difference?' Then he continued, trying once more in this lifetime, to help me get it right. 'Well, one way of understanding that difference, is that I'm in the bardo of dying and you're not.'
A few months earlier Rick had written [on] 'The Bardo of Dying' in his journal. . . . The bardo of dying begins when you are diagnosed with incurable illness [and only ends when you enter the bardo of after death]. Rick had come across these same teachings many times, but he wrote that this time, they 'clearly revealed where I am, where I live in the cycle of existence — the

endless wheel of life and death. . . . To realize this replaces ignorance with knowledge, perhaps even wisdom, or its beginning at least. Ah, *this* is where I am.' (23)

"It's interesting that Fields hadn't found much to read about this particular bardo. I suppose it's only recently that the bardo of dying, as opposed to that of after death, has become for many people a sufficiently extensive space to invite a lot of elaboration. Or political éclat—think how much the impact of early AIDS activism came from the stunning novelty of seeing young adults with a fatal disease who were nonetheless physically strong enough, and for a long enough time, to undertake the project of their own, forceful representation. AIDS and cancer are among the grave diseases where, in the absence of cure, modern medicine has offered ever-earlier diagnosis along with, at least for AIDS, delayed mortality. Whether it be through early diagnosis or more effective treatment, at any rate, the bardo of dying has expanded for many of us to a period that can encompass several years or even, sometimes, many. Tworkov remarks that Rick Fields valued 'the companionship of those who inhabit the same bardo,' a companionship that can even generate a new kind of public sphere, as in the case of AIDS and increasingly, I hope, of people with advanced cancer. These may be years of good health or ill health, of pain or its relative absence, of lassitude or energy; more likely all these are mixed together unpredictably, intermittently, though on a worsening trajectory.

"A few months ago, getting a checkup, I mentioned to my oncologist an academic conference on death and dying, and remarked that as far as I could tell from the program, I was the only sick person involved in it. He said, 'You know, it's a nice philosophical question at this point, in exactly what sense you can be said to *be* sick.' He meant his comment to be cheering, and it actually was—I'm feeling very well, and I liked his acknowledging that.

"At the same time, what's harder to explain is the sense of recognition that comes, as Fields put it, with being able to see and say, 'Ah, *this* is where I am'—in this bardo, the one of dying. Fields also noted how others, such as the healthy, who 'live in different bardos, move perhaps at different speeds, perceive, think, feel perhaps at different frequencies.' To say that there seem to be distinctive psychological and spiritual tasks to accomplish in the bardo of dying, for anyone lucky enough to be able to focus and be present to them, is only another way of saying that there are special freedoms to be claimed here: freedoms both of meaning, relation, and memory, yet also from them.

"When Sherwin Nuland, the physician author of *How We Die* (New York: Vintage, 1993), writes about the way metastatic cancer behaves in the human body, he does so in a chapter entitled not 'The Malignancy' but rather 'The *Malevolence* of Cancer' (emphasis added). It's clear that he simply disapproves of such behavior, essentially on civic grounds. Cancer cells, he points out, reproduce promiscuously while they are still immature, becoming drains on society. 'Cancer cells are fixed at an age where they are still too young to have learned the rules of the society in which they live. As with so many immature individuals of all living kinds, everything they do is excessive and uncoordinated with the needs and constraints of their neighbors. . . . Malignant cells concentrate their energies on reproduction rather than on partaking in the missions a tissue must carry out in order for the life of the organism to go on. The bastard offspring of their hyperactive (albeit asexual) "fornicating" are without the resources to do anything but cause trouble and burden the hardworking community around them' (209). The 1980s–1990s image of the demonized welfare mother and her terrorizing brood, as sinister as Milton's Sin and Death, is all but explicit; he [Nuland] even refers to the tumor cells' rapacious behavior as 'wilding' (208). Yet however immature, they deserve to be tried as adults. 'A cluster of malignant cells is a disorganized autonomous mob of maladjusted adolescents. . . . If we cannot help its members grow up, anything we can do to arrest them, remove them from our midst, or induce their demise — anything that accomplishes one of those aims — is praiseworthy' (210).

"Setting aside the phobic and, still more, the unreflectively anthropomorphic nature of this language, it's true that the progress of this disease is extremely unpredictable and antinomian. Each type of metastatic cancer has particular sites that it's most prone to seeking out and devouring, in no particular order — breast cancer, for instance, besides often going to bone, has a tropism toward liver, lungs, eyes, brain — but there is no organ, vital or vestigial, including the little toe and the heart, where it won't take hold if the tide of contingency and sheer unorganization drops it there. The disease's course depends much on the thinnest fabric of whimsy, and not at all on any law — except for the one law, of being fatal.

"It's thus that a certain Buddhist problematic becomes so heartfelt in the face of advanced cancer: the coming to terms, and ideally terms of love if not of dignity, with a process where endless underdetermination continues to arise and arise in the face of one single overdetermination, whose narrative coherence will only be retrospective. 'The point's not what becomes you, but what's you' — if one isn't going to cling desperately to a self, however, another point might be to become *it*; to identify with the fabric and structure of this discohesive fate itself."]

2. Dudjom Rinpoche, quoted in Soygal Rinpoche, *The Tibetan Book of Living and Dying*, ed. Patrick Gaffney and Andrew Harvey (New York: Harper Collins, 1992), 49. All further citations from Soygal Rinpoche are from this source.

3. Robert Thurman, trans., *The Tibetan Book of the Dead* (New York: Bantam, 1994), 34.

4. Ibid., 138–39.

5. Ibid., 141.

6. See Stephen Batchelor, *Buddhism without Beliefs* (New York: Riverhead, 1997).

Index

Abrams, M. H., 40 n. 44

Activist politics, 137, 169, 191; gay lesbian queer, 137–39, 166–69, 171, 183–86, 188–89, 195–203

Affect theory, 12, 57–58, 126, 129, 145, 146, 159–61

Agency, 20, 83, 130, 170, 209

AIDS, 137–39, 202–3, 214 n. 1

A la recherche du temps perdu: Albertine in, 7, 10, 19, 32, 151, 153–55, 162 n. 13; art in, 33; Aunt Leonie in, 24; barometer in, 8–9, 13; Bloch in, 15, 46; Buddhism and, 6, 113; Charlus in, 10, 17, 38 n. 23, 47; demystification in, 4–5, 48; Duchesse de Guermantes in, 17, 36 n. 3, 47; father in, 8; Françoise in, 22–31, 35, 39 n. 41; Gilberte in, 20–21; gods in, 6, 15–18, 20–21, 35, 43–48; grandmother in, 7, 13–14, 26, 27–30; Habit in, 23; homosexuality in, 15, 17, 36 n. 7, 45, 46; Hubert Robert fountain in, 1–2; Marie Gineste and Céleste Albaret in, 35, 40–41 n. 49; Mme d'Arpajon in, 3; mother in, 12, 19, 26, 28, 30–31; mysticism of, 4–5, 32, 35, 40 n. 45, 48, 113; narrator in, 7–10, 12, 14, 20–22, 25, 31–33, 151–55, 159, 161, 162 n. 13; Neoplatonism and, 14–15, 18, 35, 40 n. 45, 48; Oedipal in, 29–31, 48; omnipotence in, 20, 48; reincarnation in, 2–3, 6–7, 16, 26, 33; Sedgwick's textile art and, 84, 113, 120–21 n. 8; sleep and dreams in, 7; Swann in, 10, 17, 47, 48; Theory of Mind and, 151–55; Vinteuil sonata in, 17–18, 47–48; weather in, 7–9, 34–35

Anna Dalassini (Cavafy), 65

Arabian Nights, 18–19, 151

Austin, J. L., 51–53, 58, 63, 65

Autism, 146, 156–59

Balint, Michael, 10–13, 26, 34

Baron-Cohen, Simon, 146

Barthes, Roland, 10

Batchelor, Stephen, 212

Benjamin, Walter, 96

Bersani, Leo, 37 n. 10, 168

Blackburn, Jared, 157, 159

Bloom, Harold, 137

Bohm, David, 100–101

Boletsi, Maria, 52–53

Bollas, Christopher, 40 n. 46

Botticelli, Stephen, 166, 177–81
Breuer, Lee, 21
Brontë, Charlotte, 44
Buddhism, 6, 14, 37 n. 11, 70, 75, 79, 101, 105–6, 113, 129, 134, 141–42, 179, 206–12; bardos in, 210–12, 214 n. 1; bodhisattvas and, 93, 102–5; Buddha images and, 75, 102, 104; prayer flags and, 106; psychoanalysis and, 209. *See also* Guanyin
Butler, Judith, 52, 174

Cameron, Julia Margaret, 96
Camp, 66
Cavafy, C. P., 43, 45, 60; gods in, 43–45, 49–50, 53, 67; homosexuality and poetic vocation in, 45, 50–51; performative and peri-performative utterances and, 45, 51–53, 57–68. *See also individual poem titles*
Chaos/Complexity, 3–4, 84
Closet, 13, 56
Come Back (Cavafy), 51
Comes to Rest (Cavafy), 51
Cornell, Joseph, 66
Craig, Larry, 54–55
Crompton, Louis, 195
Cyanotype, 93

Daimon, 16, 46
Dante, 56
Dark Victory (Goulding), 27–28
Davis, Bette, 27
Deconstruction, 75, 212; Buddhism and, 207, 209
Dennett, Daniel, 161
Derrida, Jacques, 53
Dualism: language and, 79, 105; middle ranges of agency and, 20; politics and, 133; psychoanalysis and, 5. *See also* Non-dualism

Eliot, George, 155–56

Ferenczi, Sándor, 10, 126
Fields, Rick, 213–14 n. 1

Flatley, Jonathan, 68 n. 1
Footsteps, The (Cavafy), 43–44, 49, 66
Foucault, Michel, 133–34, 138, 182 n. 8, 185
Fractals, 90, 93
Frank, Adam, 143 n. 9
Freud, Sigmund, 5, 10, 12, 19, 20, 30, 130–31, 170, 196. *See also* Psychoanalytic concepts
Friedman, Richard, 173
Frith, Uta, 146, 159

Gay Left Collective, 167, 168. *See also* Activist politics
Gender, 105, 168, 171–72, 175–77, 192, 195–96; transgender, 175–76
Genet, Jean, 167, 170
Genius, 15, 36, 46; génie and, 18; genies and, 18–19; *genius loci* and, 16, 46–47; Jinni and, 16
George, Elsa, 158
Gettysburg Address (Lincoln), 54
Girard, René, 10, 36 n. 8
God Abandons Antony, The (Cavafy), 67–68
Godwin, Jocelyn, 38 n. 29
Going Back Home from Greece (Cavafy), 62–63
Greek Anthology, 63–64
Growing in Spirit (Cavafy), 56
Guanyin, 102, 104–5
Guss, Jeffrey, 166, 168–77

Hadot, Pierre, 34, 37 n. 9
Hamilton College, 191
Hardy, Thomas, 6–7
Hartmann, Heidi, 194
Hawarden, Lady Clementina, 96
Heart Sutra, 75, 105, 120 n. 3
He Had Come There to Read (Cavafy), 50
Hertz, Neil, 156
Hinshelwood, R. D., 125, 136
Hoch, Paul, 167–68
Hocquenghem, Guy, 166–67, 169, 175

Holmes, Dave, and Dan Warner, 172–73

Holomovement, 101

Il ritorno d'Ulisse in patria (Monteverdi), 21

Irwin, Robert, 39 n. 34

Isay, Richard, 173

James, William, 40 n. 45

Japanese Death Poems, 111, 113

Johnson, Barbara, 11, 37 n. 22

Kentridge, William, 21

King Lear (Shakespeare), 26

Klein, Melanie, 5, 12, 17, 19, 20, 24–26, 30–31, 47, 83, 124, 126–28, 130–32, 134–37, 181. *See also* Psychoanalytic concepts

Kleitos' Illness (Cavafy), 60–62

Kristeva, Julia, 37 n. 10

Ladenson, Elisabeth, 29

Likierman, Meira, 125–27

Meyerding, Jane, 158

Mieli, Mario, 166, 167

Myris: Alexandria, A. D. 340 (Cavafy), 57

Neoplatonism, 2, 6, 14–15, 26

Newman, Barbara, 38 n. 29

Nietzsche, Friedrich, 34, 134, 137

Non-dualism, 35–36, 96, 125, 190, 207; affect and, 129; agency and, 79, 90; art–craft and, 79; Buddhism and, 75, 106, 207, 208; deconstruction and, 75, 207; folded–unfolded and, 98; implicate–explicate order and, 101; inner–outer and, 13, 32, 45; language and, 79; Neoplatonism and, 2, 5, 14–15; reality and, 208; texture and, 84; touch and, 90

Nuland, Sherwin, 214–15 n. 1

Obama, Barack, 169

Of the Jews (A. D. 50) (Cavafy), 61

Omnipotence, and language, 79

Peat, F. David, 90

Performativity, 52, 105, 133, 169

Periperformative, 53–55, 57–58, 65–66

Photograph, The (Cavafy), 61

Plotinus, 2, 14, 16–17, 36, 37 n. 11, 37 n. 13, 38 n. 27, 46

Prayer (Cavafy), 58–60

Proclus, 38 n. 26

Proust, Marcel, 45, 177; George Eliot and, 155–56. *See also A la recherche du temps perdu*

Psychoanalytic concepts: activist politics and, 166–67; depression/depressive position, 25, 127, 136, 139–42; drive, 11–12, 132, 170; mourning/melancholy, 30–31; object relations, 5, 10–11, 13, 17, 30, 33–34, 47, 126, 136; Oedipal, 3, 5, 10–11, 19, 30–31, 129, 173–74; omnipotence, 19, 24, 83, 130; paranoid/schizoid position, 24, 30, 131–32, 134; projection/introjection, 124, 127, 132, 135; projection/splitting, 24, 26; repression, 30, 131, 167; transference, 10–11, 26

Puppet theater, 21–22, 66

Queer, 188–89, 198–203; art and, 66–67; gay, lesbian, and transgender politics and, 69–70, 139, 175; psychoanalysis and, 5; sexual identity and, 176–77, 188; theory and, 69, 128–29, 134, 137. *See also* Activist politics

Rinpoche, Dudjom, 209

Rinpoche, Sogyal, 210

Roilos, Panagiotos, 68

roman-fleuve, 2, 45

Ronsard, Pierre, 15, 38 n. 29

Rose, Jacqueline, 155

Rubin, Gayle, 192, 194

Sally-Anne test, 149, 156

Sedgwick, Eve Kosofsky: artwork by, 69–122; autobiographical re-

Sedgwick, Eve Kosofsky (*continued*)
flections of, 42, 69–75, 79, 83, 106,
111, 118–19 n. 1, 123–25, 137–39,
177–78, 191–92, 210; *Between Men*,
192–97; *Epistemology of the Closet*,
144–45, 185–86, 197–98; poems by,
x–xi, 128
Sexuality, 166, 170, 186–88, 197–98;
anal, 167–69, 179, 181; gay male,
173, 177, 180, 195; gender and, 172,
175–77, 193, 194
Seznac, Jean, 38 n. 29
Shaw, Gregory, 38 n. 28
Shibori, 96, 98, 100–101, 111
Smith, Barbara Herrnstein, 119 n. 1
Souls of Old Men, The (Cavafy), 49
Spenser, Edmund, 44
Suminagashi, 83–84

Textile art, 70, 100; middle ranges of
agency and, 83; texture and, 84, 90.
See also *Shibori*; *Suminagashi*
Theory of Mind, 145–46, 148–49,
156–61

Thoreau, Henry David, 125
Thurman, Robert, 210–11
To Call Up the Shades (Cavafy), 51
Tomkins, Silvan, 37 n. 19, 129, 132,
140–41, 144–49, 160–62 n. 6, 162
n. 8, 170, 182 n. 7
Trojans (Cavafy), 49

Unreliable narrator, 150, 152

wabi-sabi, 79
Wada, Yoshiko, 96
Walls (Cavafy), 55–56
water cycle, 3
weather, 3, 9
White, Hayden, 2, 36 n. 2
Whitman, Walt, 175, 177
Wilson, Edmund, 39 n. 44
Winnicott, D. W., 11–12, 27, 34, 181
Wordsworth, William, 7

Zunshine, Lisa, 149–50

EVE KOSOFSKY SEDGWICK (1950–2009)

WAS DISTINGUISHED PROFESSOR OF ENGLISH AT

THE CUNY GRADUATE CENTER.

→⤚

JONATHAN GOLDBERG IS ARTS AND SCIENCES

DISTINGUISHED PROFESSOR OF ENGLISH

AND THE DIRECTOR OF STUDIES IN SEXUALITIES

AT EMORY UNIVERSITY.

Library of Congress
Cataloging-in-Publication Data

Sedgwick, Eve Kosofsky.
The weather in Proust / Eve Kosofsky Sedgwick ;
Jonathan Goldberg, editor.
p. cm. — (Series Q)
Includes bibliographical references and index.
ISBN 978-0-8223-5144-3 (cloth : alk. paper)
ISBN 978-0-8223-5158-0 (pbk. : alk. paper)
I. Goldberg, Jonathan. II. Title.
III. Series: Series Q.
PS3569.E316W43 2012
814'.54—dc23   2011027555